Somme
1914–18

Somme
1914–18

Lessons in War

Martin Marix Evans

For the women and children –
Gillian,
Louise and Polly,
Cherry, Ruby, Olivia, Minnie and Stanton

May they never have to endure events
such as these.

First published 2010

The History Press
The Mill, Brimscombe Port
Stroud, Gloucestershire, GL5 2QG
www.thehistorypress.co.uk

British Library Cataloguing in Publication Data.
A catalogue record for this book is available from the British Library.

ISBN 978 0 7524 5525 9

Typesetting and origination by The History Press
Printed in Great Britain
Manufacturing managed by Jellyfish Print Solutions Ltd

Contents

List of Maps and Diagrams   6

List of Illustrations   8

Introduction   10

Acknowledgements   12

1 First Fights on the Somme   15

2 A New Kind of War: 1915–16   47

3 The Somme 1916: The First Day   81

4 The Somme 1916: Experiment and Attrition   111

5 The Somme 1917: A False Quiet   151

6 The Somme 1918: Operation Michael   175

7 Advance to Victory: May to November 1918   199

8 Hindsight   241

Bibliography   244

Index   249

List of Maps and Diagrams

	Pages
The opposing armies in August 1914	17
The situation on 5 September 1914	24
The situation on 9 September 1914	27
The railway system and the Western Front	30
The situation on 21 September 1914	33
The situation on 30 September 1914	41
The Western Front from Nieuport to Nancy	46
The Hébuterne–Serre area	57
Diagram of a German defence trench	59
British trench map: Albert and La Boisselle, 1916	82
British trench map: Beaumont-Hamel and Hamel, 1916	86
British trench map: Serre, 1916	91
British trench map: Thiepval, 1916	94
German trench map: Thiepval, 1916	95
German machine-gun fields of fire, Thiepval, 1916	95

Key to British Maps

Enemy { Any trench apparently organised for fire...... *Breastwork*

Enemy { Other trenches..........

Enemy { Disused trenches..........

British front line trench..........

Entanglement or other obstacle..... XXXXXXXXXXXXXXXXXXXXXXXXXXXXXX XXXX X XX

Ground cut up by Artillery fire ....

Mine craters.   Mine craters fortified ..

Hedge, fence or ditch. (Unknown which)..........

Hedge ....

Ditch with permanent water.... ....

NOTE.—The fact that an obstacle is not represented on the map does not necessarily mean that there is none there. It is often impossible to distinguish obstacles or to identify their character. It may be assumed that there are obstacles in front of all fire trenches (shown by thick line).

List of Maps and Diagrams

British trench map: Gommecourt, 1916	101
British trench map: Fricourt – Mametz – Montauban, 1916	105
The Somme front, 1–5 July 1916	109
British trench map: Bazentin-le-Petit – Longueval, 1916	118
British trench map: the Pozières Ridge, July 1916	125
British trench map: Martinpuich – Flers, 3 September 1916, annotated 15 September	137
The Hindenburg Line, Lens to the Chemin des Dames	153
The Second Battle of the Somme, March–April 1918	179
Operation Gneisenau, June 1918	201
US 1st Division attack on Cantigny, April 1918	211
British map: the artillery plan for the action at Le Hamel, 4 July 1918	213
British trench map: the Australian front, the Battle of Amiens, August 1918	217
The Third Battle of the Somme: August 1918	224, 225
British trench map: the Hindenburg Line, Bellicourt – Bellenglise, September 1918	232
The advance of the Allies, 18 July to 26 September 1918	237
Artillery sound-ranging film, 11 November 1918	240

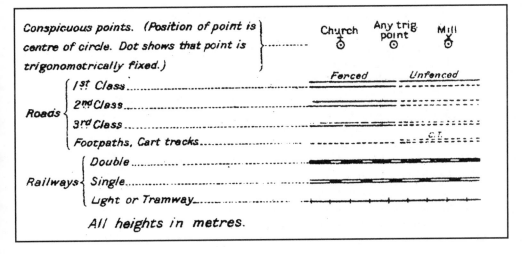

List of Illustrations

Black and White Illustrations (between pp. 96–97)

1 Terrain overview of the Western Front from Lens to Soissons
2 French Colonial Troops, 1914
3 British and Belgian troops retreating from Mons, 1914
4 The Indian Corps arrive in Amiens, 1914
5 German troops in Belgium, 1914
6 Germans carry a biplane wing through St Quentin, 1914
7 German trenches before Arras, 1914
8 A French trench, 1915
9 German deep bunker entrance, 1916
10 German trenches near La Boisselle, 1916
11 Reversed German trench at Orvillers, July 1916
12 Canadian troops with Vickers machine-guns on Vimy Ridge, 1917
13 German troops with 1-inch Maxim anti-aircraft gun
14 US 26th Infantry with Hotchkiss machine-gun, 1918
15 A Lewis gun mounted as an anti-aircraft weapon
16 Captured German field gun and light and heavy machine-guns
17 A French heavy artillery piece, 1914
18 A French 75mm gun mounted for anti-aircraft use
19 'Big Bertha', a German heavy gun taken by US 33rd Division, 1918
20 A German LVG CI biplane
21 A German lateral aerial photograph of Thiepval, 1916
22 Thiepval Château, 1915
23 A British Mark I tank on the Somme, 1916
24 A French Schneider tank demonstrated to US 26th Division, 1918
25 A British Mark V tank of the US 305th Tank Battalion, 1918
26 British 'Whippet' light tanks, 1918
27 German A7V tanks, 1918
28 A battery of the French 85th Heavy Artillery at Curlu, 1916
29 Curlu first aid post, 1916
30 Georges Marix in his dugout, 1916
31 Supply delivery by donkey, near Cléry-sur-Somme, 1916
32 85th Heavy Artillery command post, near Cléry-sur-Somme, 1916

33 Hindenburg Line trench
34 Scorched earth tactics in the retreat of March 1917
35 German shock troops in mud-filled trench, 1916
36 German storm-trooper training
37 US 28th Infantry, 27 April 1918, before Cantigny
38 Aerial photograph of the attack on Cantigny, 28 May 1918
39 German prisoners of US 105th Infantry issued with stretchers, Ronssoy,
     27 September 1918
40 Troops embark for England at Boulogne-sur-Mer

Colour Plates (between pp. 224–225)

1 Newfoundland Memorial Park
2 Thiepval Memorial and cemetery
3 Beaumont-Hamel cemetery from Hawthorn Crater
4 Australian memorial at Pozières windmill site
5 Mametz halt from the graveyard
6 The river Somme at Curlu
7 Lochnagar Crater, La Boisselle
8 Riqueval Bridge, St Quentin Canal
9 The St Quentin Canal
10 US 28th Infantry memorial, Cantigny
11 The American memorial, Cantigny
12 Cantigny village from the American start line
13 The American cemetery at Bony
14 Serre Road Cemetery No. 2
15 The CWGC cemetery at Caix
16 The German cemetery at Caix
17 The French cemetery at Caix
18 German map of the British lines, Bullecourt to Bellicourt, March 1918
19 Sketch map of US 301st Tank Battalion's attack on the Hindenburg Line,
     September 1918

Introduction

People of many nations fought and died on Somme battlefields – it is not only the British who revere this land. In the early days of the First World War, the Germans, French and British disputed the territory, and by British I mean the English, Irish, Scottish and Welsh. The French Army included troops drawn from North Africa and West Africa. Very soon, citizens of the British Empire arrived, from India, South Africa, Canada, Australia and New Zealand as well as the colonies and dependencies. In the later stages of the war the Americans arrived, and while their battles elsewhere have had greater attention, they also fought valiant and vital actions on this front. This diversity, and the experiences of men and women on opposing sides, is reflected in this book.

Located between Paris and Calais, Picardy and the battle theatre of the Somme are easily visited by both continental and inter-continental travellers, and here the evolution of warfare between 1914 and 1918 can be studied in full. Technical innovation was sometimes seen on the Somme for the first time and almost every new development was eventually demonstrated here. Moreover, the area is quite small; you can drive from Amiens to St Quentin by autoroute in an hour, and the same time will suffice for the north to south traverse of the region. The high-speed railway from the Channel to Paris crosses the fought-over ground. It is easy to access the Somme.

What happened on the Somme is set out, inevitably, partly with the benefit of hindsight, but an attempt has been made to show what the participants, from the bravest to the most fearful, and from private soldier to army commander, knew and thought at the time. The answers these participants found to the questions they thought they faced were in their outcome often less successful than they would have wished, but it is often possible to see why they thought that they were right at the time. It can also be seen how these questions changed and innovated in the face of terrible events. The same thinking has informed the selection of maps. All are contemporary with the events studied here. Trench maps convey a good deal about the real situation but also illustrate the perceived facts. The maps from publications of the time show the terrain, roads and railways as they existed during the war, and they can easily be related to the modern touring maps used by the visitor.

All of this brings the courage and sacrifice of these warriors into sharper focus.

Acknowledgements

Since I first wrote on this subject in 1996, new and revealing work has been published. In particular, Jack Sheldon's research within German archives has provided another dimension to the possible appreciation of the battles of this war and I recommend his work to serious students of the conflict. The other authors to whom I have turned with particular attention for vivid impressions of the experience of the Western Front are Lyn Macdonald and Martin Middlebrook. I am grateful to Cleone Woods for permission to quote from the work of Geoffrey Malins, Ian Parker for allowing me to quote from his father's book, Robert Burton for access to his father's unpublished papers and to Fanny Hugill for allowing me to quote from her father's correspondence. I have used the words actually written in the sources quoted; spelling and grammar are unaltered and the intrusive use of the word 'sic' has been avoided. At the time of going to press the copyright holders of some texts have not been identified, and the author would be glad of information to correct the deficiency. The greater part of the American and French material is from my own research in France and the USA, and is reproduced with the permission of the institutions detailed below and cited in the bibliography. The translations from the French are my own. In seeking to understand aspects of how the British fought, I have learned much from the work of Paddy Griffith and of Gary Sheffield.

The constructive and patient assistance of Marie-Pascale Prévost-Bault, Jean-Pierre Thierry, Frédérick Hadley, Sabine Belle and Nathalie Legrand at the Historial de la Grande Guerre (HGG), Péronne, variously over several years, of Jan Dewilde of the Documentatiecentrum In Flanders Fields, Ieper (IFF), of David Fletcher of the Tank Museum, Bovington, Dorset (TM) and his former colleague, Graham Holmes, Dr Tröger of the Bayerisches Haupstaatarchiv, Munich (BH), of Teddy and Phoebe Colligan of the Somme Association, 36th Ulster Division Tower (UT), of David Stanley and the volunteers of the Oxfordshire and Buckinghamshire Light Infantry Archives, Horspath, Oxford (Ox & Bucks) and of the staff of the Photograph Archive of the Imperial War Museum, London (IWM) is most gratefully acknowledged. Assistance in accessing and understanding the material at the US Army Military History Institute, Carlisle, PA (USAMHI) was most constructively given by Dr Richard Sommers, David Keough, John Slonaker, Michael Winey and Randy Hackenburg. Ashley Ekins and Libby Stewart made work at the Australian War Memorial, Canberra, very productive. I am deeply grateful to the late Major General Tim Cape, CB, CBE, DSP, Australian Master-General of Ordnance for his explanation of the history and officering of the Australian Imperial Force, made in a private meeting in 2002. John Kliene has contributed his picture editing skills to render various images legible, and I am most thankful for that.

The illustrations in this book are subject to copyright and are reproduced by kind permission of the institutions listed above where identified by their initials. The modern colour photographs are mine and any unannotated illustrations are from my collection. British Ordnance Survey maps of the battlefields are Crown Copyright.

Martin Marix Evans,
Blakesley, Northamptonshire,
December 2009

Chapter 1

First Fights on the Somme: 1914

On Sunday 28 June 1914 Gavrilo Princip shot and killed the Austrian Archduke Franz Ferdinand in Sarajevo and set in motion a chain of events that led to the outbreak of war, not only in Europe, but across the world. During the next five weeks massive armies assembled in Germany, Austria, Russia and France and lesser armies mobilised as well, including the relatively small British regular army. Roger Charlet of the French 87th Regiment of Infantry wrote home from Ham, south of Péronne, on 25 July to report that war had been declared between Austria and Serbia and that Germany was mobilising. His leave was cancelled. His 2nd Company was mobilising and being issued with field equipment. 'I still hope to be able to come and see you,' he signed off. Maurice LePoitevin, 329th Regiment of Infantry, was unenthusiastic on being mobilised. 'It's not the rehearsal the optimists think,' he remarked.

When war broke out in the west with the German invasion of Belgium on 4 August, both adversaries, the Germans and the French, thought it would soon be over. The Germans had complete confidence in the Schlieffen Plan, the strategy of sweeping through Belgium to take Paris, while the French relied equally on Plan XVII which involved a strike to the east through Lorraine and Alsace, the lands lost in the Franco-Prussian War. Neither succeeded.

In the summer of 1914 the principal opposing forces in the West were arrayed as follows. On the German side, from north to south, were the First Army, 320,000 men under General Alexander von Kluck, north of Aachen, and the Second Army, 260,000 men under Field Marshal Karl von Bülow, facing Liège and southern Belgium, poised to tackle the forts at Liège and Namur, while the more northerly force was to thrust westwards at all speed.

The plan was hugely ambitious as the distance to be covered by the First Army, passing east of Lille and Amiens to envelop Paris, demanded much from an army reliant on horse-drawn transport and marching men. The Third, Fourth, Fifth, Sixth and Seventh Armies were to hold territory to the south. The Third, 180,000 men under General Max von Hausen, and Fourth, 180,000 men under Albrecht, Grand Duke of Württemberg, were to advance between Rheims and Verdun, while the Fifth, 220,000 men commanded by Crown Prince Wilhelm of Prussia, would surround the iconic stronghold above the river Meuse. The Crown Prince Rupprecht of Bavaria had the 220,000 men of the Sixth Army and General August von Heeringen the Seventh, 125,000 men, to attack on the Moselle and in the Vosges mountains.

The French Fifth Army with 254,000 men spread itself from Sedan in the direction of Maubeuge on the river Sambre, between Valenciennes and Charleroi and was commanded by General Charles Lanrezac. Lieutenant Edward Spears, 11th Hussars, had been attached to the French War Office that summer, and, bring fluent in French, was now with the Fifth Army as liaison officer. The British Expeditionary Force (BEF), 103,691 men under Field Marshal Sir John French, commenced embarkation on 9 August and by 20 August was concentrated at Maubeuge. In Belgium the 117,000-strong army under King Albert, stood from Namur to Diest on the river Gette, but two divisions were sent forward to protect the fortified areas of Namur and Liège, an awkward deployment which was directly attributable to Belgian reluctance to be seen as allies of France. The Belgian forts were garrisoned only by some 90,000 men. Usually forgotten is the space between the BEF and the coast. On 14 August 1914 a Territorial Divisions Group was formed under General Albert d'Amade. It consisted of three divisions, the 81st, 82nd and 84th, comprised of older men, unfit for front-line service and known to regulars as 'grandads'. Their task was to protect the railways against possible raids by enemy cavalry on a front that was not expected to see serious action.

To the east the French had four armies numbering 817,000 men in all. The First was commanded by General Auguste Dubail, the Second by General Noël de Castelnau, the Third by General Pierre Ruffey and the Fourth, east of Sedan, by General Fernand de Langle de Cary.

Sir John French, arrived to meet General Lanrezac at Fifth Army headquarters in Rethel on the river Aisne on the morning of 17 August. The interview was not a success. The two men lacked a common language and suspicion and incomprehension doomed their alliance. Lieutenant Edward Spears wrote of the event:

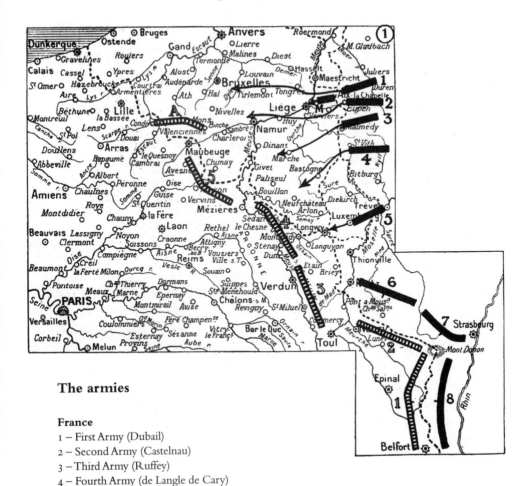

The armies

France

1 – First Army (Dubail)
2 – Second Army (Castelnau)
3 – Third Army (Ruffey)
4 – Fourth Army (de Langle de Cary)
5 – Fifth Army (Lanrezac)
A – BEF (French), from 22 August

Germany

M – Army of the Meuse (von Emmich)
1 – First Army (von Kluck)
2 – von Bülow
3 – von Hausen
4 – Duke of Württemberg
5 – Crown Prince Wilhelm
6 – Crown Prince Rupprecht
7 – von Heeringen
8 – von Deimling's detatchment

From l'Illustration, *Paris, 1915. (HGG)*

Sir John, stepping up to a map in the 3ème Bureau, took out his glasses, located a place with his finger, and said to Lanrezac: '*Mon Géneral, est-ce-que –*' His French then gave out, and turning to one of his staff, he asked: 'How do you say "to cross the river" in French?' He was told and proceeded: '*Est-ce que les Allemands vont traverser la Meuse à – à –*' Then he fumbled over the pronunciation of the name '*Huy*' ....'What does he say? What does he say?' exclaimed Lanrezac. Somebody explained that the Marshal wanted to know whether the Germans were going to cross the river at Huy? Lanrezac shrugged his shoulders impatiently. 'Tell the Marshal,' he said curtly, 'that in my opinion the Germans have merely gone to the Meuse to fish.'

What was even more damaging than this rudeness was that Lanrezac's appreciation of his own front was not sufficiently detailed, for there were bridges over the Sambre of which his men were not aware. On 21 August the German 2nd Guard Division crossed at Auvelais, between Charleroi and Namur, and part of the 19th Division did the same a little to the west. On that day the bombardment of Namur began. In the next four days all of the forts would fall, putting the hinge of the defence line under German control. In the meantime Lanrezac's staff persisted in the expression of a determination to move north and the British therefore planned to advance into Belgium. D'Amade moved to take positions centred on Lille, putting eleven battalions in forward positions and twenty-five, supported by six groups of artillery, on the main line of resistance on the river Scarpe, to the British left. On 22 August Lieutenant Spears went to report to Sir John French at Le Cateau. In trying to return to the French Fifth Army forces on the British right, Spears found them falling back and he immediately returned to BEF headquarters with the news. He recalled:

Never have I felt more tired, but the feeling of being well-nigh spent was due far more to the news I bore, and of the responsibility of the report I had to make, than to actual lack of sleep. I felt more and more miserable: if I were mistaken in my deductions or in my observations the result might be terribly serious. Yet the situation, if I understood it rightly, was so perilous that I felt I must convince Sir John of two things; that General Lanrezac was not going to attack whatever happened, and that the position of the Fifth Army was dangerously exposing the British.

The British then decided to stand on the line of the canal at Mons.

II Corps, under General Sir Horace Smith-Dorrien, was on the left between Condé and Mons, and on the right, between Mons and the river Sambre at the French border to the south-east, was I Corps under Lieutenant General Sir Douglas Haig. Each had two divisions comprising three brigades of infantry with mounted troops, artillery and engineers. In addition the BEF had the Cavalry Corps under Lieutenant General Edmund Allenby with one cavalry division to the rear of II Corps. In all there were about 72,000 troops with some 300 guns to hold against von Kluck's First Army's 135,000 men and 480 guns.

The battle took place on Sunday 23 August and although the Germans were startled by the ferocity and speed of British rifle fire, their advance was relentless. By evening, the BEF was pulling back, having suffered 1,600 casualties. As midnight drew near and the defenders of Mons gained a little rest, Lieutenant Spears arrived at the BEF Headquarters at Le Cateau with the news that Lanrezac had issued orders for his Fifth Army to retreat. D'Amade's 'grandads' had taken the force of von Kluck's right wing and the poor men of the Territorial Group's 88th Division were either dead, wounded, taken prisoner or in retreat to the river Escaut. The BEF's position at Mons had become untenable and confidence in their ally on their right had been severely shaken. Sir John French issued the order to retire at 0100 hours on 24 August, but gave no indication of by what route or to which location Smith-Dorrien and Hague should take their Corps. The Germans were, fortunately, ill-informed about the Allies' positions and, fearful of an attack on the flank of his Second Army, von Bülow insisted that von Kluck's First Army should maintain close contact with him instead of swinging west to outflank the BEF. That day Lille was declared an open city and d'Amade pulled back to a line through Douai.

By the time that Sir John's orders had reached front-line units, daylight had come and, unable to achieve a clean break with the Germans, the British were obliged to conduct a fighting retreat. On the way south-west towards St Quentin, the Forest of Mormal split their route. Smith-Dorrien's II Corps took the route along the north-western side of the woodland and Haig's I Corps the road along the south-eastern. The Germans, assuming the British were running as hard as they could, advanced on a broad front but no significant renewal of combat ensued; both sides were exhausted by long marches and heavy fighting. The weather was hot and the ways dusty and filled with refugees. I Corps was also sharing the road with French troops, the left wing of Lanrezac's army, which compounded the confusion and discomfort. The German advance through and to the east of the Forest of Mormal led to a clash late at night and the precipitate withdrawal of I Corps the next day. II Corps was in serious trouble.

Two Roman roads cross this open terrain. One runs south-west, to the west of the Forest of Mormal, to the canal north of St Quentin at Riqueval – a place the British would next visit in September 1918. The other road, coming south-east from Cambrai, meets its fellow route near Le Cateau. From Cambrai the river Escaut runs northwards into Belgium. Small streams cut north-west across the plain to join the Escaut, among them the Selle, which rises south of Le Cateau and flows through the town. Also through this little town comes the railway from St Quentin, heading off north-east along the river Sambre towards Liège, with a junction taking a line to Cambrai. In the south, near St Quentin, the river Somme rises to snake its way westwards, through open, chalk country. Here there is space to manoeuvre. (*See* b/w plate 1)

Sir John French ordered Smith-Dorrien to continue the retreat of II Corps the following day, 26 August. The order was received at 2100 hours on Tuesday, 25 August, three hours before the march south to Le Cateau was completed. The ridge at Solesmes, north of Le Cateau which General Allenby had planned to hold with his cavalry to cover further withdrawal, was occupied by the Germans, and, in addition, there was a real threat of a successful outflanking movement on the west. In his defence, Allenby had had the additional problem of the dispersion of his cavalry in a series of running actions throughout Tuesday. Fortunately the 4th Division, under Major-General Sir Thomas Snow, had arrived on Monday, by train, at Le Cateau and other nearby stations, and without Snow what followed would probably have been impossible. Snow and Allenby placed themselves under Smith-Dorrien's orders. The II Corps commander concluded that there was no alternative but to let the men get as much rest as possible and to stand and fight on the ridge that carried the Le Cateau to Cambrai road. As dawn arrived they hastened to dig what trenches they could. The Royal Field Artillery (RFA), of primitive fire control in these days, was immediately behind them.

On the left, 4th Divison faced north-west in the direction of Cambrai to secure the flank. Along the Roman road, 3rd Division were positioned in the centre and 5th Division and XXVIII Brigade, RFA, were holding the spur over-looking Le Cateau and the Selles Valley where the German 5th Division was already advancing. The progress of the Germans on the right flank during the day, as I Corps withdrew towards St Quentin, eventually forced the artillery to turn at right angles to their original line of fire. By 1400 hours it was clear that Smith-Dorrien's men could hold no longer and orders were given to retreat. The orders did not reach some units, who fought to a standstill. Three VCs were won in the efforts to pull the guns out. By nightfall the disengagement was complete, and the last troops were making their own way back as best they could. On the left, General Jean Sordet's Cavalry Corps and d'Amade's territorials had prevented the German First Army turning the 4th Division's flank. Indeed, d'Amade had planned to use his reserves, the 61st and 62nd Divisions, to attack the German right, but the ferocity of the German attack on the BEF gave him too little time. II Corps had held that army for a day at the cost of 5,212 killed and wounded, 2,600 taken prisoner and thirty-eight guns. The German First Army did not pursue them as von Kluck was under the impression, as he reported, that he had been fighting the entire BEF – six divisions, a cavalry division and several French Territorial divisions. While the British fell back by way of St Quentin, d'Amade pulled back to Bray-sur-Somme to create a defence along the river from Amiens in the west to Péronne in the east. Von Kluck thought that the entire BEF was facing east and on the march for the Channel, so he sent General Georg von der Marwitz and his cavalry corps on a sweep westwards to cut the British off. The whole situation remained uncertain in what was still a war of movement. Writing in 1918, Marwitz recalled seeing Péronne on his left. As IV Corps was attempting to get there, he took II Corps to Cléry to attempt a crossing of the Somme. He found the marshy valley too wide. Here the 'grandads' had succeeded in turning back a German force.

In St Quentin the mood was so depressed that, encouraged by a mayor eager to avoid fighting in his town, two British lieutenant-colonels were ready to surrender their forces to the Germans. Major Tom Bridges of the 4th Dragoon Guards would have none of it however, and swore to evacuate every living British soldier. The exhausted and demoralised troops were hard to rouse to action, but a toy drum and penny whistle bought from a shop still open for business sparked a reaction when Bridges marched his skeleton military band round the square, and by midnight, the last of the BEF had quit the town.

That same day a frosty meeting chaired by the French Commander-in-Chief, General Joseph Joffre, took place in St Quentin from which Sir John French and Lanrezac both departed with their poor opinion of each other confirmed and little else settled, other than the announcement of Joffre's plan to form a defence line along the Somme and Oise rivers. Simultaneously, significant numbers of troops were being rushed by railway train from the Lorraine front to form a new French Sixth Army in the west which was to be commanded by General Michel-Joseph Maunoury.

As the BEF fell back from St Quentin on 27 August, the Royal Marines were landing at Ostend to take part in the defence of Antwerp. The Royal Naval Air Service Squadron, under Commander Charles Samson, was with them.

The marines were recalled four days later, and Samson's unit was moved to Dunkirk with the intention, in England, of ordering it back home. Before that, however, on 29 August, Samson was asked to use his support vehicles to make a reconnaissance towards Bruges which gave him a taste for undertaking forays into debateable territory that he was able to indulge in the weeks that followed. When they came, instructions to fly back across the Channel were fended off with excuses about adverse weather conditions or any other pretext Samson could offer in order to stay and fight.

To allow the shift of French troops from the east to take place, any further advance by von Bülow and von Kluck had to be held up, so on 27 August Lanrezac was ordered to counter-attack to the west, against von Bülow's Second Army which was now pushing more south-west than due south. The order was resisted and only executed when, the next day, Joffre repeated it, face to face with his subordinate, and backed it up in writing. Meanwhile the British were retiring swiftly to Noyon from Lanrezac's left flank. This attack required a massive realignment on the Fifth Army's front and the danger of exposing a flank to the north. Lanrezac was encouraged to learn that Haig, with I Corps, was ready to act in support and infuriated when French withdrew his subordinate's offer. On the morning of 29 August, along the river Oise where it runs east to west through Guise, Fifth Army's X and III Corps faced north and to their left, where the river turns south-west and is joined by the canal from the Sambre, XVIII Corps was ready to attack west. In reserve was I Corps under General Louis Franchet d'Esperey. The German Guard and X Corps were surprised to meet the resistance along the Oise at Guise, but towards the end of the day they had managed a modest advance. To the west the French attack had got nowhere. It appeared that the Germans were on the brink of a breakthrough but then Franchet d'Esperey launched I Corps northwards, rallying X and III Corps in the process, and threw the Germans back. Lieutenant Spears recorded the event:

> It was not until 5.30 in the afternoon that everything was ready, and General d'Esperey, riding at the head of the 2nd Brigade, surrounded by his staff on horseback, gave the order for the general attack. It was a magnificent sight. Strange, but very gallant, the bands were playing and the colours were unfurled. The I Corps troops, deployed in long skirmishing lines, doubled forward with magnificent dash on either side of the X Corps. The X Corps and the right of the III were carried forward in the splendid victorious wave, the men frantic with joy at the new and longed for sensation. The Germans were running away, there was no doubt about it.

The British withdrawal from St Quentin was not uneventful. On 28 August there was a gap between I and II Corps into which the Germans were threatening to move. The western arm stopped the Germans near Benay with a combination of cavalry and artillery, but 3 miles (5 kilometres) east, near Möy-de-l'Aisne there was a more dramatic encounter. Where the autoroute now swings down a valley to cross the river and canal, the old road to La Fère crossed the Cerizy to Möy road at La Guingette, to the south of a ridge that marks the edge of a mile-wide valley running east to west. Here, the British prepared to offer battle. The pursuing Germans entered the valley in late morning and attacked the Royal Scots Greys, two machine-gun sections and J Battery, RFA. At Möy were the 12th Lancers, of which two squadrons were sent around to the north to fire on the Germans. J Battery also engaged them. C Squadron, 12th Lancers was led forward, out of sight of their adversaries in dead ground, until close enough to charge. The engagement was settled with steel-tipped bamboo lance and with the sword. The Richthofen Cavalry Corps was comprehensively beaten. That it was a minor action did not prevent the British press portraying it as a major victory, not least because a charge by lancers invoked memories of imagined romance in warfare.

The Times newspaper reported the 'brilliant action' and, on the same page, published a message of support and solidarity to the Royal Scots Greys from the Tsar, for the Russian monarch was Colonel-in-Chief of that regiment.

The BEF was by now desperately tired, badly mauled and seriously demoralised. Sir John French sought to pull out of the line to allow his men to rest and recover, but the German advance appeared to be rolling on to Paris and to victory. Joffre was struggling to maintain control. It took the intervention of Lord Kitchener to stiffen Sir John's resolve to fight on and the replacement of Lanrezac by Franchet d'Esperey to convince French that the BEF was truly part of Joffre's team. On 2 September he agreed to take up a position southeast of Paris to complete a defensive line with the Sixth Army under General Maunoury north-east of the French capital. The Sixth Army was made up of units of various sizes and differing levels of professionalism. It included the VII Corps, transported from Alsace, two reserve divisions, the 55th and 56th, and was later joined by the 61st and 62nd from d'Amade's group. To these were added the Moroccan 45th Brigade and, from 7 September, Sordet's Cavalry Corps, with Bridoux in command. To Maunoury's right was the BEF, and, running eastwards, the Fifth Army and the new Ninth Army, created on 28 August, under General Ferdinand Foch, and then the Fourth Army under General de Langle de Cary. Joffre had been vigorous in making changes in the

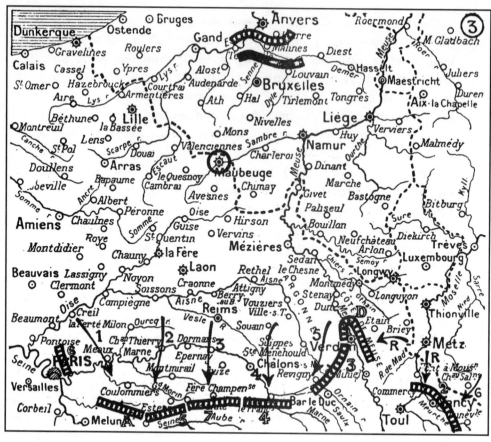

The situation on 5 September. The Sixth Army is forming in front of Paris, the BEF (A) is on the left of the Allied line facing the Marne, while Maubeuge and Antwerp (Anvers) are under siege to the north. *From* l'Illustration, *Paris, 1915. (HGG)*

French commands, replacing those he decided had under-performed and, as with Foch, promoting those who had impressed with their leadership.

The appearance of massive strength given by the Germans was just that: an appearance. In fact German control of their invading armies was becoming tenuous. Whereas Joffre was rushing about visiting his commanders in person, German Field Marshal Helmuth von Moltke was still far away from his armies, even after moving from Koblenz to Luxembourg on 29 August. A radio signal sent from von Kluck's HQ at 2100 on 31 August passed through so many relay stations that von Moltke only got it early on 2 September. The orders in response were received by the First Army in Compiègne on 3 September; the orders were to proceed south-eastwards. The Schlieffen requirement to reinforce the right wing was being forgotten amid the multitude of tasks that the German armies had to perform. The sieges of Antwerp and Maubeuge were still in progress, the requirements of the Russian front had drawn away the Namur siege train, supply lines were stretched and Samson's Royal Naval Air Service aircraft had raided Düsseldorf, though it was not until 8 October that the intended target, Zeppelin *Z IX*, was hit by Flight Lieutenant Reggie Marix. Adding to these difficulties, von Kluck was now marching south at a pace that was opening a gap between the First and Second Armies. On 30 August von Kluck began a move to the south-east to close up with the Second Army. General von der Marwitz was denied the opportunity to employ his cavalry, as every time he saw an opportunity to release it to outflank the French, the Army Corps insisted he remain on their wing to prevent the French outflanking them.

The change in direction was a welcome relief to the battered divisions of d'Amade's Territorial Group. The 61st Division had been severely mauled near Péronne and by 28 August had reached Combles, where its commander, General Vervaire, was evacuated, too ill to continue. The 62nd had been harried back by way of Arras to Doullens from where the shattered remnants were able to depart for Paris where they, and the 61st, were to rest before joining the new Sixth Army. Regiments had been reduced to a mere 500 men, cavalry divisions to a couple of squadrons, artillery batteries had run out of ammunition and the infantry's supplies were almost gone. The 'grandads' had paid heavily for their defiance. They blew the bridges over the Somme and fell back towards Neufchâtel-en-Bray, between Amiens and Dieppe. The 81st, 82nd and 84th regrouped there, followed by the shattered 88th. D'Amade reported that he had 'covered' Rouen and that, when the men were rested, he would attack the communication lines of the German IV Corps, but the speed of events outran his powers.

In Dunkirk, Commander Samson received a satisfactory message: his squadron was to remain there to carry out reconnaissance duties. On 2 September he was asked to take the British Consul to Lille and they set off, accompanied by a Jesuit priest, Cavrois O'Caffrey, in two cars, one of which was armed with a machine-gun. As they reached the suburbs of Lille at La Carnoy they were stopped and told that the Germans had entered the city. They telephoned the Prefecture to find out if it was true and, on being told the enemy were actually in the building, a series of calls were then made to see if a rescue operation could be undertaken. It was deemed too risky for the civilian population, but in the meantime O'Caffrey had taken the tram to the city centre to find out more.

He returned to report the presence of about a thousand German infantry in the main square, so Samson's little force withdrew.

On 4 September two cars drove to Cassel, a town some 16 miles (25 kilometres) from Dunkirk, perched on a hill rising abruptly from the plain and the scene, in 1793, of the noble Duke of York's famous march up and down again. News came of the approach of German vehicles from the east, so Samson hurried his little force down to the Armentières road as the enemy came into view. His memoirs record:

> As soon as they saw us, the German who was driving the car applied his brakes, skidded half-way round, and started reversing to turn completely. There appeared only one thing to do or they would escape us, and that was to stop and open fire. We couldn't use the Maxim whilst the car was moving, so I gave the necessary orders and Harper opened fire with commendable promptness.

The machine-gun and rifles were brought into action, putting the Germans to flight. The British waited for two hours in case of a renewed approach, but then a telephone message arrived to say that the German automobile had returned to Lille carrying wounded men. The victorious party withdrew to an enthusiastic welcome in Cassel.

On 5 September General Bidon sent for Samson and asked him to verify the news that the Germans had quit Lille. He set off with four automobiles, three with machine-guns, and a mixed force of French artillerymen and his own RNAS. They moved with care, the vehicles taking turns to go forward, take up a firing position and cover the progress of the others while an aircraft scouted ahead of them. On the way they passed a squadron of cavalry. Arriving once more on the outskirts of the town they found the Germans had indeed departed and so they carried on, to be welcomed by cheering crowds and cries of '*Vive l'Angleterre!*' Apparently the Battle of Cassel had been interpreted as a sign of the approach of a large British force. In order to ensure the later safety of the town's administrators should the Germans return, Samson gave them a note saying he had 'occupied Lille with an armed English and French force', and signed it 'C R Samson, Commander RN, Officer-in-Command of English Force at Dunkirk' which he hoped would give the enemy cause for alarm if they came back. It was still, at this stage, a curious kind of war in Picardy and Artois; almost a nineteenth-century experience.

The situation on 9 September. Maubeuge has fallen, making another railway route available to the Germans. *From* l'Illustration, *Paris, 1915. (HGG)*

The German reaction to their experience was different. They had had a much harder time than they anticipated. Hauptmann (Captain) Walter Bloem of the 12th Grenadier Regiment wrote:

At this early period ... our ideas of war ... were based entirely on the 1870 campaign [the Franco-Prussian War]. A battle would begin at 6 am and end ... at 6 pm ... early the next morning the pursuit would begin and be continued for two enjoyable weeks with two rest-days in comfortable billets, followed by another good, healthy battle in the grand manner. But this was something entirely different, something utterly unexpected. For a month now we had been in the enemy's country, and during that time on the march incessantly ... without a single rest-day. How many miles had I covered the last few days on foot, being so tired that if I got on my horse I fell asleep at once and would have fallen off? How many anxious discussions had I had with Ahlert regarding the company's boots? ... a few more days on the road and my Grenadiers would be marching barefoot.

On 4 September a fresh instruction was sent, stipulating that the German First Army should face west against an attack from Paris, which was reinforced by sending Lieutenant-Colonel Richard Hentsch, von Moltke's intelligence chief, on a tour of the army commanders to rebuild some coherence of frontage. The strain was telling on the German commander-in-chief, but the French and British were unaware and struggling to create an effective opposition.

The fight developed into a conflict on a fragmented line, away from the Somme, running east from Paris to Châlons-sur-Marne and on to Verdun. By the late evening of 6 September it was clear that the French Sixth Army was in a perilous position. While it had advanced, it was at great cost and the Germans were hurrying up their reinforcements. The commander of the Paris garrison, General Joseph Gallieni, ordered the 7th Division, newly arrived from the east by rail, to be sent to Maunoury's aid. When told of the lack of rail capacity to move them, Gallieni ordered the 14th Brigade to be taken by taxi cab. All over the city police stopped cabs, threw out the passengers and sent the vehicles to the Esplanade des Invalides. During the night, taxis, private cars and buses moved five battalions of infantry, some 4,000 men, to the front.

In the centre the German Second and Third armies worked together to put Foch's Ninth Army under almost intolerable pressure. Reinforced by X Corps from Franchet d'Esperey's Fifth Army, Foch counter-attacked from an almost untenable position. The Germans, lacking supplies of food, ammunition and fresh troops, had to fall back. That same day, 8 September, the British were shelling retreating Germans crossing the Marne northwards at La Ferté-sous-Jouarre, and the next morning Haig's I Corps was over the river between that town and Château-Thierry to the east. II Corps fought their way over on Haig's left and by evening the French were across in Château-Thierry. It was clear to the Germans that they were now in the gravest danger and the decision was made to pull back to the north to establish a new line on the river Aisne. On 14 September von Moltke resigned. He had been unable to turn the hugely ambitious Schlieffen plan into a reality.

Kaiser Wilhelm had, in fact, ordered von Moltke to report sick and in his place appointed the Prussian Minister of War, Erich von Falkenhayn. The situation he inherited was one of increasing stabilisation of the line in eastern

France, but with a wide open flank in the west. His long-held opinion that a breakthrough in the east was the solution had become, he realised, no longer appropriate, but with part of his force facing Antwerp and a gap between St Quentin and Belgium, the extent of the terrain outstripped the numbers at his disposal. His eventual decision was to attempt to envelop the French in the west while discouraging them from reinforcing their power there by mounting assaults in the east and on the Aisne. The challenge for both sides was to concentrate sufficient force on this flank, from Paris to Picardy and Belgium.

The key to the problem lay in the unglamorous discipline of logistics. The movement of large bodies of men and munitions depended on the railway system. The German rail connection between east and west ran through Trier, Liège, Brussels and Valenciennes to Cambrai. The line coming south from Belgium to St Quentin passed through Maubeuge, which was held by the French until 7 September, and even then it was of no use until the blown bridge at Namur had been brought back into service. Both routes were in need of repair because the Belgians and the French had destroyed various signalling systems and other minor parts of the infrastructure as they retreated. The French, on the other hand, were in full possession of their Paris–centred rail system, which enabled them to carry troops from the eastern front and transport them west and north to the Somme and towards the Channel coast. On 15 September, Joffre brought General Castelnau from his Second Army in the east to form a new Second Army in the west while von Falkenhayn moved the German Sixth Army under Crown Prince Rupprecht from Lorraine to the St Quentin front on 18 September. But these are the starting dates and the action took time. The German armies were organised into two corps, each of two divisions. The capacity of the railway limited them to moving one corps in four days at the very best. The armies therefore reassembled unit by unit while the situation in the field threatened all the time to outstrip the capabilities of their increasing strength.

The French order for the movement of the XIV Corps of Dubail's First Army to join Maunoury's Sixth gives the scale of the challenge. The instruction, No. 650 of 17 September 1914, says that the operation is to commence at 5am on 18 September. The departures were to take place from Bayon (using one platform), Charmes (two platforms) Châtelmouxy (one platform) and Thaon (one platform). In all there were to be up to thirty departures from each platform in twenty-four hours. This would require 109 trains and the diversion of regular traffic to other routes to free up the railway for the XIV Corps. This was a race to build power in the west in order to outflank the enemy rather than a 'race to the sea'.

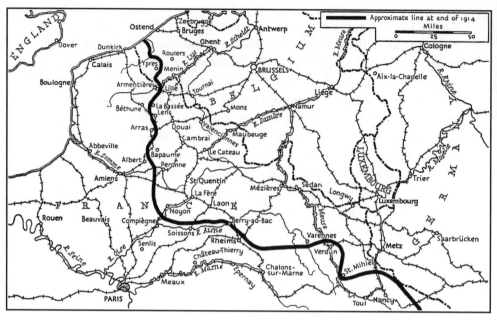

The relationship of railway communication to the eventual line of the western front at the end of 1914 shows the pivotal position of Paris and the importance of the Amiens junction to the Allies. The Germans have a line from Saarbrücken in the east via Mézières all the way to Lille in the north fed by lines emerging from Germany. *From C.R.M.F. Crutwell,* A History of the Great War, *OUP, 1934.*

While the principal action was taking place on the Aisne, the open country conflict in Picardy continued. On 8 September Commander Samson had been joined in Dunkirk by 250 Royal Marines under Major Armstrong. He was also given the assistance of Captain Richard and the men of the Boulogne Gendarmerie in order to clear the country of bands of German cavalry and cyclist troops roaming from their bases in Arras, Albert and Douai. Attempts to surround the enemy with their automobile-carried force failed; there was simply too much room for manoeuvre. For example, the foray Samson undertook on 12 September took him from Cassel to the suburbs of Lille, down to St Pol and thence towards Arras. Some way short of the town they had a brush with a party of 'uhlans' (lancers, but the British tended to use the term for any German horse). No damage was done to either side and the German cavalry rode off. The night was spent at Hesdin. The next day, now with reinforcements – a patrol of eleven vehicles – they drove south-east passing through Doullens. As they left the town on the road for Albert they almost literally ran into a group of six uhlans whom they engaged with rifle fire as they retreated across the fields. Three were killed and one wounded, later dying without recovering consciousness.

From his papers they discovered that he had served with the 1st Squadron, 26th Württemberg Dragoons. In his pocket he had a miniature school atlas, in which the map of France was about three inches square, as an aid to navigation.

On 15 September the Second Army's formation was accompanied by an order to the Territorial Group to force the Germans to cease their activity in 'the north' and cover the Allies' left wing, to police the area already freed of the enemy and to harass the German lines of supply. This tall order required operations to range over territory from the west of Compiégne all the way north to Douai. Two days later d'Amade was replaced, for no apparent reason, by the venerable General Brugère, who was wheeled out of retirement with the order to hold a line between Bapaume and Péronne with the 'grandads' of the battered territorial divisions.

Castelnau's new Second Army began to assemble from 18 September onwards. From the First Army on the Moselle came XIV Corps, by way of Montdidier to Amiens. From the Fifth Army most of Conneau's Cavalry Corps and the associated 45th Regiment of Infantry moved from the Compiègne area to the Sixth Army's left wing. The XIII Corps, including the 3rd Moroccan Brigade, and the XIV and XX Army Corps from the east also came under Castelnau's orders. Meanwhile German army movements were, imperfectly, observed. D'Amade had estimated that the arrivals at Valenciennes reported by French Intelligence, the Deuxième Bureau, amounted to at least an army corps, but there was puzzlement about their destination. Movement from Valenciennes towards St Quentin was at first seen, mistakenly, as a strengthening of the line north of the Aisne.

The movement of Crown Prince Rupprecht's Sixth Army was planned at a conference with von Falkenhayn in Luxembourg on 18 September. The orders were to destroy the French infantry, thought to be quite few, between Roye and Montdidier using the XXI Corps, and then, with the entire army, to envelop the Allies' left. Rupprecht and his Chief of Staff General Konrad Kraft von Delmensingen, were not happy with the scheme as, when XXI Corps arrived on 21 September, they would be on their own – the next arrival, XIV Corps, would be two days away. In addition, the rest of the army would continue to trickle westwards, subsequently forcing Rupprecht to feed his troops into action piecemeal. Meanwhile, they decided, Joffre would be speeding his armies to the west with ease, so a simultaneous German attack on the Aisne, or more exactly between Compiègne and Reims, was vital to detain the French in that sector, and a push to create a salient at St Mihiel would concurrently add to French worries in the east.

In the third week of September the fight moved to the Somme front. The French XIII Corps and the German IX Reserve Corps disputed the difficult terrain around Lassigny, between Compiègne and Roye. Castelnau's XX and XIV Corps were on a line between Villers-Brettoneux, east of Amiens, and Rosières-en-Santerre, north of Roye while at some distance from them, the I Bavarians were close to Péronne and the XXI Corps were to their south, near Ham, on the eastern side of the Somme. Castelnau, on the basis of reports from his reconnaissance aircraft, had pulled the Péronne garrison back to Albert. The French cavalry under Conneau clashed with von der Marwitz's horse near Chaulnes, west of the river, and pushed them back, but the hardest fighting took place east of Roye. The French IV Corps was pushing up towards Nesle and ran into the van of the German XXI probing across the Somme. A sharp action followed in which the French had the advantage, but Castelnau was cautious and ordered them to dig in rather than to advance in haste on Nesle. To their right the XIII were also told to hold their positions. Further west Castelnau had the XX straddle the Somme east of Amiens and the XIV advance towards the river.

The Germans had to decide which alternative to use to finish off their enemy – use the II Bavarians to break through on the left to isolate Castelnau from Paris, or swing around to the right to roll his army up. They decided to concentrate their efforts on Roye, assaulting the French IV Corps on 24 September from the east with their XXI Corps and a division of the 1st Bavarian, and from the north, the direction of Chaulnes, initially with the XXVIII Corps and two days later with the II Bavarian Corps. The first assault forced the French 8th Division to retreat more than 5 miles (8 kilometres). The losses were substantial; indeed, an entire battalion of the 124th Regiment of Infantry became casualties – killed, wounded or made prisoner. An attempt by Castelnau to hit the I Bavarians in the flank with his XIV Corps was frustrated by the sluggishness of his subordinate, General Baret, who brought only a single regiment, the 140th, into action to take Chaulnes. The gap between the IV and XIV Corps was plugged by the 3rd Cavalry, and a line from Roye to Bray-sur-Somme was stabilised. Blocked, Rupprecht decided to employ the II Bavarians on his right.

While renewed assaults on the severely stretched French IV Corps at Roye took place, the Bavarians were to make a huge encirclement by way of the Somme and the Ancre. The French held at Roye and Chaulnes, and in attempting to get round the north of Chaulnes the Germans were stopped at Lihons, west of the town. Reserve Hauptmann Karl Weber of the 5th Company, 16th Bavarian Regiment, wrote that in the late afternoon of that

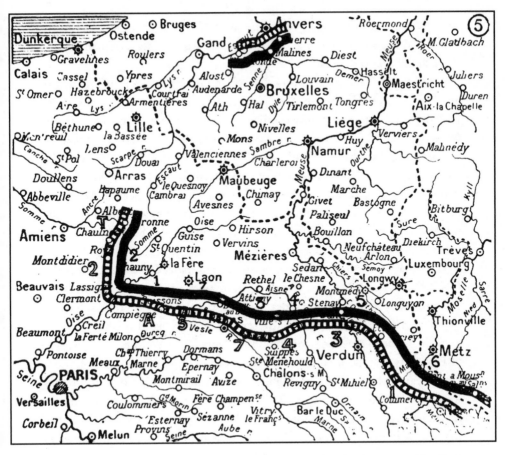

The situation on 21 September. The French Territorial Group is on the river Somme and the German Sixth Army has not quite arrived. *From* l'Illustration, Paris, 1915. *(HGG)*

day, 24 September, they had been ordered into bivouac, but that the destination might have to be fought for – not an attractive prospect. The 1st and 3rd German battalions made a cautious advance in as much silence as possible. Flames enveloped the church in Chaulnes, lighting the gloom. As they reached the marketplace the French opened fire. The battalions pulled back and called up their artillery to destroy the château from which the fusillade had come. Next morning they went in to clear the town, but found determined resistance, which took all morning to overcome. Advancing much further beyond the town proved to be impossible.

Closer to the river Somme at Herbécourt, west of Péronne, on 25 September, the Bavarian Infantry Liebregiment was actually retreating under orders from the 2nd Division headquarters. Hauptmann Graf

33

Armansperg said that in Herbécourt he was told of a heavy fight that I Army Corps had been involved in and that a retreat was possible. German cavalry was falling back to the east.

Meanwhile German reconnaissance aircraft observed reinforcements de-training at Longeau, on the south-eastern outskirts of Amiens – the XI Corps was arriving from Compiègne. Castelnau put other new arrivals under General Balfourier of the XX Corps on his mobile left – the 11th and 45th Infantry divisions and Conneau's cavalry corps. Unfortunately the Germans had come into possession of vital information. The body of a French staff officer was searched and the complete strength of the Second Army was thus revealed as well as the limitations in its ability to extend its line northwards. Castelnau informed Joffre that, on the evening of 25 September, he held a line to the Somme near Bray-sur-Somme, but had no reserves.

The situation further north had not remained static. On 20 September the First Lord of the Admiralty, Winston Churchill, had attended a conference in Dunkirk at which Commander Samson was also present. It was decided to create a special force under the second-in-command of the Dunkirk garrison, General Plantey, to operate from Douai. This consisted of a brigade of French territorial infantry, a squadron of Goumiers (Algerian volunteer cavalry) and a battery of 65mm guns. Samson and his force of automobiles were attached to this force, while he came under the formal command of Brigadier-General Sir G. Aston who had arrived in Dunkirk with both the Brigade of Royal Marines, previously been sent to Ostend, and the Queen's Own Oxfordshire Hussars. On 22 September they moved by road and train to Douai. Samson was sent out on the Valenciennes road and had covered about a quarter of the distance to that town, as far as the village of Lewarde, when he was informed that there were Germans in Aniche, halfway to Valenciennes. He attempted to creep around the town to cut the Germans off, but the clamorous welcome the citizens gave his little force revealed their presence and a brisk action took place. Samson won the skirmish, but withdrew to Lewarde with his wounded when German reinforcements were reported. A steam tram ran between Lewarde and Aniche, and Samson asked the driver for news of the enemy there. The tram plied its regular route, bringing back fresh intelligence with each trip – there were about 300 Germans in Aniche who withdrew that evening. On 24 September the battalion of the 6th Territorials in Orchies, north-east of Douai, came under fierce attack. Samson was sent to lend support with his small, nine-automobile force and joined a detachment of some forty 'grandads' outside the town. This combined force did what they could with great valour, but by the end of the day had to pull back to Douai. A further Allied foray the next day had some small success, but was recalled when Douai itself came under attack. Arras was Samson's next destination and there he found a battalion of infantry and a squadron of cavalry apparently acting as flank guard for a French division marching to Lens. General Plantey knew nothing of their presence, typical of the confusion that made operations so difficult in the region.

In the Somme region, 26 September saw a renewal of the German attacks south of Péronne as far as Roye, and north of Péronne as far as Bapaume, where the 2nd Bavarians went into action. For the French the morning went well; north of the river Somme itself the 11th Infantry Division of XX Corps seized Combles, but later in the day the newly arrived Bavarians gave them serious problems. The French High Command's reaction to Castelnau's claim that the situation remained volatile was to question the wisdom of de-training troops as far away as Amiens to strengthen the front at Bapaume, but the movement of French troops from the east continued to Amiens, Arras, Lens and towards Lille as the operations of the Second Army became defensive. The BEF was still on the Aisne front, but now Sir John French asked Joffre to agree to moving it to the Flanders area, closer to the supply lines from England.

On 28 September the fighting on the Second Army front was in the Mametz to Montauban area and Contalmaison was lost to the Germans. On 29 September Fricourt was taken by the German 40th Reserve Infantry Regiment. When they had entered the village, having endured shellfire as they advanced, Oberleutnant Gutsch recalled how pleased they had been with themselves; they had made a satisfying advance under heavy fire and were buoyant with anticipation of fresh victories. They were, he noted, to be disappointed.

The French experience of fighting here in September and early October was terrifying and exhausting, as Marcel Riser of the 329th Regiment of Infantry wrote to his father, Albert, on 8 December:

> While on the Marne everyone had terrible diarrhoea – even boiling all water was no good. On the Somme we are not much troubled by illness – more by simple fatigue. We left Lisieux on 13 September, via Paris, marching to the Gare de l'Est, cheered by the Parisians… On the Somme we had no rest for three weeks, fighting hard. The whole 53rd Division was moved by motor car by way of Compiègne – we went to the Albert/Fricourt/Mametz sector. We did fourteen days in the front line trenches without a break. The food was cold because the cook-house was four kilometres to the rear, at Méault [just south

of Albert]. We had rain and fog, maybe not because of the time of year but of the proximity of the marshes of the Somme. We twice attacked the village of Mametz and twice were met with tough resistance. The 'Caïsonette' [pillbox] at the cemetery was occupied by German machine-gunners we thought we had destroyed. We hadn't.

Riser went on to send the news of his appointment as an auxiliary medical orderly and closed telling how cold the weather was and how he needed warm clothes. There are few indications of dates or places in his, or many others' letters home, which makes it difficult to relate first-hand witness to precise events, but the nature of what he experienced is clear.

On the other side of the Bapaume to Albert road both the French and the Germans closed on the Ancre valley and the village of Thiepval to the east, standing on the edge of the abrupt drop to the river. The French territorials had arrived on 27 September in the morning mist. As they advanced into and through Authille, tense with apprehension of a possible German presence, a grey figure was seen banging in a fence support on the ridge to the north, and the nervous 'grandads' opened fire. It was not until evening that they learned they had killed Boromée Vaquette who had merely been safeguarding his cattle. The German 51st Reserve Infantry Brigade were moving into Thiepval at the same time. The village itself was not disputed, but the Germans found that the river crossings had been secured and the French were firmly installed in Thiepval Wood. The villagers, Leutnant Koehler reported, were anxious but not particularly hostile. Indeed, the priest gave them quite useful information about the Ancre valley. However, their attempt to advance into Authille met vigorous resistance and the commanding general himself was forced to retire by French shellfire. Koehler also wrote:

> Every one of us who was in the park and château of Thiepval on this day will always have pleasant, somewhat nostalgic, memories of this property. In the excellently maintained park, dotted with magnificent trees, which was entered via great wrought iron gates, the château rose behind a broad expanse of lawn... Its interior bore witness to the best of French taste and refined elegance.

During the following night an officer who had been reconnoitring the river valley rushed back to report a French advance from the direction of Hamel. In the early hours of the next day gunfire broke out and the Prussian cavalry which had turned up the previous evening made itself scarce, but their machine-guns were made over to the infantry. Nothing more happened that night. The next day attempts by the French XI and XX Corps to take the plateau above the river Ancre at Thiepval failed. On the Somme front the old men of the Territorial Group, the 81st, 82nd, 84th and 88th Territorial Divisions, faced von Marwitz's cavalry and the German XIV Reserve Corps infantrymen and while they failed to gain the plateau or retake Fricourt, they held their line. Castelnau's forces had stalled. Joffre had lost confidence in him, and in order to maintain movement on the left wing appointed General Louis Comte de Maud'huy to command a 'detachment of the army' independent of Castelnau. He was given Conneau's cavalry corps and four divisions, some hurried to this sector from the east. The 19th and 20th Divisions joined his force and the 'Division Barbot', 12,000 men strong and named after its chasseur general, quit the Vosges front on 30 September to travel to Artois. These were mountain fighters, men of the 97th and 159th Chasseurs Alpins in their vast black berets, and four battalions of Chasseurs à Pied with them, the men who had halted the crack Gebirgsjäger regiments in the east above Colmar. Finally there was the 70th Reserve Division, General Marie Emile Fayolle's men who had stopped Rupprecht before Nancy. Maud'huy's orders were to base himself on Arras and attack the German flank. It is clear that Joffre was ill-informed about the developments in northern France.

On 29 September Major Armstrong telephoned Commander Samson to tell him that the situation at Douai, which was defended by 5,000 infantry and a battery of artillery, was becoming unsustainable. Samson set off at once with two armoured cars and three touring cars. General Plantey sent him to reconnoitre Orchies, where he had a brief encounter with an unseen enemy before returning to Douai. The defenders were all within the walls of the town and there were virtually no outposts. Plantey decided to pull out of Douai to defend the high ground to the west, but while most of his force was assembled in the great square, the Germans got into the town and opened fire on them. Late in the afternoon news came that the Pont d'Esquerchin, the bridge carrying the road west over the river Scarpe, had been taken. Samson undertook to retake it. With French infantry declining to follow, his automobiles set off for the bridge. Samson later wrote:

> I must confess that as we went along this road I certainly thought that here was the end of our little party; and I felt very guilty at bringing Armstrong, Goode, and the other fine fellows to death for no purpose except to keep up the Pride of the Service.

They were in fact so angry with the French infantry that they were in a ferocious mood. The Marines spread out and a hail of rifle and machine-gun fire was showered onto the Germans. Passion did not lend itself to accurate marksmanship, but the very volume of fire forced the enemy to fall back. Pushing forward, they ran into another fire-fight which lasted a quarter of an hour. In the meantime, behind them, French infantry were pouring out of Douai; about half of the garrison escaped the trap. Samson, with eight men wounded then returned to his base near Béthune and reported to Major-General Sir Archibald Paris, who had taken over from General Aston. In November that year Samson received a letter from General Plantey, thanking him for his action and conveying the thanks of General Maud'huy as well. Arras, however, was now facing encirclement.

Von Falkenhayn was energetically thinning his armies to the east in order to build his right flank in Belgium and northern France, still hoping to outflank the French. From von Kluck's First Army came the IV Corps, the 18th Brigade from the Seventh Army and, from von Bülow, the Prussian Guard. From the Lorraine front came the XIV Corps, destined for Arras, the IV Cavalry Corps and the Bavarian cavalry division together with, similar to the French, various battalions of mountain troops, which were moved to Mons.

The movement of the British was, Joffre felt, too leisurely, and he urged Field Marshal French not to wait until his reinforcements were all present but to proceed with all speed to General Maud'huy's left flank. The BEF was recovering from the retreat from Mons and the battles on the Marne and the Aisne during which it had sustained 15 per cent casualties. Sir John French was deeply concerned for his men and sought to give them respite. The 6th Division had arrived on the Aisne on 16 September and the Indian Corps disembarked at Marseilles on 26 September, but more troops were needed. The battle for Arras raged in the first week of October, but the BEF did not move from Abbeville to St Pol until 9 October. Meanwhile, on 6 October, General Sir Henry Rawlinson's 7th Division, together with the 3rd Cavalry Division and sixty-nine guns, was disembarking at Ostend and Zeebrugge in Belgium on their way to relieve the siege of Antwerp, which fell three days later. Rawlinson then had to command a retreat to what would become the Ypres Salient. The British, therefore, would have no hand in the developments around Arras and the Vimy Ridge, which helped to shape the Western Front.

The German attack on 2 October from Douai was intended to come from both north and south using the 1st Bavarians and von Marwitz's cavalry. In the north, near Lens, Fayolle's 70th Division opposed them, and in the centre and on the right was Barbot, with X Corps to the south. The fight was terrible in its ferocity. German artillery inflicted massive casualties on the mountain troops, but they held. The territorials of X Corps faced the Prussians and also held. From all sides Maud'huy was beset with pleas for reinforcements – reinforcements that he did not have. The battle continued on 3 October, with a Bavarian assault towards Vimy and Notre-Dame-de-Lorette. Fayolle had received fresh troops, but their chief task was to cover the arrival of a new army corps, the 21st, which Joffre had sent to Maud'huy's force. On the X Corps front to the south, Courcelles-le-Comte and Achiet-le-Petit were lost and General Brugère begged to get relief for his exhausted territorials who had now been in the thick of the battle for eight days. Rupprecht's eyes were on his right flank where arrivals from the eastern front could make the difference, and from where von Marwitz could penetrate between Lens and Lille. Indeed, the optimism encouraged Kaiser Wilhelm II to visit St Quentin, Rupprecht's headquarters, on 4 October to enjoy the anticipated success. By ten o'clock that night the heights of the Vimy Ridge were in German hands. Arras was now threatened with being entirely surrounded, and the liaison between the infantry and cavalry on the French left had broken down. On the town's southern flank a gap was opening between the Territorial Group and X Corps. The Prussian Guard had virtually broken the poor 81st Territorial Division and its commander, General Marcot, had been killed. With the Bavarians to the north and the Prussians to the south, Maud'huy exclaimed that he was facing a Sedan – the ghastly French defeat during the Franco-Prussian War in 1870.

Marshal Joffre took immediate and dramatic action. From 4 October Maud'huy's 'detachment' was formally severed from Castlenau's command to become the Tenth Army. Further, Joffre created the Northern Army Group and put General Ferdinand Foch in command – a man dedicated to the concept of the 'offensive spirit'. He was energetic and flexible and had had the task of conducting the pre-war discussions with the British Army, which was a vital adjunct to the force for which he was now responsible. His mission, acting as assistant to the commander-in-chief, was to coordinate the actions of the Second Army of Castelnau, the Tenth Army of Maud'huy and the Territorial Divisions Group of General Brugère. By 9.30am on 5 October Maud'huy had planned to order the 31st Infantry Division to cover an evacuation of Arras. At that moment Foch arrived at his headquarters in Aubigny. The exchange between the two men was dramatic. 'I know of only three ways to fight!' cried Foch. 'Attack, resist or scram! Choose between the first two!'

The mood at Rupprecht's headquarters had darkened; reports from the front line had become infrequent and unclear. The impetus was falling away and the expected progress was not coming to pass. The summit of Bouvigny, the north-western end of the Vimy Ridge, had not fallen. The Kaiser departed. The 1st Bavarians suffered heavily under French artillery fire and consolidated round Balleuil, 5 miles (8 kilometres) north-east of Arras. On the southern flank the Prussian Guard gathered itself to break through but was redirected by Rupprecht who feared that this flank would become disorganised. The alternatives soon became irrelevant when the advance stopped short at Beaumetz, south-west of the town and the Bavarian effort expired at Carency, south of Souchez. Both flanks of the new Tenth Army had stiffened their resolve and on the evening of 6 October von Falkenhayn decided his energies were best directed further north, through southern Belgium. The losses of the Tenth Army had been very great. Of the 12,000 men comprising Barbot's mountain troops for example, only 3,000 remained in the field.

On 10 October Antwerp finally capitulated and the Belgians were forced back to the south-western coast of their ravaged country. The action developed in Belgium and the extreme north of France, where Falkenhayn still hoped to achieve victory by outflanking his opponents rather than by seizing the coast. The Belgians, French and British had to fight to the very limits of their resources before they stopped the Germans during the First Battle of Ypres. By mid-November the shape of the front had been formed, running from the Belgian coast at Nieuport, around a salient centred on Ypres, east of Arras and Albert, on southwards to the Aisne and east past Verdun to the Swiss border. The war of movement was over, but neither men nor commanders appreciated that the trenches they were now digging were anything more than a temporary expedient from which they would spring forth once more to experience what the German writer Wilhelm Groener called 'fresh, joyful open warfare.'

The effect of the creation of this front was a disaster for France. The great concentration of her industrial strength was now behind the German line. Three-quarters of French coal and coke production, eighty per cent of her iron, sixty per cent of her steel and a substantial portion of other heavy industrial output came from the occupied territory. It was mandatory for the future growth and health of the country that the enemy be ejected as soon as possible. The material losses of the first few weeks of the war had been massive. Ten per cent of French field guns were gone and half a million rifles were missing. What is more, shortage of ammunition for the artillery and the infantry had hampered recent operations. This was a crippling blow to continued resistance,

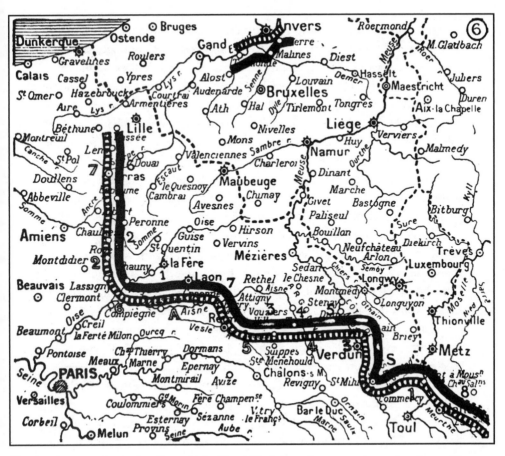

The situation on 30 September. General Maud'huy's Tenth Army is erroneously numbered 7 on this map. *From* l'Illustration, *Paris, 1915. (HGG)*

but resistance, attack and ultimate victory was the only policy that could be accepted. The French had only fifteen days' supply of shells by the end of September, but fortunately for the Allies the German situation was no better – by mid-November Falkenhayn estimated that only four days' supply remained. It had become evident that the industrial abilities of the opposing sides would play a crucial part in deciding the outcome of the conflict.

In place of the shallow scrapes that the men had made in the first days here, both sides deepened and improved their shelter. This sometimes involved repositioning the line as the original diggings were the result of the accident of battle and often failed to give an outlook of advantage or cover from enemy fire. The topsoil on the rolling uplands of the Somme region is clay, peppered with flints, overlying the chalk beneath, with alluvial soil in the river valleys.

The thickness of the topsoil varies between 3 feet and, in some places, 20 feet. The design of trenches became a matter of importance. A continuous, straight line of trench would have maximised the damage of a shell exploding in it, so trenches ran for a short way – a 'bay' eighteen to thirty feet long – before a buttress was left, taking the trench in a U-shaped diversion between 9 feet and 12 feet long, to stop enfilade fire (someone shooting from the flank, along the line of the trench) or shell blast sending shell fragments rattling along it. When the terrain permitted, the same effect could be obtained by digging in 'dog-legs', or if the position required it, the buttress could be made to jut forwards to give an opportunity of enfilading fire being brought to bear on an attacker. This front line fortification was joined to a support line trench by communication trenches, and in front of the complex, barbed wire was strung in bands up to 30 feet wide, with narrow spaces left for patrols to get out into the no-man's-land that divided one side from the other. The trenches were furnished with dugouts and, where possible, deeper chambers for sleeping, shelter from shell-fire and for daily living. The Germans, intending to stay in place, used a good deal of concrete to make pillboxes and observation posts. Both sides revetted their diggings, that is, faced the exposed soil with wood or corrugated iron, where necessary. The French did this more rarely, perhaps deeming it to be smacking of long-term occupation. The systems developed by the different armies reflected their approaches to the task before them. French lines had a front line and a single support line trench, with the front line divided into fully manned and sentry-only sections, the former using enfilading fire to defend the latter. These were positions from which they planned to attack and drive the invader from their land. The British manned their front lines continuously, and were dissatisfied with the defences that their allies left for them when taking over a new front. Further, the French had superior provision of field artillery and so were content to rely on two trench lines plus supporting guns, while the British preferred to dig themselves a third support line. The terrain, of course, had an effect. In the waterlogged area of Flanders it was sometimes impossible to dig down at all, so sandbags and earth-filled gabions formed parapets. In the mountains of the Vosges, trenches were either cut in the living rock, or a series of pillboxes were built to form the front. The chalk terrain of the Somme permitted deep and elaborate diggings to those who sought to build permanent defences; but permanence was not the Allies' wish – they planned to throw the invaders out. As the lines grew in complexity and sophistication, the inhabitants of the area were forced to leave, their fields despoiled and their villages flattened by artillery.

The last of the villagers were evacuated from Thiepval on 1 November. The German 26th Reserve Division had thirty-five men, forty-five women and twenty-five children taken away, leaving the 180th Infantry Regiment in sole occupation. Orders were given to avoid being seen or heard moving about in the village, not to make smoke by cooking in the houses and to avoid gathering in a vulnerable group in the village church.

The topsoil formed a water-retaining cap to the free-draining chalk. On 5 November Corporal Gustav Sack of the 1st Bavarian Infantry wrote to his wife from Hardecourt-aux-Bois, south-west of Combles to complain of the muck and the labour of digging through the clinging mud in continuous rain – he had been a week in this mire.

German defences at Thiepval were already well developed. Here the overlying *Limons des Plateaux*, the clay-with-flint cap on the chalk, is thicker than elsewhere, making the area notably muddy in wet weather, but the critiques of the works completed so far made no particular mention of drainage. On 10 November the full inspection of the defences resulted in a list of necessary improvements. The chalk thrown up in digging trenches had to be covered in soil to conceal the positions, banked-up earth rounded to disguise the defences and the communication trenches dug deeper. All trenches were to be brick-lined and all overhead cover for dugouts and machine-gun positions made thicker. The signposting was to be improved and the troops trained to know their way about, who their supporting units were and what the range was of key reference points to their front. The wire in front had to be strengthened and the listening posts connected to the command posts by bell-pulls to give the alarm. The sanitary arrangements came in for severe censure. Already it was clear that the position was planned to be as comfortable as possible to occupy and as effective as could be devised for defence.

These precautions were soon put to the test. On 17 December the French Tenth Army was launched in an attack on the Arras front and a secondary assault by the Second Army was undertaken on the Somme front. Near Montauban a signals corporal of the 3rd Battalion, 40th Infantry Reserve Regiment, found himself virtually isolated in a storm of French shellfire. The town hall was destroyed and doors and windows blown out. The phone wires to the front line were cut, but Fernsprechunteroffzier Elperstedt managed to get through to his artillery to plead for shellfire to be directed on the French troops attacking Carnoy Copse. The artillery were reluctant to use more ammunition, but eventually complied. Several salvoes followed and Elperstedt remarked that the French were scattered, making excellent targets for their machine-gunners.

A private soldier in the 111th Reserve Infantry Regiment wrote of that day after coming out of the line just before Christmas. Xavier Schilling had been close to Fricourt and reported that he had heard a French trumpet call at about six in the morning and that the attackers had been revealed in the searchlights, coming ever closer, bayonets gleaming. The Germans fired frantically, but the French came as close as thirty metres before they were halted. The shellfire continued for six hours. All they could do was cower in their trenches and hope. The following day more shelling resumed. By the end of the fourth day half a dozen of Schilling's comrades were crouched with him in a single hole, the rest of their trenching entirely destroyed.

The fighting enveloped La Boiselle, Mametz and Fricourt and caused substantial casualties. In terms of territorial gain, the effect on the German line was negligible and the French had lost perhaps as many as 500 men killed and hundreds wounded to no purpose. Near Mametz an informal truce was agreed. Leutnant Westermann of the 40th Reserve Infantry Regiment saw a Red Cross flag and cautiously stood up to investigate. He feared a trick, but as the flag drew closer he went forward, making a show of stepping over his own barbed wire to impress the fact that it had not been comprehensively smashed. A French medical orderly accompanied by two teams of stretcher-bearers approached and said they were going to collect wounded in no-man's-land. Westermann consented to a short truce and the French went about their task, collecting five wounded who had been lying out there for more than a day. The German officer occupied himself with making observations about his enemy's defences. After a little while both returned to their own lines.

Maurice Le Poitevin and the 205th Regiment saw service on this front late in the year. His regiment was at Vaux, south of Maricourt. When they got there, the villagers told them of their surprise when the Germans had arrived there in the summer. They had mistaken the invaders for British troops, and welcomed them with open arms. 'Yes, English!' the Germans had responded, roaring with laughter. The French position overlooked the river Somme where it flowed south from Curlu before turning west once more at Eclusier, where, from the east, the canal joined the river. The valley here is a broad, marshy feature through which the river meanders and digresses through countless side-streams around innumerable little islands. As a front line it is ideal – the enemy cannot approach. Indeed, Le Poitevin's sentinel duty consisted of listening and looking for boats which might have been carrying attackers. While there, Le Poitevin recounts:

The section was chosen to furnish a squad for the execution of some poor fellow who had shot himself in the hand to get out of this job… Luckily I was not picked… When they got back Leroy told me about it down to the last detail with complete indifference.

At Christmas Le Poitevin became a stretcher-bearer and his companions joked that he'd now have an even worse time picking up their remains.

Christmas came. Parcels and letters arrived. Soldiers made the best of things to celebrate the festival, which for the Germans was an especially moving occasion. Grenadier Thimian of the 1st Grenadier Guard Regiment wrote of the 24 and 25 December, telling of the brewing of hot toddy and the eating of cakes before going on watch. The night was cold, frosty and star-lit, and the next day clear:

Up until the afternoon of Christmas Day, everything was noticeably quiet, then occurred something I shall never forget. I was on guard, when I suddenly noticed a Frenchman had climbed onto the parapet of his trench. I had just taken aim when I noticed one of our men had climbed out too. The two of them advanced step by step towards each other and shook hands. The others from both sides followed their example. The Frenchmen, who were mostly old, looked ill-nourished and poorly clothed. They begged for tobacco. We chatted for forty-five minutes then we all returned quietly to our respective trenches.

From Mametz, to the south, the greeting the French sent came in the form of more shellfire. To the north, halfway between Albert and Arras at Bucquoy, the New Year's Eve sermon being preached to the 1st Grenadier Guard Regiment was cut short by the outbreak of shellfire. Captain von Graese was hurrying back to his house when a shell hit it. Groping about in the smoke of the explosion he stumbled across the corpse of one of the musicians from the Elizabeth Regiment. His head was missing. The shell had killed twenty men and left another thirty wounded. Not a happy new year.

The casualties suffered had been heavy on both sides, but comparisons are not easy because of differences in designations and methods of reporting. 'Combat casualties' means, in official records, the numbers killed, wounded, missing or made prisoner; that is, losses of all kinds to an army's strength excluding sickness, desertion and the like. In operations in France in what became known as 'the race to the sea', and thus excluding the Battle of Ypres, it appears that the British lost some 16,000 men and thirty-eight guns; of these

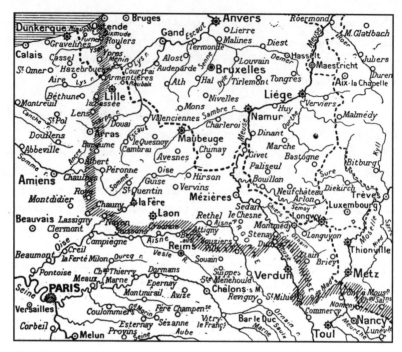

The Western Front from Nieuport to Nancy. *From* l'Illustration, *Paris, 1915. (HGG)*

casualties 1,700 were attributed to the Battle of the Marne. The French figures are disputed. At the Marne they probably came to some 80,000. It was a figure close to this that was first given as the total for the whole of 1914 on this front, listing the casualties in the east separately. Later figures raised that to 104,000 but in 1919 Louis Marin announced in the Chamber of Deputies, that 140,000 men had become casualties, 125,000 of them in October and November. For all fronts the French loss was nearly 300,000 men in 1914. The German right wing suffered about 66,000 from total losses in France of some 235,000. They also lost about sixty guns. While the British figure is small in comparison, it is significant when considered in the context of a total force numbering only about 120,000 men. What is more, nearly 650 officers had been lost. All this to create nothing but deadlock – a continuous line of trenches from the North Sea to the Swiss border.

Chapter 2

A New Kind of War: 1915–16

A static war was something for which the generals on both sides were unprepared. Their experience was of wars of manoeuvre – combinations of infantry and cavalry movement with artillery support. The impact of new weapons on military thinking was still superficial although the immediate practical use of such weapons was understood. They had at their disposal artillery of a power formerly undreamed of: heavy field guns and even huge naval guns mounted on railway trucks, capable of firing immense explosive shells with uncanny accuracy for many miles. Indeed, so impressed were they that reliance on artillery power and an over-estimation of what it could achieve led to serious tactical errors. It was, however, the invention of the American, Hiram Maxim, that made the trench system so easy to defend. Maxim devised a gun in which the recoil on discharge both powered the ejection of the spent cartridge and reloaded the weapon, which was thus capable of continuous fire. From this, the British developed the Vickers, the Germans the Maxim and the French the St-Etienne. All three had water-cooled barrels and were capable of firing at a rate of 500 rounds per minute. This rate was somewhat academic as the Vickers and the Maxim feed belts held 250 rounds and the St-Etienne's 300, but all were capable of laying down a withering hail of bullets. Their weight, with their mountings, made them hard to handle in mobile situations (the Vickers weighed in at 30.8 kilograms, 68 pounds, and the Maxim at a massive 52 kilograms, 115 pounds) but for beating off an infantry attack they could scarcely be bettered. Other systems were also employed, such as the gas-operated Browning perfected by Colt and adopted by the Americans by the end of the war, and the French Hotchkiss, an air-cooled gas-operated weapon brought into service before the war.

Lighter machine-guns, such as the British Lewis, a gun invented by another American, Colonel Isaac Lewis in 1911, were suited to more mobile use and were also mounted in aircraft. This gun had the advantage of using the same .303 ammunition as the British Lee-Enfield rifle and the Vickers machine-gun, fed from a circular pan. This simplified the problem of supplying ammunition to troops in the firing line. By the end of the war the Germans had introduced the first sub-machine-guns for use by the storm-troopers. The French light machine-gun was the Chauchat, which was issued to the Americans when they joined the war in 1917. Sergeant Donald D. Kyler of the 16th Infantry, 1st Division wrote about it in his memoir and gives a good idea of what such weapons were like to use:

We were issued one French chauchat machine rifle to each squad. By machine rifle, I mean those weapons which shoot continuously as long as the trigger is pulled or the ammunition supply lasts. The term, automatic rifle, means those weapons which when fired, automatically load another cartridge into the chamber ready to be fired again when the trigger is pulled.

The chauchat rifle weighed over twenty pounds and was recoil operated. Ammunition was supplied to it in spring loaded magazines. The magazine could be quickly attached to the gun by spring latches, and held twenty rounds of French rifle cartridges. One gun could shoot more shots than all the rest of the squad combined for short periods. So it added a lot to our fire power. But it was not accurate at over a few yards, was too heavy, too clumsy to aim, and in general not effective except against very close concentrated targets. About a year later those rifles were replaced by American made Browning machine rifles, which were an improvement.

The Browning weapon was lighter than the chauchat, with an adjustable rate of fire, could be shot singly or in short bursts, and used our own rifle cartridges. The regular magazine held twenty rounds, but magazines were available that held forty rounds. It was a good weapon, but with the same limitations as the chauchat, and had a few faults of its own. One was that it fired too fast on automatic, resulting in the loss of very effective aim. Another was that of frequent jams in the mechanism, and the loss of its use until the jam could be corrected. A little sand or mud getting into the chamber or magazine could cause a malfunction. Also, the gas port sometimes became clogged, causing failure of the extraction and ejection mechanism, which was gas operated. However, in spite of their faults, those weapons were very effective at close range concentrated targets.

In the early years of the war the heavy machine-guns dominated the trench lines and their power was not countered until a new fighting machine was deployed.

Fortifying the Somme

The new year, 1915, began with severe frost so although uncomfortable for the troops, it was at least dry underfoot. It did not last. Heavy rain was soon turning the trenches into streams and the unrevetted sides into landslides. Lieutenant Franz Demmel of the Bavarian Infantry-Liebregiment recalled that communication trenches were often knee-deep in water and the dugouts leaked so badly that many men took the risk of remaining in the open. Attempts to do repair and improvement work were frustrated by the downpour. Luckily, he pointed out, the French were in exactly the same situation. Their supplies were being brought up across the open country, avoiding the flooded trenches, and each side turned a blind eye to the work of the other in the performance of basic survival tasks.

Work on German trenches introduced improved drainage and more sophisticated design, whereas the French were less keen to make their fortifications any more than jumping-off points for attacks. The Germans sometimes detected the preparations for these raids and mounted their own assaults on the gathering enemy before they could move. On 17 January an observer of the German 60th Infantry Regiment noticed that the French trenches were becoming more crowded than normal and the call went out for volunteers – the chance to win an Iron Cross. Armed with daggers and grenades, three men, Koch, Wonziakowski and Selden, crawled out into the darkness of no-man's-land near Chaulnes, using the railway embankment for cover. The grenades were hurled into the French trench, from which shouts, screams and a blaze of gunfire emanated as the raiders sped back to their own lines. In the morning a white cloth fluttered from the French barbed wire where Musketeer Selden had tied it to taunt his adversaries.

Particularly foul was the human debris of the previous year. No-man's-land, the narrow strip of ground between the opposing trench lines, was defiled with the bodies of the slain. Not only was the scene demoralising in the extreme, but the corpses were attracting hordes of rats. In the heavily disputed area near Lihons, west of the town of Chaulnes, the 6th Company, 269th Reserve Infantry tried to do something about their fallen comrades of the invasion force. The French, Musketeer Wassilowski alleged, would not cooperate, though he does not explain how they tried to arrange matters. On a day when fog shrouded the area, permission was given for small groups to go out to gather up personal possessions, identify the fallen and see what could be done to bury them. On 11 February Sergeant-Major Manthey of 1st Company managed to bury thirty-six rotting corpses, most of whom they succeeded in identifying.

With the lines of trenches winding across the Somme country, both sides began to seek ways to penetrate and pass the enemy defences. The raids across open country were terribly costly and the action moved underground. The terrain in the northern sector, from Beaumont-Hamel past La Boiselle and south to Fricourt and Mametz was particularly suited to tunnelling as the chalk that underlies the clay is easily worked. On the plain south of the Somme, similar conditions encouraged similar activity around Dompierre. The task was dangerous and the conditions appalling. The work began in December 1914 and by January, near La Boissele, the farm the Germans called La Granathof (later known to the British as the Glory Hole) on the road coming from Albert became a subterranean battleground. The sappers of the 1st Bavarian Engineer Regiment dug eight tunnels at shallow depth towards the objective and, on 5 January, heard French sappers at work close by. They loaded 300 kilograms (660 pounds) of explosive into their gallery and, having filled in 9 metres (30 feet) of tunnel, blew it up. The French workings were destroyed, together with another German tunnel. New diggings were undertaken and on 12 January the French were caught a second time with a charge twice the size. Bodies and parts of bodies were hurled through the air. That was not the end of the fight here; on 18 January the 120th Reserve Infantry Regiment attacked the French 65th Infantry, wiping out the 7th and 8th Companies and capturing three officers and 104 men. No ground of significance was lost or gained.

The French did not let the matter rest. A new gallery was made and filled with explosives, but on the night of 8–9 March a breath of fresh air was felt in a gallery being worked by the Bavarians. Officer Deputy Heinz was summoned to investigate and discovered a narrow gap through which the draught was coming from a large open space beyond. He made the hole bigger and saw a stack of packets marked with the name of a French explosive and the tunnel beyond closed off – a mine ready to be ignited. The surrounding galleries were cleared and eight volunteers went into the tunnel, enlarged the hole through to the French mine and began work. The device might be blown at any minute. Hand to hand came the packets. Time ticked by. Sweat ran into their eyes. All that was to be heard was their quiet breathing. At last, after forty-five minutes of incredible strain and tension, the firing cables were exposed and cut.

The tunnelling and counter-tunnelling continued. On 12 April the French succeeded in blowing a mine south of Fricourt. Dr Niedenthal, the medical officer with 1st Battalion, 110th Reserve Infantry, witnessed the result. A vast roar filled the air and the ground shook beneath their feet. The roofs of their dugouts began to cave in. The German sappers scrambled from their workings but left fifteen dead behind them. The crater was 20 metres (65 feet) wide and 8 metres (26 feet) deep. The communication trenches had been wrecked and Dr Niedenthal was forced to hazard the open ground as he rushed forward to assist the wounded. The largest dugout had been blown in with more than a dozen men in it. Their comrades worked furiously to free them. Soon they came across the body of their platoon commander, smothered by the earthfall. Then, as they dug deeper into the buried shelter, their hopes soared at the sight of twelve men sitting in a row against the wall. Their horror and dismay felt at finding that these unmarked men were all dead can be imagined.

The Germans' industry in developing their defences continued without pause. With a stable front line and steadily growing complex of entrenchments, they were able to plan for the protection of a known frontage. Each artillery battery was responsible for a specific defensive fire zone and the infantry officer holding the relevant trench frontage knew which battery that was. Swift liaison could bring down a curtain of protective fire on an attacker, it was hoped. In the early days the artillery was not dense enough to cover the whole of a given fire zone, so exercises were held to train the infantry to supply precise information about the target to be engaged. As liaison officers were in short supply, promising men were promoted from the ranks to link up with their gunner comrades, developing understanding and confidence. Communications were steadily improved to become effective by day or night.

As spring arrived the German trench systems grew even more sophisticated and powerful. Trenches were fitted with drainage and dugouts were made even deeper, while the extent and complexity of the second and third lines and the connecting communication trenches spread across the countryside. Trench mortars and grenade launchers were added to the defences. Barbed wire was strung in cunning formations to herd attackers into channels covered by machine-guns ready to fire on fixed lines. Reserve Lieutenant Franz Demmel of the Bavarian Infantry Liebregiment described the conditions facing Maricourt in early April as being relatively satisfactory for physical protection against shellfire, but plagued with rats, which were half the size of rabbits, he claimed.

As the digging, shelling and sniper fire continued on this 'quiet' front, attempts to break out of the stalemate were being made elsewhere in the enduring challenge of mastering a new kind of warfare.

Learning to Attack Trench Lines

The German line on the Western Front was sustained by the railway network they had managed to secure in 1914, extending from Antwerp in the north, through Lille, Cambrai, Hirson and Sedan to Metz in the east. As part of a plan to disrupt it and win back an area of economic importance, Joffre required the British to go east of the Aubers Ridge. The village of Neuve Chapelle was the first objective.

The new British First Army, under General Sir Douglas Haig, was to attack with Sir Henry Rawlinson's IV Corps and Sir James Willock's Indian Army Corps. Air photography and careful targeting of artillery helped in a thirty-five minute preparation for the infantry advance at 0805 hours on 10 March. High explosive shells were in short supply, and the shrapnel that was used instead only destroyed the barbed wire in random sections of the line, so it happened that the Garhwal Brigade and 25th Brigades were able to advance quickly, but the 23rd was halted by the wire and became a helpless target for German fire. The artillery barrage, which was intended to prevent German counter-attacks, also prevented the British and Indians from exploiting their advantage. Messages could only be sent to the rear by a runner. When the barrage lifted, the Germans had been able to reinforce the flanks and their artillery shelled the men now crowded into the centre where they had waited for orders to advance. It was too late in the day when, at 1500 hours, Rawlinson was well enough informed to order the attempt to reach Aubers. Strong-points set up by the Germans had already stopped them.

The assault was renewed the next day, but fog obscured the field for artillery spotters and the British shelling was largely wasted. Some costly progress was made, but as there was no provision for liaison between neighbouring units in the front line, messages had to be sent back to HQ, across to the next unit's HQ and back to the front to coordinate operations. On 12 March the Germans themselves attacked, but their artillery fire at 0430 hours was no more accurate than that of the British the previous day. As the German infantry, in drill-book lines, assaulted the untouched British trenches, they were methodically shot down. The British took an important strong-point, Mauquissart, and sent a message back to say so. The British artillery fire continued as if the Germans were still in occupation and the position had to be abandoned. Eventually the message reached British HQ and at 1430, with fresh artillery support, the attack on the Aubers Ridge began, too late to surprise the enemy. Haig soon called it off.

The experience had shown that, with surprise and speed, an attack could succeed in the first instance, but that keeping it up was prevented by poor communications and excessive centralisation of control. Sir John French complained of the lack of heavy shells, and the newspapers in England took this up, contributing to the misleading idea that longer and fiercer artillery barrages, rather than better artillery and infantry coordination, were the solution. Haig, on the other hand, demanded a lighter machine-gun for use by infantry on the move. The Lewis gun would supply this need. The battle's limited success held many lessons. It had cost the BEF some 13,000 casualties and the Germans a similar number.

General Rawlinson noted his own conclusions:

> The enemy are not yet sufficiently demoralised to hunt them with cavalry... What we want to do now is what I call, 'bite and hold'. Bite off a piece of the enemy's line ... and hold it against counter attack. The bite can be made without much loss, and, if we choose the right place and make every preparation to put it quickly into a state of defence, there ought to be no difficulty in holding it against the enemy's counter-attacks, and in inflicting on him at least twice the loss that we have suffered in making the bite.

Six weeks later the Germans made one of their rare attacks, experimenting with a new weapon, in the Ypres Salient. The Allies' front was held by the French – the 87th Territorial Division and the 45th Algerian Division – alongside the Canadian Division. At 1700 hours on 22 April the Germans opened the valves of 5,730 cylinders of gas, releasing 160 tons of chlorine to drift onto the French. A mild dose of this gas causes intense irritation of eyes and lungs; a heavy one fills the lungs with fluid and drowns the victim. The French had no defence and either fled or died. In half an hour the north of the Salient past Kitchener's Wood and down to the canal was open to the Germans. At Steenstraat they crossed over the canal and severed the link between the French and Belgians. The Canadians and some 500 Zouaves created a front north of St Julien and news of the huge gap in the line reached British Second Army headquarters where General Smith-Dorrien at once began sending whatever units he could find to Lieutenant-General Sir Edwin Alderson, who was in command of the Canadians. The Canadians fought stubbornly and, supported in the following days by a mixed, ad hoc force hastily thrown into battle, they prevented a German breakthrough and stabilised the line. The experiment with gas had shown its power, but also its limitations – more sophisticated chemicals and tactics would develop.

The experience of Neuve Chapelle suggested that a well-directed short bombardment could open the road for a penetrative attack. In May and June the French and British renewed their assaults on the Artois front – the French in an attempt to regain Vimy Ridge and the British to support them by making another attack on the Aubers Ridge. Two short British bombardments were to cut the wire before them at locations 3 miles (4.8 kilometres) apart, with the British VI Corps striking towards Fromelles while the Indian Corps was to advance immediately south of Neuve Chapelle to attain the ridge and then encircle the German positions on it. General Haig noted in his diary on 6 May that all commanders were satisfied with the adequacy of artillery fire provided.

The German defence line had, however, been transformed since March. Then there had been a single, unsophisticated trench line to break. In the weeks since, the trench had been reinforced with thousands of sandbags to create a robust parapet in the soggy landscape, barbed wire had been added generously to impede attackers and a series of v-shaped machine-gun emplacements had been spread all along the German front line. Aerial reconnaissance was still in its infancy and British intelligence had provided no indication of how formidable German defences had become.

The shelling began at 0450 hours on Sunday 9 May. After only forty minutes of bombardment by 637 guns, the infantry advanced. The 2nd Rifle Brigade, in front of Fromelles, suffered from 'shorts' – their own shellfire falling short and inflicting casualties on them – but none the less two companies dashed forward, found the wire destroyed and entered the German front line trench. Captain R. Berkeley said:

> ... B and D companies ... swept across to the German trench taking it in their stride and pushed on to the battalion objective, followed by A and C companies who occupied and consolidated the German trench. Battalion Headquarters crossed immediately behind the support companies but the enemy machine-gun fire was terrific and they had heavy casualties. The battalion machine-guns were unable to get across. Battalion Headquarters

were dispersed and the bombing [grenade] and blocking parties, so carefully organised beforehand, were at once broken up and could not be reassembled. Nevertheless, the task had been performed swiftly and well, and they were just enjoying the afterglow of success when they suddenly realised that, apart from a handful of the Royal Irish Rifles, they were entirely alone.

To their right the 1st Sherwood Foresters and 2nd Northamptonshires had been less fortunate; they were caught in the open against largely uncut wire. On the Rifles' left, the 2nd Lincolns suffered the same fate. Machine-gun fire forced them to ground and shellfire found them there.

South of Neuve Chapelle, the Indian Corps attack fared no better. The 1/4th Seaforth Highlanders assaulted the German positions at 0530 hours and were lying where they had fallen when the 2/3rd Gurkha Rifles had worked their way forward to the front line through shattering shellfire later in the day. The only gain from the action was the short section of line taken by the Rifle Brigade at the outset of the battle, which was regained by the Germans with a counter-attack on 10 May. Haig cancelled plans to renew the assault. British casualties, killed, wounded and missing, came to 458 officers and 11,621 men.

The brief bombardment and its alleged cause, the shortage of shells, led to reports in *The Times* newspaper that British soldiers (the loss of Indian lives appears to have been ignored) had died for lack of shells. It was a mighty public scandal. This added to the difficulties of the government in London and contributed to the growing belief at home that if enough shells and guns could be supplied the German lines could be reduced to ruins before the infantry even had to leave their trenches. The need for counter-battery fire to destroy enemy artillery, the need for a means of advancing against machine-gun fire and the need for improved intelligence received less attention.

General Haig drew his own conclusions, writing on 11 May that the German defences were so well built and the machine-gun deployment so complete that a long, methodical bombardment was needed to destroy them. To destroy the German supplies heavy guns would be used. Finally, to undermine enemy morale, the bombardment would go on all night. The attack at Festubert on 15 May followed a four-day bombardment. The day before the attack a ruse was attempted when the British put down a three-minute bombardment with rifle and machine-gun fire added to the howitzer shelling, followed by two minutes of silence and then two minutes of shrapnel and rifle fire in an attempt to hit the defenders who had manned the parapets during the silence. The result was not clear. The genuine assault took place half an hour before midnight in some confusion, but the German first and second lines were broken on a 3-mile (5-kilometre) front. But no breakthrough was achieved.

To the south, on the French front, Maurice Le Poitevin's medical unit was struggling to deal with the result of the assault on Vimy Ridge. He worked 'to take the broken bodies that had escaped the gruel of the battlefield and prolong their suffering in appalling transportation.' Then, moving forward to a captured trench, 'in shattered holes, amid a bloody soup and pulverised limbs, seek for what might still be living.'

The comparative quiet of the Somme front was shattered in June. The Second Battle of Ypres had ended in May, a month that cost the British 65,730 casualties. The French attacks on Vimy Ridge and the Aubers Ridge had been made at the astounding expense of 102,533 casualties, of whom only 2,463 had been made prisoners. To draw German strength away from these northerly fronts, the decision was taken to reduce a salient remaining in the line in the Somme sector. Between Serre and the village to the northwest across the valley, Hébuterne, the Prussian Guards had taken the farm of Toutvent in 1914. If the French could retake the position and the ridge to the east, their situation would be improved. Preparations for the assault did not go unnoticed. The Germans observed the increase in aircraft activity, the ranging of guns and the digging of approach saps in front of the farm. Their 52nd Infantry Division and 26th Reserve Division gathered their strength to resist.

The French shelling of the German trenches became heavy on the evening of 3 June and continued relentlessly through to Sunday 6 June, when the barrage falling on the 52nd Division's positions, and those of the 170th Infantry Regiment near Toutvent, became yet more intense. The division sent the message: 'Trenches utterly smashed. Expect attack tomorrow. Request artillery support.' On Monday morning the valley was shrouded in fog and, by the time the Germans were able to assess the situation, the French 137th Infantry Regiment had taken the farm and were advancing towards Serre. They were held off, and the next day an attempt to take the farm of La Louvière, a little to the north, also failed. But General Castelnau was not giving up. A new assault was planned from the direction of Mailly-Maillet, to the south-west, by men of the 101st Infantry Brigade.

Fog was thick on the morning of 10 June, and the French artillery failed to cut the barbed wire in front of the enemy positions. By now the Germans were fully prepared and, as the light improved from 5am onwards they brought down a heavy fire on the French assault trenches. The attack was delayed for a full twelve hours, and it was apparent that it would have to go in across a wide

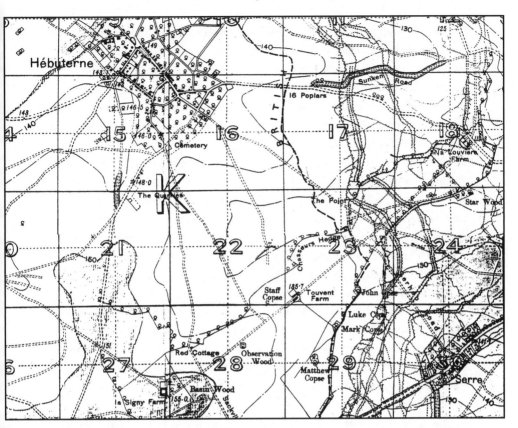

A British map of the Hébuterne–Serre area dated 16 May 1916. 'Touvent' Farm, as the British mark it, is in square 23 and La Louvière Farm remains within German lines at square 18. Only 'enemy' trenches are shown in detail. (TM453)

valley and in clear daylight. The commander of 5th Battalion, 243rd Infantry, Commandant Lequeux foresaw, with considerable apprehension, that his men would be exposed to German fire for all of 380 yards (350 metres). At 5pm the French attacked. The leading companies suffered greatly. Almost all of their officers were killed. The 6th Battalion were thrust into battle in their turn and the first trench line fell to them. The next day they withstood both shellfire and three counter-attacks and on 13 June yet another assault was mounted to take part of the second line of defences. The cost was great. One and a half miles (2.5 kilometres) of German front line had fallen for a loss of about 650 French dead and 1,000 wounded. The ridge at Serre remained in German hands and the French front line, later to be the British line, now ran through the valley below.

The initial attack had been successful – it was based on careful preparation and was able to take advantage of poor visibility. The success of the second attack had been dearly bought as a result of inadequate artillery support and preparation and the clear visibility of the assaulting troops. What lessons the French drew from this is not known, but the German view is clear. General Freiherr von Soden of the 26th Reserve Infantry Division said the battle 'was an extremely instructive preparation for the Battle of the Somme, during which the experiences gained at Serre were of the greatest value.' Within a fortnight the German Second Army commander, General von Below published the instruction *Army – Oberkommando 2 Ia No. 96* – of 27 June. It pointed out that the deep dugouts, shellfire-proof though they might be, made it difficult to man the trenches quickly in case of a surprise attack, as had been shown at Hébuterne when defenders had still been underground when the enemy swarmed in. Therefore it was ordered that the entrances to the dugouts were to be widened and each dugout was to have two of them. They were not to dig too deep – 3 metres (10 feet) was enough. Methods of sounding the alarm should be considered and regular alarm practice carried out to ensure a swift transition from passive sheltering to active resistance.

On 1 July the French took delivery of the first batch of steel helmets – 180,000 of them. In the following month 55,000 were produced, but with their army now at the zenith of its strength with 4,978,000 men mobilised, it would be many months before all were equipped. The British were not issued with their steel helmets until 31 October. The Germans issued their 'coal-scuttle' steel helmet in 1916.

The defensive constructions ordered by General von Falkenhayn in January 1915 had already shown their worth on the Aubers and Vimy ridges in the summer, and work continued apace to complete the complex of first and second line entrenchments. The quality of the defences was described by Captain Eric Gore Browne of the 1/8th London (Post Office Rifles) Regiment after the Battle of Loos:

> This trench had been bombarded by high explosives for five days, and it was practically unhurt, only the dugout blown in. Most of these are at least seventeen feet deep, and quite impregnable. The trench itself was floored throughout with fascines [bundles of cut wood], and revetted and showed signs of deliberate and skilful carpentry. Everything was neatly labelled: directions, limits of sectors, officer dugouts etc., all clearly marked… I found a lot of explosive bullets, and kept a clip as a trophy …

The defensive tactics the Germans had decided to follow were to use the artillery to disperse any concentrations of Allied troops preparing to attack, and then to shell them fiercely in no-man's-land as they came forward. Those who survived would be dealt with by machine-gunners. Browne gave his wife an explanation of the German front line defences in his letter of 23 September:

> You ask me about our front – or rather the Hun [German] line in front of us. It certainly has the advantage of ground – it slopes up from us here – but it has several dangerous salients in it …which are a danger to them I think and then salients are interesting for this reason. There is nothing in the ground to have made it necessary for them to have a dented line, but a dented line makes for <u>economy in men</u>. Do you see the idea? If you have a dented line you hold it like this:

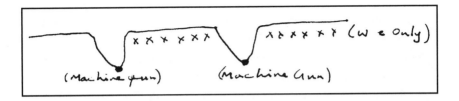

and quite a handful of men with machine-guns or at worst without then can hold quite a long line. On this system you do not occupy the trenches between the dents at all but you [barbed] wire it strongly to make entrance difficult and occupy the heads of the dents only.

If the front line was penetrated the area to its rear had to be crossed in the face of fire from machine-gun-equipped pillboxes before the second line could be assaulted.

French determination to eject the Germans from their land had not diminished since the summer and two fresh assaults were planned. The BEF was to take over the front as far south as the river Somme in order to release General Pétain and the Second Army he now commanded to go east. The British and French together were to attack in Artois while the French alone were to strike in the Champagne. General Haig was unhappy with the scheme. The shell shortage had still not been overcome and, in spite of the arrival of the first divisions of the 'New Army' – Kitchener's volunteers of 1914 – now at least partially trained, he argued that greater numbers of men were needed. Further, the flat terrain around Loos favoured the defensive machine-gun. When it became clear that his views were to be set aside, he welcomed the use of gas to support a six-division attack. If the use of gas was not practical, the attack would proceed with two divisions on a narrow front.

The preliminary bombardment began on 21 September and lasted until 25 September. Captain Browne wrote to his wife on Thursday 23 September as he prepared his company for the attack:

> On Tuesday night Tom Morris and I walked up to our new trenches to have a last look at them and to see everything was right before we go into them tomorrow.
>
> It was a lovely moonlight night, the same strange lifeless scene that I know so well now, the dim lines of the Hun trenches and behind them the Terra Incognita which perhaps we shall know one day as well as we know these parts...
>
> We walked round to see one of our parties under Jim which was working in the ruined village of N. Maroc and had a little chat with him and a cigarette under the shadow of a ruined house. Our guns were very active and shells came over thick and fast. The slow, lazy, liquid-sounding heavy shell and the fussy little shrapnel which came so quick and suddenlike, that it is difficult to know whether they are friends or enemies.

They went back by a different route, passing two of their artillery batteries. He described the effect of a heavy gun firing:

> ... a sudden burst of flame and the roar of the departing shell and a noise that goes right through your ears while the air for twenty yards around seems to collect in a heavy mass and bang you in the chest.

What he does not describe, presumably because of the great secrecy of the weapon, was the plan to use gas – known by the code name 'the accessory'. Seventy tons of chlorine from 2,400 cylinders handled by specialist gas officers were in place. The weather was monitored continuously as the wind had to be westerly, between north-west and south-west, and Haig himself watched cigarette smoke drifting off towards the north-east at 0500 hours before he gave the order to use the gas. In some locations, particularly in the north near the Hohenzollern Redoubt, there was scarcely any wind and the gas officer's decision not to release the gas was overruled by his local commander. Robert Graves, an officer in the Royal Welch Fusiliers, was caught up in the confusion that followed the failed gas release in his sector:

The answer came back: 'Accessory to be discharged at all costs.' The span-
ners for unscrewing the cocks of the cylinders were found, with one or two
exceptions, to be misfits. The gas-men rushed about shouting and asking
each other for the loan of an adjustable spanner. They discharged one or two
cylinders ... the gas went whistling out, forming a thick cloud in No Man's
Land, and then spread gradually back into the trenches... Then [the German]
batteries opened on our lines.

The men of the Middlesex Regiment, choosing between being gassed and
moving forward, rushed into the attack only to be held up on the German wire
and then hit by their own shelling which had been intended to cut the wire.
The Royal Welch moved up in support, but could not make progress.

At 0630 the infantry to the south moved forward through a murk of gas and
smoke. On the right, the coal-mining waste tip known as the 'double crassier'
was quickly taken by the 47th Division. Captain Browne of the Post Office
Rifles took part in that attack:

Loos was about half a mile to our left, and between us and it another brigade
of our Division. On our immediate left was the main Lens-Béthune road.
Our Division was ordered to take the two lines of German trenches, and then
face right and form the right of the Southern defensive flank...

The feature of the German line to our immediate front was the double
crassier – two huge slack heaps thrown up by a mine at their Eastern end.
These were about fifty feet high, and ran parallel E & W and the German
front line ran round the western end, or nearest edge to us.

The attack was timed to start at 05.40 and punctually at that hour our
initial steps [i.e. the gas release] were taken, which I may not tell you about
yet, but I do not think they helped us much.

At 05.50, the Germans, who must I think have been fully aware of what
was coming – opened a tremendous fire upon us. Rifles, guns and shells of
all kinds seemed to pour down all this time. Our guns were going all out too,
and the noise was awful.

I sat in the trench feeling very frightened, and occasionally took trips along
my company to pass the time of day. They were all cheery and we had only
about six casualties here, wonderful luck ... The other companies, who were
on my right, got off even easier. At 06.20 the whole line in front of us got
up, and over, and went straight for the German line. From my line I saw the
Scots [15th Scottish Division] to my left going straight line after line to Loos,

in front of me the 6th and 7th [London (City of London) regiments] in four waves of men went straight for their objective, the double crassier, and the ground to the left of it.

The 8th, the Post Office Rifles, moved up to the support trenches and news came at about 08.30 that the 6th and 7th had taken both the front and second German trench lines. Three companies of the 8th went forward immediately, leaving only Browne, with 4th Company, in the support line with orders to occupy the double crassier that evening. That afternoon, at about 1500 hours, the Germans counter-attacked. The three Post Office Rifles companies' commander sent back to Browne for supplies:

> I got very busy about this and raised six boxes each containing thirty bombs [grenades], and all my company bombers and sent them over ... Thomas went over with my ten men, and I hear he was splendid.

Next came a request for a machine-gunner to man a captured German Maxim, which Browne fulfilled, and at 1700 hours came a message about bombs – 'Send no more for pity's sake!' Another Post Office Rifles officer wrote of the German counter-attack:

> The Germans are coming down the slag heap throwing bombs at us. Owing to being short of bombs we are being driven back. Our supply of bombs gives up, so we throw lumps of stone and coal. Situation getting serious. One of our signallers manages to signal with flags for support. Men of the 15th Civil Service Rifles come across open country with boxes of bombs, but they are just mowed down, most of them were killed. Our bombers came running across open country with the officer in front, Lt. Thomas. They get across without casualties and chase the Germans up the slag heap hitting out with their coshes [iron-topped clubs].

At 1900 Browne led his men forward across the battlefield.

> ... on this walk I went right through it all; the profusion of dead and wounded makes one's heart stand still. We got over safely, a machine-gun to our right had a go at us, but shot too high, and I reached the old hun front line without a casualty.

The 15th Division had circled and taken Loos itself. In the centre the remaining part of Rawlinson's IV Corps, the 1st Division, had advanced as far as Hulluch but in insufficient strength to hold it. Gough's I Corps to the north had themselves suffered from the gas as Graves recounted, and so did not make similar progress, but overall, by 0900, it was clear that the attacks had gone well. It then remained to reinforce success, but the reserves, the 21st and 24th Divisions, Kitchener volunteers, were under the control not of Haig but of Sir John French some 15 miles (24 kilometres) to the rear. Sent forward only at 1230 hours, they marched until night, covering two-thirds of the distance, and it was not until the afternoon of 26 September that they attempted to attack the German second line. It had, by then, been reinforced and machine-gun fire cut into the gallant but inexperienced troops. Of the 15,000 men who made this assault some 8,000 fell killed or wounded. Only the timely arrival of the Guards Division steadied them enough to permit a retreat and that was abetted by the Germans, who humanely ceased their fire.

The attack seemed to have failed because of the handling of the supporting troops by Field Marshal French – a fatal delay in sending reinforcements to exploit early success. The fiasco at the northern end of the line paled into insignificance in comparison to the initial success of the 15th Scottish and 47th London Divisions at the start of the day – their men advancing in succeeding lines after ample artillery preparation. That the right lessons were being learned is questionable. Encouragement was given to the employment of infantry attacking in waves, line after line. The military historian Paddy Griffith points out in his book on battle tactics:

> Within the 9th Scottish Division, for example, the attack at Loos was made by four battalions in line on a frontage of 1,600 yards, with each battalion split into three waves, one behind the other. Behind each battalion followed a second one in the same formation, ready to leapfrog through; and behind that came a whole brigade in general reserve. The depth of attack at any given place was therefore at least six lines of men, at intervals of perhaps two yards between each man.

In short, the formation adopted had worked well at Loos, it appeared, and should work just as well in future.

Erich von Falkenhayn, Chief of the German General Staff, wrote after the war:

Although the terrible gunfire [of the preparatory bombardment] had caused hitherto unheard-of destruction both in and far behind our positions, in addition to very heavy losses in men, the French were unable to gain any vital advantages on the 24th in Champagne. The English, on the other hand, on the first day of their attack, by the employment of gas, succeeded in occupying our foremost positions at Loos over a breadth of seven and a half miles. They were, however, unable to develop this success. Incessant counter-attacks of the brave defenders not only prevented this, but also recovered substantial portions of the lost positions.

He goes on to praise the quality of German troops and also say of the Allies:

If the French and English cannot be placed on the same level [of valour] as the defenders, they certainly did their duty nobly. Their losses are best proof of this. The lack of success was due to no failure of theirs. It was probably due to the plan of operations.

He attributed the French failure to break through in the Champagne to a conviction that numerical superiority on a grand scale could succeed against modern defensive systems and weaponry. In summary, he saw well-developed entrenchments and strong-points, coupled with machine-gun and artillery skills and the courage of German infantry as being sufficient to defy attack. At this stage of the war he was arguably correct.

The Black Hole of Verdun

On Friday, 10 December, Sir Douglas Haig wrote in his diary:

About 7pm I received a letter from the Prime Minister [Asquith] marked 'Secret' and enclosed in three envelopes! It was dated 10 Downing Street, 8 December 1915 and ran as follows: 'Sir J. French has placed in my hands his resignation of the Office of Commander in Chief of the Forces in France. Subject to the King's approval I have the pleasure of proposing to you that you should be his successor...

Haig assumed his command on 19 December at noon. He found himself heir to the decision taken by the Chantilly Conference of 6–8 December, at which Sir John French had agreed that the Allies, including Russia and Italy, would undertake coordinated offensives in the following year. It fell to Haig to negotiate exactly what this meant for the British and Empire forces and where the attacks would take place. First, on 8 January, he conferred with his immediate subordinates, the three army commanders. He told them to:

> … work out schemes for (a) preliminary operations to wear out the Enemy and exhaust his reserves and (b) for a decisive attack made with the objective of piercing the Enemy's lines of defence.

He saw the first of these as being necessary at once. On 15 February he wrote to the King to tell him that Marshal Joffre was encouraging him to attack in April and also to take over the French Tenth Army's frontage. He evaded giving a clear answer, although he had already agreed with Joffre on 20 January to undertake a substantial attack in the Ypres Salient and a lesser assault together with the French on the Somme, and the two men had changed this scheme, as the Russians could not act earlier, to a massive joint effort on the Somme in July 1916.

At Christmas 1915 Falkenhayn drafted a document as a basis for his report to the Kaiser, reviewing the situation on all fronts and making recommendations for action in 1916. He stated that the French were close to exhaustion and that the English were hoping to starve Germany out of the war by means of blockade. He said it was necessary to damage the English cause on the continent of Europe as only indirect damage could be inflicted elsewhere, but action in Flanders could not, because of the condition of the terrain, be undertaken until the middle of spring. The opportunities to hurt England reduced to two, one of which was submarine warfare to deny her supplies. Falkenhayn continued:

> As I have already insisted, the strain on France has almost reached the breaking-point – though it is certainly borne with the most remarkable devotion. If we succeeded in opening the eyes of her people to the fact that in a military sense they have nothing more to hope for, that breaking-point would be reached and England's best sword knocked out of her hand. To achieve that object the uncertain method of a mass break-through, in any case beyond our means, is unnecessary. We can probably do enough for our purposes with limited resources. Within our reach behind the French sector

of the Western front there are objectives for the retention of which the French General Staff would be compelled to throw in every man they have … the forces of France will bleed to death … whether we reach our goal or not… The objectives of which I am speaking now are Belfort and Verdun… the preference must be given to Verdun.

One part of his plan was not adopted: unrestricted submarine warfare. It would have meant being prepared to torpedo American ships. For the time being attacks would be limited to armed enemy merchant ships.

The target had been selected with care – one they believed that France would give everything to defend. The huge forts above Verdun were to be Falkenhayn's killing-ground.

The French Commander-in-Chief, Marshal Joffre, was in fact willing to yield this ground; strategically it was of no importance to his campaign. Politically, however, the fortifications created after the humiliation of the Franco–Prussian War were of enormous symbolic significance, and the soldier was overruled by his political masters. Thus, when on 21 February 1916, the 1,400 guns of the Germans opened fire on Verdun, the French resisted. The prevailing defensive philosophy that guided them was *l'attaque à l'outrance* – all-out attack – any position taken by the enemy must be counter-attacked at all costs and regained. Falkenhayn relied on this to tempt the French to bleed themselves white at Verdun. For the Allies the German attack spelt a revision of their own plans for the Somme.

To some extent Falkenhayn had misjudged his move. Given the low priority accorded to the position by Joffre, the defences were lightly manned and many of the guns of the forts had been withdrawn. Success came more easily than expected, drawing the Germans into the hand-to-hand fighting the original plan had intended to avoid. By 25 February Fort Douaumont had fallen to the Germans, taken by nine men of the 24th Brandenburg Regiment who climbed through an undefended embrasure and overwhelmed the fifty-seven men inside. The expected counter-attack did not come. The new commander here, General Pétain, husbanded his soldiers' lives and his more cautious approach drew the Germans in. Nevertheless, by March France had suffered 89,000 casualties and the Germans 81,000. Here was France, heroically defending her homeland, and what were the British doing?

As the hills above the little town in the Meuse were ground into a wilderness of mud and blood, and as French reinforcements were swallowed up in the apparently never-ending maelstrom, the demand on the British commander, General Sir Douglas Haig, to relieve the pressure by launching an attack in the west became irresistible. Any attack, anywhere would do, so long as it drew off the power of the Germans in the east, but in order to do this, it had to be soon – by the end of June at the latest. Haig agreed, although he would have preferred to have until September to build up his forces and complete their training. The waterlogged terrain of Flanders was uninviting, and the southern end of the British line where it met the French in Picardy, was chosen. The battle would take place on the Somme.

While Haig made his preparations the horror at Verdun continued. On 19 April Pétain was promoted to command the Central Army Group and General Robert Nivelle replaced him. His style was much more to the public taste – dramatic attacks and resounding utterances such as his general order of 23 June: '*Ils ne passeront pas!*' ('They shall not pass!') More Frenchmen were poured into the battle.

The Germans attacked Fort Vaux on 1 June. It was defended by 250 men under the command of Major Sylvain-Eugene Raynal. The outer defences fell on the first day, and the dogged Frenchmen were forced back though the dank passages over the next week. Their only method of communicating with the outside world was by pigeon, of which they had four. Their appeals for support went unanswered and the last of the birds flew through gas clouds to head-quarters on 4 June, dying on arrival. The drinking water ran out the next day, but it was not until 7 June that Raynal surrendered. It was to be in July that the Germans suffered their first reverse at Fort Souville, and they were slowly forced back thereafter. By the end of August the French casualties at Verdun were to reach the incredible figure of 315,000 men. Up to and during the Battle of the Somme the carnage at Verdun exerted its influence, and the scale of the French losses coloured the attitude to casualties in Picardy.

The Armies on the Somme

Unlike Germany and France, Britain had no conscription before the war. The small Regular Army was composed of full-time professionals, backed up by the part-time Territorials for home defence in Britain. The Regular Army was terribly mauled in 1914 and 1915 and the Territorials were drawn into over-seas service. The wisdom of the Minister of War, Lord Kitchener, in appealing for fresh volunteers at the start of the war was proved. The response had been massive. These men became Kitchener's New Army.

Conscription had given Germany and France a vast pool of trained manpower, ready to be called to the colours and quickly brought up to operational fitness. The 500,000 volunteers who responded to Kitchener's call had no such military experience. Clerks and labourers, miners and farm workers enlisted in a torrent of patriotic enthusiasm, but they knew nothing of war. What was yet more problematic was the lack of officers to lead them. Five hundred Indian Army officers in England were found and a further 2,000 young men who had just left school or university were invited by the War Office to apply for commissions, untrained and inexperienced as they were. Non-commissioned officers were in equally short supply. These deficiencies were to have terrible consequences.

The hasty enlistment of so large a number produced strong regional characteristics in the bodies of men recruited. Whole battalions were made up of men from a single town; indeed, the objective of the recruitment drive became the formation of such groups – the Grimsby Chums, the Manchester Pals. They were anything but an instant army, for there were no uniforms for them to wear and no weapons with which to train. In spite of all these difficulties, as the months passed, disciplined units emerged from the ant-heap of volunteers. Their competence at parade-ground drills outstripped their abilities with their weapons and their unquestioning willingness to obey orders their fighting initiative, but by the spring of 1916 General Haig had a growing force of new, unproven but eager and dedicated troops with which to reinforce his more experienced army in France.

Added to these were the Empire's forces – units of the professional Indian Army, the tough and casually courageous ANZACs from Australia and New Zealand, the Canadians who had already shown their mettle at Ypres and their neighbours, the men of Newfoundland. Simple manpower was becoming less of a problem, but skill and battlecraft were in short supply. Indeed, Australian laws forbade their regular army to serve outside their own territory and the units that rallied to the cause in Europe were officered by territorials. Many regular officers resigned their commissions and re-enlisted so as to be able to go to war.

Supply of matériel was building as well, but not as fast as desired. The factories of Britain were turning out increasing quantities of heavy guns and ammunition, though the quality of the shells, or more precisely their detonators, was to prove poor. By the autumn Haig calculated he would have what he required, but he could not wait until then; the French had to have relief by the end of June.

An advertisement issued by the War Office,
8 August 1914: 'A Call to Arms'.

**Your King and Country
Need You.**

A CALL TO ARMS.

An addition of 100,000 men to his
Majesty's Regular Army is immediately
necessary in the present grave National
Emergency.

Lord Kitchener is confident that this appeal
will be at once responded to by all those
who have the safety of our Empire at heart.

TERMS OF SERVICE.

General Service for a period of 3 years or
until the war is concluded.
Age of Enlistment between 19 and 30.

HOW TO JOIN.

Full information can be obtained at any
Post Office in the Kingdom or at any
Military depot.

GOD SAVE THE KING!

The Germans held the initiative after the advance of 1914 and thus could choose their ground. In planning their lines of trenches they could afford to retreat a little if necessary to take maximum advantage of the lie of the land to create the finest defensive positions against Allied attack.

The line the British were to assault in 1916 ran from the north of the Ancre, around Gommecourt, southwards by way of Beaumont-Hamel and Thiepval, in front of La Boisselle, Fricourt and Mametz to the marshy flood plain of the Somme. Here the French faced and fought the Germans for more than a year. Both sides were concentrating on the battles on other fronts, so life was relatively quiet on the Somme before the British arrived, and the Germans had continued to develop their positions without cease. The western edge of the ridge had become the first line of defence, its projecting spurs fortified to cover the little valleys and the trenches sited to provide the best fields of fire. Behind this two more lines of trenches had been constructed and key villages turned into strong-points connected by a network of communication trenches. The ground was painstakingly surveyed to give their artillery the precise range of the probable routes of an attacking force. Most important of all were the deep bunkers the Germans excavated beneath their surface fortifications all along the line. Here they could survive the inevitable bombardment that would precede an Allied attack. The winter had been harsh, and an officer in the 119th Reserve Infantry, Lieutenant M. Gerster wrote of the consequences. The water soaking into the ground caused many trench sides to collapse and unceasing effort was needed to keep the front line in operational condition. The shelters deep underground were equipped with stoves and so the men had some comfort, but the growing complexity of the trench system placed a heavy load on troops ostensibly withdrawn for rest but actually tasked with building and maintaining the diggings.

The British had come to Picardy in 1915, taking over the line from the overstretched French, northwards from the river Somme. The virtually unopposed Royal Flying Corps was able to observe and photograph the long lines of chalky spoil from the German trenches and the Ordnance Survey prepared detailed maps of the complex defences visible from the air. The bunkers went undetected. Lieutenant Gerster noted that in mid-July, there was unusual activity behind what they knew as the French line. Artillery movements, marching men, cavalry riding by – something was up.

> Suddenly a new battery firing from the flank opened up. The firing signature and explosions on impact sounded different... the entire style of firing was quite different... the new opponents made use of a great deal of airburst shrapnel... The French 75 millimetre shell disappeared. For the first time shells with burning fuzes appeared... The British artillery had relieved the French.

The Germans reacted immediately, giving warnings to the front line troops to beware of cunning ruses that they said the British used; pretending to surrender and drawing men out of the opposing trenches to be shot down or coming over to the Germans in simulated submission, but with weapons hidden about them to be used as soon as their innocent 'captors' relaxed. Real prisoners taken from the 6th Black Watch and from 1st East Lancashires, yielded more information.

This was no longer a quiet sector. Lieutenant Gerster wrote that there were no large-scale operations during the autumn of 1915, but incessant minor clashes between patrols took place, escalating into serious trench raids involving large numbers of men. Artillery fire developed into a recognisable tit for tat habit; one side shelled here, the other retaliated by shelling there.

The British believed in keeping the enemy on the hop with constant, small-scale probing attacks. While these revealed useful information about the obstacles they faced, they were also a strain on the troops who had regularly to be relieved. Much of what they learned was thus wasted, while the German policy of keeping the same formations in the same position gave them complete familiarity with their ground.

Preparations for Battle

The British General Headquarters (GHQ) had been set up in Montreuil-sur-Mer, close to Boulogne and the Channel coast, because of its central position, the midway point in the journey between London and Paris and a short drive by automobile from the front. Here a staff numbering only 1,700 controlled the massive forces now assembled. The town found space for these and the 3,000 or more supporting personnel required.

General Haig had favoured the joint operation with the French on the Somme originally planned, but the crisis at Verdun meant that the British had to shoulder almost the entire burden of the action, and significantly sooner than seemed prudent. The main attack was to be undertaken by General Sir Henry Rawlinson's Fourth Army, with supporting attacks by the French to the south and by the Third Army, essentially mounting a diversionary action, at Gommecourt in the north.

The Fourth Army were to attack on a front from Serre in the north to Montauban in the south to take the Pozières ridge and to open the way for three cavalry divisions under Lieutenant-General Sir Hubert Gough to sweep forward to Bapaume. If that plan succeeded, Gough would hold the eastern flank while Rawlinson would turn his forces northwards, rolling up the German lines. Between Serre and the Gommecourt salient there was a gap of a mile, which was not to be attacked, leaving General Sir Edmund Allenby's Third Army unsupported. The battle was to commence on 25 June.

Rawlinson lacked confidence in the New Army. He doubted that inexperienced troops could be controlled in rushing the enemy trenches and decided that, following the example of the successful German offensive at Verdun, artillery could reduce the German trenches to ruins and wipe out their defenders, allowing his forces to advance unopposed to occupy the ground in much the same way as certain of the attackers had succeeded at Loos. The heaviest artillery bombardment of the war, lasting five days, was to achieve this, and the troops could therefore proceed in line, weapons at the port, strolling forward to their objectives and mopping up the few surviving pockets of resistance. At least, that was the theory. They would then destroy the inevitable German counter-attack before repeating the process. Haig was troubled. He suggested rushing the enemy after a much briefer bombardment thus gaining some element of surprise, and he also advocated attempting to take two lines of German trenches immediately instead of the more deliberate day-by-day shell and advance schedule Rawlinson proposed. He recorded in his diary on 5 April:

> I studied Sir H. Rawlinson's proposals for attack. His intention is merely to take the Enemy's first and second system of trenches and 'kill Germans'. He looks upon the gaining of 3 or 4 kilometres more or less of ground immaterial. I think we can do better than this by aiming at getting as large a combined force of French and British across the Somme and fighting the Enemy in the open!

Haig remained devoted to achieving a breakthrough, but he also adhered to the maxim of leaving the decision to the man in command. Rawlinson's plan was, by and large, confirmed, but Haig was still pressing for an intention to break through to underlie Rawlinson's approach a mere four days before the attack. He had held a conference with his commanders on 15 June to reinforce his orders.

> ... I explained the scope of the offensive by the Fourth and two divisions of the Third Armies and enunciated certain principles.
>
> The length of the bound forward by the infantry depends on the area which has been prepared by the artillery. The <u>infantry</u> must for their part, capture and hold all the ground ... prepared with as little delay as possible.
>
> <u>The effect of the artillery</u> depends on (a) 'Accuracy of fire and (b) 'concentration'...
>
> The advance of <u>isolated detachments</u> (except for reconnoitring purposes) should be avoided. They lead to loss of the boldest and best without result: Enemy can concentrate on these detachments. Advance should be uniform. Discipline and the power of subordinate Commanders should be exercised in order to prevent troops getting out of hand.
>
> As regards the objective of the Fourth Army attack, it was,
> <u>Firstly</u>, to gain the line of the Pozières heights, organise good observation posts, and consolidate a strong position. Then, <u>secondly</u>, (a) If Enemy's defence

broke down, occupy Enemy's third line …push detachment of cavalry to hold Bapaume …and work northwards so as to widen the breach in Enemy's line … (b) <u>If Enemy's defence is strong</u> and fighting continues for many days, as soon as Pozières heights are gained, the position should be consolidated, and improved, while arrangements will be made to start an attack on the Second Army front.

Perhaps it is as well to keep in mind the fact that all the British commanders were in a new world. Their experience and expectation was that of relatively small-scale operations against fairly unsophisticated opposition. None had ever handled so large an army and nor had their Staff College training contemplated anything more demanding than an Expeditionary Force situation such as in 1914. Now Haig found himself in command of a force ten times the size, and his subordinates had to up their game to a similar proportion – the direct result of expanding the British army to this unprecedented size. French and German generals by contrast had a very different preparation and a comparison of performance perhaps suggests that, for all their faults, the British did well in learning to become their equals.

The men were gathering for the 'Big Push' – over half a million of them. The first attack was to be carried out almost exclusively by the British, with Indian, Australian and Canadian troops in reserve. Haig's force numbered twenty-five infantry and three cavalry divisions and to his right, straddling the Somme and ready to attack over the plains beyond the swampy river valley, was General Marie Emile Fayolle's Sixth Army but only fourteen infantry and four cavalry divisions were available, given the pressure at Verdun. Vast stores of munitions were assembled. Dispositions were made to deal with the casualties expected; 10,000 per day was the estimate. With the help of Royal Flying Corps observers, the artillery registered its targets and fourteen observation balloons were readied to report on the fall of the shells. Yet more tunnels were dug under no-man's-land to place explosives under the German lines. Haig thirsted after the very latest in weaponry to gain an advantage. He wrote on 14 April during a visit to London:

I … saw Colonel [Ernest] Swinton … regarding the 'Tanks'. I was told that 150 would be provided by the 31 July. I said that was too late. 50 were urgently required for 1 June. Swinton is to see what can be done, and will also practise and train 'Tanks' and crews over obstacles and wire similar to the ground over which the attack will be made. I gave him a trench map as a guide and

impressed on him the necessity for thinking over the system of leadership and
control of a group of 'Tanks' with a view to manoeuvring ...

The Germans were well aware that an attack was imminent, but they could
not know exactly where or when. Their Second Army, under General Fritz
von Below could not be reinforced as von Falkenhayn wished because of
the situation on the Eastern Front. The Russian General Alexei Brusilov had
launched a massive assault on the Austrian Seventh Army on 4 June compelling
the Germans to send reinforcements. The German Second Army therefore had
only six front-line divisions and four and a half reserve divisions on the Somme.
The cancellation of the Whitsun Bank Holiday in England to keep the factories
going in full production, protested by the Unions and widely reported in the
English newspapers, gave a clue that the attack would be soon. The digging of
new forward positions in front of Gommecourt suggested it would be in the
north. When, on 24 June, the artillery bombardment started, it was certain that
there were only a few days left.

The most numerous artillery piece the British had was the 18-pounder field
gun, with a calibre of 3.5 inches (84 millimetres) and firing a shrapnel shell
with a trivial 13 ounces (368 grams) of explosive. There were 808 of these,
supplemented with sixty French 75mm guns. There were 128 60-pounder
(5 inch/127mm) field guns and 370 howitzers of calibres between 4.5 inches
(114mm) and 8 inches (203mm) supplemented with forty French howitzers
and firing mostly high explosive shells. In addition there were another 120
pieces of larger calibres. There were also 288 medium and twenty-eight heavy
trench mortars. The French, of course, had their own artillery on the frontage
to the south, on and beyond the river Somme. The precise number of pieces
is not easy to discover, but the official history states that by 1 May 1916 the
French army had 4,254 'rapid firing' guns (i.e. using shells fixed in cartridge
cases) in a total of 6,291 pieces and that the number of these between 95 millimetre and 280 millimetre calibre, that is, heavy artillery, was 3,785.

The task of the artillery was, in general, three-fold: to destroy the trenches,
to cut the barbed wire in front of them and to suppress the German artillery batteries. For all the effort made, heavy guns were still too few, despite
the numbers being made up a little by borrowing from the French. At Neuve
Chapelle the British had one gun per 6 yards (5.4 metres) of their front and had
done well at first. Additionally at Loos the density fell to one per 141 yards and
the attack succeeded only on one part of the line. The density on the Somme
on 1 July was one gun per 15 yards (13.7 metres). Moreover, the existence of the

deep bunkers was not known and even where the trenches were smashed the defending troops had a fair chance of survival. The wire-cutting was the role of the lighter guns, using shrapnel shells, which exploded to scatter hundreds of steel balls. These could cut wire if accurately fused and fired, but if they went off too early they missed the wire, and if too late they were buried in the ground, which is what most of them did. Finally, the quality of ammunition was poor; far too many shells failed to explode and the battlefield was peppered with duds. The bombardment was, indeed, ferocious, but its results fell far short of Rawlinson's expectations.

The fourth possible use of artillery, to protect attacking troops, had been understood to a large extent in the South African (Boer) War sixteen years earlier, where Sir Redvers Buller deployed his artillery to harass Boer lines on Hart's and Pieter's Hills and support the infantry assaults that ended the Battle of the Tugela River in February 1900. He made a more elegant use of artillery at Botha's Pass on 8 June that year, using the 5-inch guns of the 16th Battery, Royal Garrison Artillery. The simple aim of destroying enemy fortifications had been augmented by fire intended to precede the attacking force and keep the enemy's men cowering under cover. The challenge was to achieve the latter without killing the former. A 'standing' barrage was a simple line of falling shells, which created a wall of successive explosions to prevent an enemy advancing. A 'lifting' barrage was the simplest solution to supporting the progress of one's own troops; a line of exploding shells falling in front of the attackers which, at given intervals, paused to be 'lifted' onto a line some 100 yards (90 metres) further on, when shellfire began again. The 'rolling' barrage was more sophisticated. It consisted of two lines of shellfire in front of the advancing troops, of which the one closest to them would repeatedly cease and be lifted beyond the further line to begin again, thus keeping the infantry covered continuously. Once the attackers closed on their objective the barrage had to stop, often moving further forward and becoming a standing barrage to prevent counter-attacks, but then exposing the assault to whatever fire the survivors of the defending force were able to bring to bear. It was thus more secure to 'lean' on the barrage even if a number of men fell to friendly fire as it shorted the opportunity for the enemy to retaliate, but the challenge of managing such tactics can easily be imagined.

The counter-battery bombardment was made possible only by careful observation and measurement of the enemy's artillery locations, and that depended largely on aerial observation. Balloons had been in use for decades, but what was revolutionary was the aeroplane. The British had conducted the annual army manoeuvres in 1913 with special attention to the coordination of infantry, cavalry, motor transport and aircraft with Brown Force based in Aylesbury in Buckinghamshire and the White Force headquartered in Daventry in Northamptonshire. Commander Samson's Naval Air Service furnished six aircraft to reinforce the army's machines. The airmen acted as observers, dropping messages in weighted bags to report enemy movements. It was this aspect – seeing what was happening as small numbers of troops moved in ample space – that was thought to be important. Now, with trench lines spread across the continent, pin-pointing static enemy positions from the air became crucial, for cavalry patrols could no longer fulfil their traditional scouting function. The first aerial photographs were taken by Lieutenant Pretyman over Belgium on 15 September 1914 and by 1916 the extensive mapping of enemy trenches by all sides was based on photographic reconnaissance. It thus became desirable to destroy the machines overflying one's own lines and the fighter plane was born. In March 1916 the Sopwith Strutter 1½ was fitted with a Vickers machine-gun synchronised to fire forward through the propeller arc by the pilot, thus adding aggressive firepower to the existing Lewis-gun defence operated by the observer in the rear seat. The Germans already had a mechanism fitted to their Fokker E.1. and the French fitted a similar device to their Nieuport fighters later in the year. Indeed, throughout the war, the machines, the associated technology and the tactics in aerial warfare developed at a dizzying pace. Now, in mid-1916, the Allies had the upper hand.

The airmen also carried out spotting duties for artillery actions. While the sophistication of the maps now being made permitted gunners to aim their weapons at targets defined in terms of a map reference, the optimum result could only be obtained by observation of the fall of shell and the consequent adjustment of the gun. This required a means of communication and a succinct mode of expression. The system developed by Major Herbert Musgrave before the war had used squares on a map as the way of indicating targets, B6, for example. The Germans used a similar system with very small, precise squaring-up of the map throughout the war. After the Battle of Neuve Chapelle the British developed the 'clock code', in which a celluloid disc with concentric rings identified by letters of the alphabet was placed by the observer on the position of the target on his map. A shell impact could then be reported by its o'clock position, say eight, and the letter of the ring, say C, to report an error of 200 yards (C) to the south-west (eight o'clock). This simple and flexible system produced a clear message which could be conveyed by radio-telegraph in Morse code. In the British system, the ground communicated to aircraft by means of panels of cloth arranged in certain patterns on the field.

Observers in balloons could make use of conventional telephone communication, but they were terribly vulnerable to enemy aircraft. Aeroplanes were preferable, but using primitive transmitters was problematical. The Royal Naval Air Service had experimented with wireless telegraphy before the war, using the French system invented by Lucien Rouzet for their air force. Among others, there were two major problems: weight and fire risk. By 1915 the weight of the Sterling transmitter the British adopted was down to some 20 pounds (9 kilograms). The spark system the apparatus used risked igniting any leaking fuel, more than likely in an aircraft under attack, and the Sterling was designed to isolate the spark. By 1916 most of the British radio sets were made by the Marconi Company. It was not to be until late 1917 that wireless telephony, transmitting the spoken word, was under development, principally for fighter aircraft unable to carry a radio operator able to concentrate on using a key to transmit in Morse code.

The Germans were a little slower in introducing wireless communication, with their first artillery spotting being undertaken on the Western Front by Lieutenant E. Neumann in February 1915. The German reporting system was based on a minute grid of map squares, each with a unique reference. Their Telefunken apparatus used an arrangement of differing lengths of metal across which a metal pencil was run to produce the effect of a keyed Morse code letter, thus avoiding the task of teaching the operator the code; an idea originally devised by Samuel Morse himself in the previous century. In June 1916 the Germans set up the Fliegerfunkentruppe, an organisation including 518 aircraft fitted with wireless telegraph, seventy-nine fighter radio stations and 320 army stations.

The British Army air force, the Royal Flying Corps, was a formation under the command of Major General Hugh Trenchard. In a year the size of the force had more than doubled to twenty-seven squadrons, and with French support over 400 aircraft were available, an advantage over the Germans of three to one. The French contribution to this Allied operation was four escadrilles of Nieuport 17 fighters including the French ace Georges Guynemer. This force was not to be used for observation alone; some 13,000 pounds of bombs were to be dropped in this battle and domination of the airspace was achieved for the whole of July and much of August. General von Below later observed:

> With the help of air spotting, the enemy neutralised our artillery, and was able to range his own guns with the utmost accuracy on our infantry trenches; the information for this was provided by uninterrupted front-line reconnaissance and photography.

While this statement smacks of an excuse for eventual German abandonment of the field, it does express the desperation land-bound soldiers felt in the
face of aerial domination.

Maurice Le Poitevin of the French 329th Infantry was at Harbonnières, west
of Chaulnes, and witnessed the build-up:

> What stupefying preparations in this desolate region behind the front line.
> As the war goes on we do not cease to be astonished! A kind of city spreads
> to infinity: camouflaged barracks, ambulances, bunkers of all sorts, aircraft
> hangars, tents, more tents, and more tents... There are armoured trains
> with their guns pointing skywards, tractors hauling squat artillery, huge and
> monstrous, carefully arranged round about. Covering the fields are stocks of
> shells of all calibres, laid out in neat rectangles. 75s, 155s, 220, 280 and 370mm,
> stacked heavy and menacing, innumerable, as if secure in their power to defy
> observation from the air. Over the horizon from all directions come the
> thin columns of blue, the troops coming to the party. Colonials, Senegalese,
> Moroccans, infantrymen occupying the last villages of the zone abandoned
> by their previous inhabitants ... leaving a discordant, melancholy note in the
> arrangement of this geometric workshop, this Babel of supplies, this monster
> of destruction where number, order and rank reign over all.

Staff Sergeant Weickel of 109th Reserve Infantry Regiment, holding Longueval,
wrote of the British bombardment starting on 22 June at five in the afternoon.
It went on through the next day and at five in the morning on 24 June rose to
a further tempest of intensity, 'drumfire', he called it. Then on 26 June orders
came to evacuate all civilians. The grieving populace gathered what possessions
they could and, with the aged, infirm and children on the few remaining carts,
left their village. They would never see it again, for Longueval was reduced to
ruin entirely in the battle that ensued.

The effect of the artillery bombardment was, according to German commen-
tators, severe, destroying trenches and dugouts and causing a steady loss of men
killed or wounded. In the French sector the greater concentration of heavy
guns inflicted even more harm. From prisoners taken the information was frag-
mentary and inconsistent in detail, but in broad terms confirmed that a major
assault on a 30-mile (48-kilometre) front was about to be made, probably on
29 June. Lieutenant Gerster described the misery of waiting under the incessant
shellfire, and the work of Allied aircraft in seeking out targets for their guns.
The German artillery did not respond; all ammunition was being conserved for

the inevitable assault. Gerster told of the collapse of the defences, the caved-in staircases of the dugouts and the eradication of the barbed wire before their position. Rubble marked the positions of look-out shelters and a tangle of wood and concrete the solidly built trench line. All the time his men had to be ready for an attack which:

> … hindered the troops from getting the sleep that they needed …Tired and indifferent to everything, the troops sat it out on wooden benches or lay on the hard metal beds, staring into the darkness when the tallow lights were extinguished by the overpressure of the explosions. Nobody had washed for days. Black stubble stood out on the pale haggard faces… All were seized by a deep bitterness at the inhuman machine of destruction which hammered endlessly. A searing rage against the enemy burned in their minds.

The 99th Reserve Infantry Regiment was at Thiepval, and Corporal Freidrich Hinkel described the desperation and impatience generated by a week's bombardment and the growing resolve to make the French and British pay heavily for the suffering they had inflicted. Fear of battle had been overcome by a thirst for revenge.

The British infantry had been issued with their equipment: full packs with necessities for several days' living during the coming advance. A rifle, bayonet, and 220 rounds of ammunition, gas helmets, two hand grenades, flares, a spade and two empty sandbags made up the load – some 70 pounds (31.75 kilograms)! With this handicap a man was expected to attack a trench under fire. The old hands quietly ditched their packs before they moved off. Those assigned to the later waves of the advance had even greater loads. There was equipment to fortify the captured trenches, rolls of barbed wire and the stakes on which to string it. There were even wooden duckboards to use as bridges across trenches. One man, Private E.G. Hall of the 1/6th West Yorkshire Regiment, complained he had to carry about 80 pounds (36 kilograms), 70 per cent of his own body weight.

Aubrey Smith, a private in the London Rifle Brigade (1/5th the London Regiment) was a driver taking horse-drawn transports of supplies up to the front. As June drew to and end, he wrote:

> The Germans were getting uneasy now. A fleet of about seven or eight aeroplanes would make an incursion over our lines and back again. Their ugly sausage balloons were in position first thing in the morning and their guns more active… The men in the trenches had a rough time, too. What with

uprooting trees and hedges, and digging new trenches, advanced gun pits, etc. and making trench-mortar emplacements, they were furnishing the enemy with ample evidence that an attack was in contemplation and he "strafed" the trenches accordingly.

Nearly every night now we were taking up stores of one kind and another – barbed wire, tools, reserve ammunition, sandbags, etc.

The smooth timetable was interrupted by rainstorms on 26 and 27 June, and the difficult decision was taken to delay the attack until 1 July to let the ground dry out. It was to start at 7.30am when it would be light enough to ensure the accuracy of the final bombardment and, unfortunately, give defenders a clear sight of their attackers.

Aubrey Smith described the Souastre camp on the last day of June.

We were still taking stores of all kinds, until Hébuterne had become a vast dump... At length the preparations were complete. The blow that would relieve the pressure at Verdun was about to be delivered... I watched the companies have their final tea in the Souastre camp, I spoke to my friends again, took field-service post-cards to post for them, watched them put their kits together... laughter and songs echoed from one end of the ranks to the other. The companies were filing out on the road, passing between several onlookers like myself, who gave them 'God-speed' and final words of cheer. A few looked straight before them, but the majority of faces were wreathed in smiles and there were all kinds of jokes and banter passing from one to another.

'Well, we're going to give it to them this time.'

...then the rest of us who had nothing more to do that night made our way back to the lines.

As daylight approached the British reassembled in the forward trenches, groping their way forward in the dark and, huddled against the enemy counter-shelling, waited for the signal.

Chapter 3

The Somme 1916:
The First Day

La Boisselle – the Thrust in the Centre

From Albert, the road to Bapaume runs ruler-straight, as the Romans built it, to the north-east. Topping a rise before descending into the Avoca valley, it then starts its long, steady climb past La Boisselle, close on the right, to the summit of the ridge at Pozières, nearly half way to its destination. La Boisselle itself projects on a little spur into the valley. It was on this front that the 34th Division was to advance.

For a whole week the shells had been falling on the German front line on the opposite hill, and two huge mines were ready to shatter what resistance might be left. In these circumstances Major-General E.C. Ingouville-Williams, who commanded the 34th Division, was confident that his men could thrust up Mash Valley, to the left, and Sausage Valley, to the right of La Boisselle, pinching out the village in the salient that remained as a routine mopping-up operation while the advance to Pozières continued during the rest of the day.

In the front line, astride the road, was 102 (Tyneside Scottish) Brigade, with the 20th and 23rd Northumberland Fusiliers (1st and 4th Tyneside Scottish) to the left and the 21st and 22nd Northumberland Fusiliers (2nd and 3rd Tyneside Scottish) to the right alongside 101 Brigade with its battalions the 10th Lincolnshire Regiment (the Grimsby Chums), the 11th Suffolk Regiment (Cambridgeshire) and the 13th and 14th Royal Scots (1st and 2nd Edinburgh) on the extreme right. In support, on the Tara-Usna line a mile to the rear,

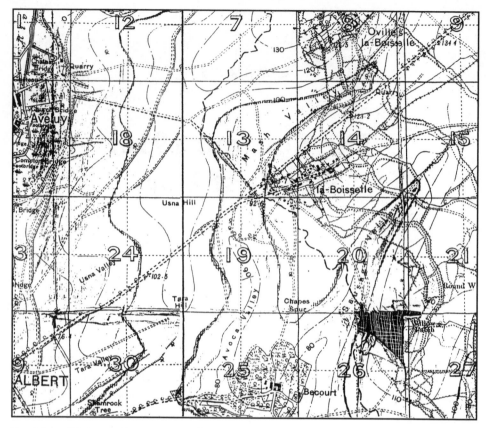

Detail from OS sheet 57D N.E. La Boisselle is in square X14, with Mash Valley to the north and Sausage Valley to the south. The Tara–Usna Ridge runs from north to south on the edge of squares 13 and 19. German trenches are shown as crenellated lines and barbed wire as rows of crosses. The British front line is shown by dashes (see square 7 for example). The original map was used at the time of the battle and the backing fabric can be seen through a tear in square 26. (TM Accn 453)

was 103 (Tyneside Irish) Brigade, composed of the 24th, 25th, 26th and 27th Battalions (1st, 2nd, 3rd and 4th Tyneside Irish) Northumberland Fusiliers.

On 1 July, at 7.28am, as the rising sun dispelled the morning mist in the valley at the start of a lovely summer day, the mines exploded. Y Sap (La Boisselle Hollow), next to the road, was charged with 46,600 pounds of ammonal, and Lochnagar (Schwaben Höhe), to the south-east of the village, with 60,000. The effect was shattering. Huge columns of earth rose into the sky and great clods of the chalky soil cascaded to earth. The strong-points they were designed to destroy were put out of action, and, as the guns stilled for a moment to increase their range, the bagpipes of the Tyneside Scottish could be heard piping the men forward. In eight successive waves the front-line troops scrambled from their trenches, and in the straight lines prescribed, officers in front, set off to traverse the half mile to the German trenches. Behind them on the gentle slope of the hill, the Tyneside Irish started down the open hillside.

Throughout the ferocious barrage of the previous week the Germans hid in their bunkers, tormented by the incessant concussions as their trenches were battered and their barbed wire subjected to artillery fire. But they survived. And so did most of the wire, untouched by the ineffectual use of shrapnel, rather than high explosive shells. The silence as the barrage lifted was the signal for them to stand to the defence of their line. Machine-guns were hurriedly hauled out of safekeeping and mounted and through the smoke they peered out on an astounding sight. Lines of men, as if on parade, plodding steadily forward.

La Boisselle on its spur overlooked the valley, exposing to view neat rows of the British in Mash and Sausage valleys on each side. Far from being wiped out by the shelling, the defenders were not only alive, but their weapons were intact and their enemies obligingly offering perfect targets. Lieutenant Kienitz of the 110th Regiment's Machine Gun Company recalled:

Silently our machine-guns and the infantrymen waited until our opponents came closer. Then, when they were only a few metres from the trenches, the serried ranks of the enemy were sprayed with a hurricane of defensive fire from the machine-guns and aimed fire of the individual riflemen.

The attackers faltered, then started to run. The fleeing men were followed by incessant fire from the German trenches. Some fell prisoner to enterprising pursuers. For a full two hours the firing persisted before some sort of silence spread over Sausage Valley.

Rockets soared into the sky to call down German artillery fire and shells began to explode amongst the survivors. Within minutes the neat rows of soldiers had disappeared, a fortunate few taking shelter in shell holes, but most either killed or wounded. And still they came, down the hillside and out onto the valley floor. Precisely according to plan the British artillery had increased their range and their shells were now falling to the rear of the German line on the next objective, leaving the front line troops free to pour their deadly fire into the ranks of the 34th.

Parade ground order was now forgotten. Small groups of British survivors pressed forward in brief rushes, diving for cover in shell holes and dying as they came. On the right, further away from the lethal spur of La Boiselle, some gained the smoking crater of Lochnagar and further over small parties managed to penetrate the German line and capture a small redoubt some 700 yards beyond.

In front of La Boiselle itself no progress was made at all. Sausage and Mash valleys were strewn with dead and wounded.

Private Tom Easton was a signaller with the 21st Northumberland Fusiliers (2nd Tyneside Scottish). They were in the third line:

> You had a dip coming from Bécourt Château to where the crater is. We were in the deep dip. You couldn't see much when the mine went up, but the noise was terrible. The fall-out was tremendous as well, but it fell short of us. Then we got orders to advance… Major Heniker was in charge. He got killed by a shell even before we started. Major Neven was Second-in-Command – a big, noble-looking fellow. He got killed too. They all got killed. All the officers… When we got to the wire, there was my Signal-Officer, Lieutenant McNeil Smith, lying dead… We climbed into the German front line. There was any amount of dead and wounded there, ours <u>and</u> theirs. We built a barrier in this line for our own defence on the La Boiselle side – the Germans were still in the trench on the other side of it.

The Tyneside Irish had set out as ordered from the Tara–Usna line, a mile to the rear of their front line, and advanced down the slope and across the valley floor, losing men all the way. On the left, before the village, they were stopped like the rest, but on the right they managed to adhere to the plan and passed through the few successful remnants of the initial wave and press on into the German lines. There were 3,000 men who set off, and now the Tyneside Irish had fewer than fifty still capable of fighting.

By the end of the day almost all of the German line was intact. The Royal Scots had managed to penetrate about half a mile on the extreme right, and the German line in front of the great Lochnagar crater was in British hands, but everywhere else the valley was carpeted with the dead and wounded with no gain whatsoever. The 34th Division lost 6,392 men on 1 July, of whom 1,927 were killed. Tom Easton was in the old German line at Lochnagar.

> We were in this sap and we'd got the telephone lines in and, late in the night, I managed to get through to my Battalion Headquarters at Bécourt Château. The dugout was full of wounded.

His sergeant was among the wounded and Easton asked permission to get him back the 50 yards to their original lines. He was too heavy to carry, so they pulled him on a groundsheet:

We had to watch what we were walking on. We were absolutely trampling on the wounded. You couldn't help it… Oh, they were crying out! I can hear them now. But there wasn't a thing we could do about it. Just get back to the sap, and hang on.

Hang on they did. The artillery kept up their fire, and the fragile foothold, which had cost so much to gain, was held through the night.

Beaumont-Hamel

The most northerly sector of the main attack was at Beaumont-Hamel, a village tucked away north of the river Ancre at the head of a little valley running up from the south-east. To the east the land rises to the broad, fertile plateau then heavily fortified by the Münich and Frankfort trench systems, while to the west the undulating country provided the Germans with excellent defensive positions along the Hawthorn Ridge. Immediately before Beaumont-Hamel itself the ridge fell steeply to a wide valley gently rising to the village of Auchonvillers behind the British line. From the height of the ridge the Germans overlooked the British front line trenches and the communication trench system, Jacob's Ladder, that served them.

Geoffrey Malins and John McDowell were the first men to be appointed to the new post of Official War Office Kinematographer. During the last days of June Malins was sent to this sector to film the preparations for attack and the action on 'the day' itself. The weather, he reports, was vile. 'A nasty, drizzly mist like a bad November day in England.' The roads were plastered with mud and the noise of the bombardment was incessant. Making his way forward, burdened with his cumbersome movie camera, he had to take shelter in a ditch as the German shells raked the approaches to the line. Much of an afternoon was spent filming the destruction of Beaumont-Hamel.

I looked out on the village, or rather the late site of it. It was absolutely flattened out, with the exception of a few remaining stumps of trees, which used to be a beautiful wood, near which the village nestled… Our guns were simply pouring shells on the Bosche. The first of the 15-inch came over and exploded with a deafening roar. The sight was stupefying… How in the world anything could live in such a maelstrom of explosive it is difficult to conceive.

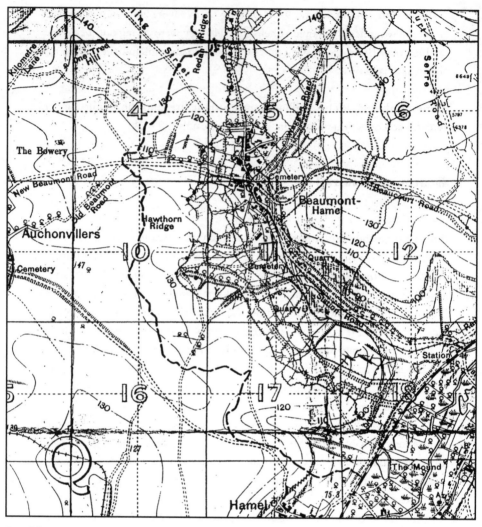

Detail from OS sheet 57D N.E, 16 May 1916. West of Beaumont-Hamel, Hawthorn Ridge is in square 10 with Y Ravine at the lower right and the site of the mine top right of the square. Jacob's Ladder came down the hill from south-west of Hamel. In square 4, between the dashes showing the British front line and the foremost German trench, is the sunken lane used by 1st Lancashire Fusiliers. The scribbled shading was added by the map's user in 1916 to clarify the contours. (TM Accn 453)

As he filmed over the next few days Malins narrowly escaped being hit on several occasions. The Germans retaliated to the Allied shelling with high explosive and tear gas. Seconds after Malins had spilled the tea they were brewing as he dived for cover, another shell killed the two angry soldiers he had disturbed. A British trench mortar unit was blown to pieces when their ammunition store was hit, destroying part of the front line and leaving a crater 30 yards (27.4 metres) across.

As dawn broke on 1 July, Malins was roused from his chilly berth in a dugout to film the men in the Sunken Road, a position created by tunnelling from the front line to reach a jumping-off point closer to the German lines. The enemy shelling was more intense than ever, and the way was clogged with wounded coming back and munitions being taken forward. He squeezed through the tunnel, scarcely wide enough for two men to pass and too low to stand upright, to find the 1st Lancashire Fusiliers crouching in what cover the old road provided and ready to advance. After filming them, he hurried back to find his vantage point for filming the firing of the mine beneath the Hawthorn Redoubt and the attack itself.

Bidding my man collect the tripod and camera, I made for the position on Jacob's Ladder...a 'whizz-bang' fell and struck the parapet ... the position was absolutely no use now. I hastily fixed my camera on the side of a small bank, this side of our firing trench, with my lens pointing towards the Hawthorn Redoubt...

Time: 7.19 a.m.... I started turning the handle, two revolutions per second, no more, no less... Surely it was time. It seemed to me I had been turning for hours. I looked at the exposure dial. I had used over a thousand feet ... my film might run out before the mine blew.

Then it happened.

The ground where I stood gave a mighty convulsion. It rocked and swayed. I gripped hold of my tripod to steady myself. Then for all the world like a gigantic sponge, the earth rose in the air to the height of hundreds of feet. Higher and higher it rose, and with a horrible grinding roar the earth fell back upon itself, leaving in its place a mountain of smoke.

I swung my camera round onto our own parapets. The engineers were swarming over the top, and streaming along the sky-line...Then another signal rang out, and from the trenches in front of me, our wonderful troops went over the top. What a picture it was! They went over as one man. I could see while I was exposing, that numbers were shot down before they reached the top of the parapet; others just the other side.

Corporal George Ashurst was serving with the 1st Lancashire Fusiliers and had started from the front line trench, heading for the sunken lane:

> Miraculously, I breathlessly reached the sunken road, practically leaping the last yard or two and diving into its shelter. Picking myself up and looking around, my God, what a sight! The whole road was strewn with dead and dying men.

Ashurst pressed on with the advance, but was quickly driven to take cover in a shell-hole:

> I could look back over no man's land towards our own trenches. Hundreds of dead lay about and wounded men were trying to crawl back to safety; their heart-rending cries for help could be heard above the noise of rifle fire and bursting shells... I noticed these poor fellows suddenly try to rise on their feet and then fall in a heap and lie very still... Over to the right I could see where our neighbouring battalion, the Royal Fusiliers, had gone over the top. Suddenly I noticed a few of them running for their lives back to their front line... This made me think that Fritz [the Germans] was counter-attacking ... I sprang from my shell-hole and dashed madly for the sunken road ...

The Hawthorn Redoubt was manned by the 3rd Battalion, 119th Reserve Infantry Regiment. Their 9th Company were the victims of the blast; the 'After Action Report' stated that most of their 1st Platoon and the left of their 2nd were buried by it. The machine-gunners on the flanks, however, were able to take up their battle positions.

Hastening forward to occupy the crater were two platoons of 2nd Royal Fusiliers, carrying four machine-guns and four Stokes mortars. They managed to get into the trenches south of the crater where part of the 119th's 9th Company was virtually trapped with only one of four entrances to their dugout remaining. As they struggled to escape, the Fusiliers called on them to surrender, and when they got no answer, they threw grenades and smoke bombs in. The fight here lasted until mid-afternoon when, lacking support, the British had to pull back. To their left the 1st Lancashire Fusiliers had attempted to advance from the sunken lane. The 1st Royal Dublin Fusiliers and the 16th Middlesex Regiment had found the wire uncut and could make no progress at all. Astride the New Beaumont Road only the handful of men in the mine crater even got as far as their enemy's front line.

As the smoke obscured the scene, Malins had been unable to see the progress of the fight. Perhaps just as well, for here, as at La Boisselle, the artillery had not destroyed the German defenders and the deadly hail of machine-gun fire and the rain of shells from the German guns prevented almost all the attackers even from reaching the German wire, let alone from taking the trenches. As the fire slackened, Malins peered forward. The British shells were now falling beyond the village, leaving the German forward positions unhampered in laying down their fire. He asked an officer how things were going:

'God knows... Everything is so mixed up. The General said this was the hardest part of the line to get through, and my word it seems like it, to look at our poor lads.'

I could see them strewn all over the ground, swept down by the accursed machine-gun fire.

To the south of Hawthorn Crater an entire brigade failed to make any progress. The 87th threw the 2nd South Wales Borderers, the 1st King's Own Scottish Borderers and the 1st Border Regiment against the German lines around Y Ravine without any gain. To their right the 1st Royal Inniskilling Fusiliers attacked with equal futility. The reserves were thrown in – the 1st Essex and the 1st Battalion, the Royal Newfoundland Regiment. The little island off the Canadian coast had raised a whole regiment in support of the motherland, and this was their first action. Their attack at Beaumont-Hamel, south of what was by now Hawthorn Crater, against a salient around Y Ravine, lasted half an hour. Of the 752 men who advanced over that ground, only sixty-eight emerged unscathed. They started from the support trenches, half a mile back from the British front line. The communication trenches were crowded with wounded and they climbed out to hurry over open ground but had to pass through the gaps in their own barbed wire. Where they bunched up, the German machine-gun fire cut them down. Still the survivors pushed forward, even up to the German lines themselves where the last few fell. The land on which they gave so much is now a memorial park, still criss-crossed with trenches.

Malins filmed on. The walking wounded staggered back, shocked and numb. The officer who had woken him that morning managed to gasp his thanks for filming his men as he was carried away, fearfully wounded. The cameraman witnessed the roll-call of one of the units he had filmed:

In one little space there were just two thin lines – all that was left of a glorious regiment (barely one hundred men)…The sergeant stood there with note-book resting on the end of his rifle, repeatedly putting his pencil through names that were missing.

Malins thought these pictures of the wounded and the pathetic little groups of survivors should be seen by everyone at home, so that they could witness the courage and self-sacrifice of the men. The War Office took a different view, and the version shown to the public was carefully cut to conceal the cost of battle.

By the end of the day, gains were heart-breakingly absent. A handful of men had managed to reach the edge of Hawthorn Crater, but the Germans had been given time to seize the opposite side and the position could not be held. It would be more than four months before a further advance could be achieved.

Serre

North of the Beaumont-Hamel sector, Redan Ridge rises and then falls away to the valley west of the village of Serre, the scene of the fierce fighting of June 1915, when the French forced the line eastwards to the position from which the British were about to launch their attack of 1 July 1916. On this front, from John Copse in the north to a position somewhat south of Matthew Copse, the British 31st Division was ready to attack and to their right the 4th Division was ready to move. A feature of the front the latter faced was the 'Quadrilateral', a fortified position projecting forward of the German line at the place where the Serre road turned north-east. This evidently vulnerable point, named the 'Heidenkopf' by the Germans, had been turned into a trap for attackers. It had been thoroughly mined and booby-trapped by 121st Reserve Infantry Regiment with a view to luring their enemies to destruction.

The 1/8th Royal Warwickshire and the left company of the Rifle Brigade swarmed around the Quadrilateral. Within, it was defended by a single German machine-gunner and a squad of engineers tasked with blowing the mines. How the mines were blown is not clear, but presumably the engineers did not do it, as they were annihilated when they went up. The German report on the action said that only the body of the commanding officer was found afterwards, and

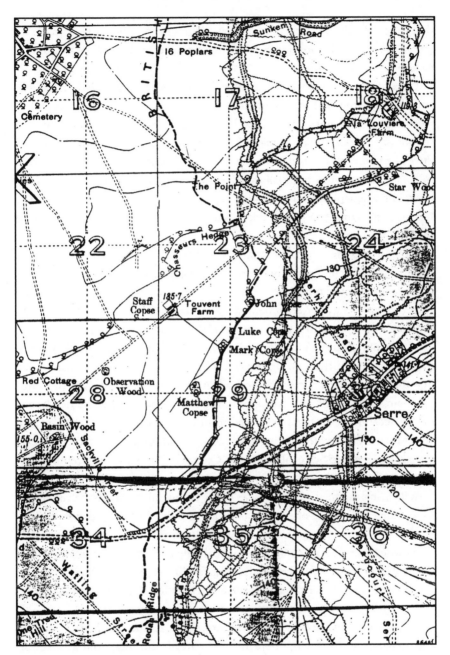

Detail from OS sheet 57D N.E., 16 May 1916. The position the French captured in June 1915, 'Touvent' Farm, is in square 23 and the Quadrilateral in 35, through which the Serre road climbs to the village on the hill. The map, which was used in the preparation for the battle, shows signs of wear and folding. (TM Accn 453)

that they thought the British had been aware of the mines as they made no attempt to assault the position head on, but passed on either side of it and tried to take it from the rear.

The dugouts were blocked and the position rendered virtually indefensible, and although the British had taken part of the German line to the rear they were not to be permitted to hold it. The German 121st Reserve Infantry, with support from 169th Infantry, massed to eject them. The fighting was long and slow. The tenacious British built barricades and brought Lewis guns into action to defend them but by nightfall they had been forced out, killed or taken prisoner. The Heidenkopf was a wasteland of the dead of both armies, with 150 German and some 500 British lying here, and over 1,700 attackers in front of the German line.

Alongside to the north, the 31st Division went for Serre. The division was composed of Kitchener's volunteers – 'Pals' regiments, raised from a particular town or area. In the front line, between John Copse and Luke Copse, was the 12th York and Lancaster Regiment, the Sheffield City Battalion. To their right the 11th East Lancashires, the Accrington Pals, and to their right, flanking the 4th Division, the 15th West Yorkshires, the Leeds Pals. At 7.20am they made their way forward through the British wire and lay down in no-man's-land. Ten minutes later they started their advance. Few got more than 100 yards (90 metres). As a result of a curiosity of the terrain, part of the line of advance of the Accrington Pals was protected from the defensive fire of the German 169th Infantry and with their comrades of the 66th to the north, they actually managed to get into Serre village to die. Corporal Otto Lais of the 169th wrote:

> Wild firing slammed into the masses of the enemy. All round was the rushing, whistling and roaring of a storm; a hurricane, as the destructive British shells rushed towards our artillery... Throughout all this racket, this rumbling, growling, bursting, cracking and wild banging and crashing of small arms, could be heard the heavy, hard and regular Tack! Tack! Of the machine-guns... That one firing slower, this other with a faster rhythm ... precision work...

The attack did not slacken. The barrel of Lais's machine-gun had overheated and a change was needed. There was no water to fill the cooling jacket, so everyone who could urinated into a container and the new barrel was fitted. As hand grenades began to fall among them, the men of the 169th resumed their fire. Belt after belt was fed into the guns. A gun jammed; frantic efforts freed it. Barrels overheated and were replaced. The disciplined slaughter continued.

The 13th and 14th York and Lancasters, the 1st and 2nd Barnsley Pals, followed the Sheffield City Battalion into this maelstrom and to their right the 16th and 18th West Yorkshires, the 1st and 2nd Bradford Pals, tried to advance as well. All were cut down. Private Reg Parker of the Sheffield City Battalion was bringing up supplies the following night:

> We could see the fires as we went up. This little country village, this Serre, were a mass of fire that night. We had to take the stuff up to a place called Basin Wood and it was an exposed position, just about 600 yards [550 metres] behind our front line. And it was full of wounded. There were three doctors there, working flat out, and you could hear the groaning in the dark and see them lying round by the flash of the guns... You could see it had been a shambles.
>
> I kept trying to find out about my brother. He'd only come to the Regiment a matter of days before the attack ... I didn't have time to wangle him onto the Transport... I kept asking, but nobody knew what had happened to him... He must have been blown to smithereens.

Thiepval

Between Beaumont-Hamel at the northern end of the attacking front and La Boiselle in the centre, the British front line was still established where the French had arrived in September 1914 to halt the German advance. Clothing the western slope down to the river, Thiepval Wood offered some shelter and the front line ran along its eastern edge, as shown on the German map. To the north the river curves away eastwards around St Pierre-Divion and to the south, below the fortification known as the Leipzig Redoubt, a valley cuts into the higher ground north of Orvillers towards Mouquet Farm beyond the Thiepval–Pozières road. Mouquet Farm itself had been converted into a fortress, and between Thiepval and St-Pierre-Divion a huge fortification had been built, the Schwaben Redoubt, together with the complex of trenches that characterised the whole of the German front line. Immediately in front of Thiepval, where the château then stood and where now the massive memorial to the missing dominates the skyline, the 15th Lancashire Fusiliers (1st Salford Pals) and the 16th Northumberland Fusiliers (Newcastle Commercials) launched the initial assault.

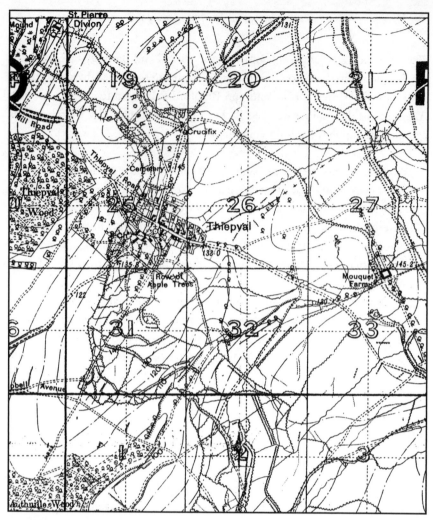

Detail from OS sheet 57D S.E. of 6 July 1916. The abbreviation of the word 'Château' in Thiepval appears beneath the number 25 identifying that square; the location is now that of the massive memorial to the missing. The Schwaben Redoubt is in square 19, lower right. The Leipzig Salient is at the lower side of square 31. (TM)

Not a man of the six waves of troops even reached the German wire. The final waves were wisely held back from futile sacrifice and, manning their trenches once more, laid down fire on the enemy.

To the south, from Campbell Avenue, men of the 32nd Division had worked their way forward before the bombardment lifted and then at 7.30am the 17th Highland Light Infantry rushed the Leipzig Redoubt, taking part of the position. Attempts to reinforce them were prevented by machine-gun fire and, in a

Detail from a contemporary German map showing the Thiepval position with the Schwaben Redoubt (*Feste Schwaben*) at the top. The 'Wundt-Werk' (wonderwork) is south of the village. The British trenches are marked and the German front zones for identifying locations and targeting artillery are shown by letter and number. (BH)

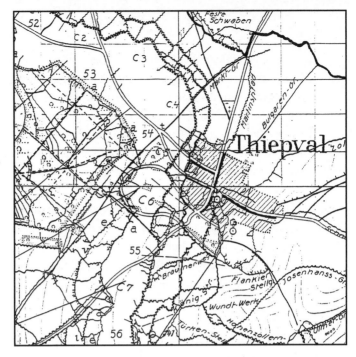

Detail from the German map showing fields of fire from machine-gun emplacements commanding the approaches to Thiepval and to the Schwaben Redoubt (*Feste Schwaben*). (UT)

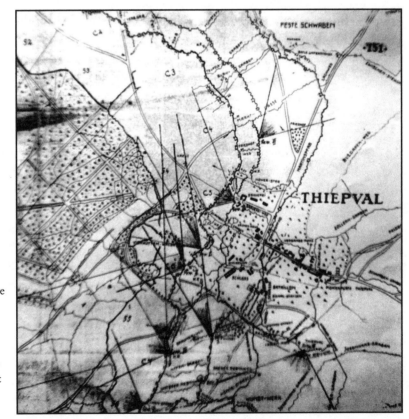

rare instance of flexibility in the use of the artillery, two howitzers were detailed to cover the consolidation of the gains. The Highlanders pushed forward, north, towards the 'Wundt-Werk' (Wonderwork) but its machine-guns forced them back to the Redoubt. The 11th Border Regiment (Lonsdale Battalion) set out to support them at 8.30am, but came under terrible enfilading fire, particularly from the 'Nord Werk', due east of the tip of Authuille Wood. One of the Lonsdales wrote:

> The wood ran up to a point and ended on our front line. We had barely gone another five yards [4.5 metres] when it seemed to rain bullets, it was hell let loose. The Corporal dropped, shot through the hand. I made one dive for a shell hole for cover. A few more dropped beside me; we stayed there for a moment, we had only got to our feet when those cursed machine-guns opened out worse than ever.

When only two of them were left, he decided to make a break for his own line and, when it seemed the fire had subsided, he ran 'like a hare.'

In Thiepval Wood the men of the 36th (Ulster) Division were in fine fighting spirits. By the old calendar, 1 July is the anniversary of the Battle of the Boyne and these Orangemen took that for an excellent omen. Before zero hour they crept forward towards the German lines and when the bugle sounded all recollection of orders to advance in line was forgotten. As the barrage was raised the 9th and 10th Royal Inniskilling Fusiliers of 109 Brigade rushed forward and before the Germans could emerge from their shelters, they had swept into the first line of trenches. From there, they, together with 11th Royal Irish Rifles on their left, pressed forward once more into the Schwaben Redoubt itself. Here the resistance was tough, as the defenders, the 99th Reserve Infantry Regiment, had not been caught in their dugouts. The German report reads:

> The enemy attack on C2 and C3 was conducted with such aggression that the two machine-guns could only fire for a short time before they were both overrun. More than half of both teams were killed or wounded by artillery fire. The remaining weapons in C1, C4 and the Strassburger Steige [Slope] were operated with outstanding effect.

Meanwhile the Germans at Thiepval, no longer faced with frontal attack, were able to turn their guns on the flank of the Ulsters, and as the next wave,

1 The Western Front terrain from Lens in the north to Soissons in the south. The hills and valleys
north-east of Compiègne contrast with the rolling plains further north which are cut through by the
valley of the Somme and its tributaries between Amiens in the west and St Quentin in the east. The
map is from *L'Illustration*, 7 September 1918. (HGG)

2 French colonial troops in North Africa preparing to depart for France. (HGG)

3 British and Belgian troops on the retreat southwards from Mons in August 1914.

4 Wagons of the Indian Corps arrive by rail at Amiens in autumn 1914 to be welcomed by French troops, clad in their traditional blue jackets and crimson trousers, and civilians and by some British soldiers. (HGG 43.1)

5 German field artillery and infantry at Visé, Belgium, in August 1914.

6 A German biplane wing being carried through St Quentin, part of an aircraft delivery in September 1914.

Above: 7 German trenches before Arras, October 1914. They lack duckboard flooring and the sides are not revetted, they are just bare earth.

Below Left: 8 A French trench in 1915 with revetting of woven panels of wood and a metal plate with a loophole for the protection of the sentry.

Below Right: 9 The entrance to a deep dugout at Montauban on the Somme front in 1916 shows the advances in trench building the Germans had made since 1914 and the formidable nature of the defences the French and British had decided to attack.

10 German trenches wind their way across the chalky Somme countryside near La Boisselle in 1916.

11 A former German trench at Orvillers, reversed in July 1916 to become a British defence. A new fire step has been dug on the right, with spoil thrown up to make a breastwork on the defended side, over which the sentry is looking. His companions sleep on the German firestep on the left and the wooden revetting shows the solidity and intended permanence of the German work. (TM)

Above Left: 12 Canadian troops in hastily dug foxholes on Vimy Ridge, 9 April 1917 deploy their Vickers heavy machine guns. (IFF)

Above Right: 13 German troops in gas masks manning a 1-inch Maxim gun, a 'pom-pom', for use as an anti-aircraft weapon. (IFF)

Below: 14 Men of the US 26th Infantry Regiment, 1st Division, training on a French Hotchkiss air-cooled machine-gun in September 1918. (USAMHI ASC 22895)

15 A Lewis light machine-gun on an improvised post-and-wheel mounting for anti-aircraft use. (Ox & Bucks)

16 Captured German weapons: a light field gun, a row of Maxim 08/15 light machine guns on the left and Maxim 08 heavy machine guns on the right. (USAMHI ASC 18849)

Above Left: 17 A gun of the French 85th Heavy Artillery on the move during the 1914 Artois campaign. (HGG 21436 G Marix coll.)

Above Right: 18 A French 75mm gun mounted on an automobile chassis for anti-aircraft use. (HGG 21436 G Marix coll.)

Below: 19 'Big Bertha' – the German gun installed on the Somme with the intention of shelling Amiens. It is being examined by men of the US 33rd 'Prairie' Division who, with the Australian 4th Division, cleared the approaches to Bray-sur-Somme from 10 to 20 August 1918, forcing the Germans to destroy the weapon. (USAMHI ASC 25211)

Above Left: 20 The German LVG C1 2-seater biplane was used principally for reconnaissance and aerial photography, both activities of great importance in this war. The accuracy of mapping and thus the control of artillery, among other tasks, depended on the data thus acquired. (HGG 165)

Above Right: 21 A German lateral aerial photograph of the Thiepval front. The village shows as a dark cross between the two large clouds, with Thiepval Wood beyond. (UT)

Below: 22 Thiepval in February 1915. The château is roofless, but still stands amongst trees and alongside the church and graveyard. By autumn 1916 only trenches through a rubble-strewn wasteland remained. The memorial to the missing now stands here.

23 A 'male' Mark I tank in Chimpanzee Valley moving up to take part in the attack of 15 September 1916, followed by a mass of soldiers. The wire shield on top was intended to fend off grenades, but its use was soon given up. (TM 243/D6)

24 The French demonstrate the Schneider heavy tank to men of the US 26th Division, 11 May 1918. (USAMHI ASC 13111)

25 A British-built Mark V heavy tank of the US 305th Tank Battalion, with Lawrence J. 'Red' Ryan indicated on the print. (USAMHI WWI-5102 Ryan Coll.)

26 British light tanks, 'Whippets', near Albert, 28 March 1918, three days after these new machines first came into action. These 14 ton tanks were armed with three Hotchkiss machine guns and could make 5mph cross country, the maximum speed being 8mph. (TM 889/A6)

27 German A7V tanks move through a shattered village.

28 The battery commanded by Major Georges Marix, 85th Heavy Artillery Regiment, at Curlu in August 1916. (HGG, 21436 G. Marix coll.)

29 The Curlu first aid post, August 1916. (HGG, G. Marix coll.)

Above Left: 30 Winter quarters. Georges Marix in his office-cum-bedroom in the dugout he occupied from November 1916 to January 1917. (HGG, G. Marix coll.)

Above Right: 31 A delivery of supplies to the 85th by donkey transport, near Cléry-sur-Somme, 1916. (HGG, G. Marix coll.)

Below: 32 The command post of the 85th built in a quarry, possibly near Cléry-sur-Somme, October 1916. From left to right, Lieutenant Payau, Adjutant Grillon, Major Marix, Aspirant Picard and Doctor Langle. (HGG, G. Marix coll.)

Above Left: 33 The substantial trench system of the Hindenburg Line with solid timber revetting. A sentry keeps watch. Note the periscope.

Above Right: 34 The retreat to the Hindenburg Line, March 1917. Communications being destroyed between Noyon and Chauny, to the north of the Oise valley.

Below: 35 German shock troops working their way to the front through a mud-filled trench, autumn 1916.

Opposite: 36 German attack training; a storm-trooper detachment. Two men on the left are carrying a heavy machine-gun and the man on the right has a flame-thrower, the doughnut-shaped fuel tank strapped to his back. This weapon had a range of 20m and its flame lasted ten seconds. (USAMHI WWI, Coll. William H Griffith, 28th Division)

37 27 April 1918: Men of the US 28th Infantry, 1st Division, smile for the camera during training with the French Schneider tanks for action at Cantigny in May.

38 An aerial photograph of the attack on Cantigny by the US 28th Infantry on 28 May 1918. (USAMHI ASC 93881)

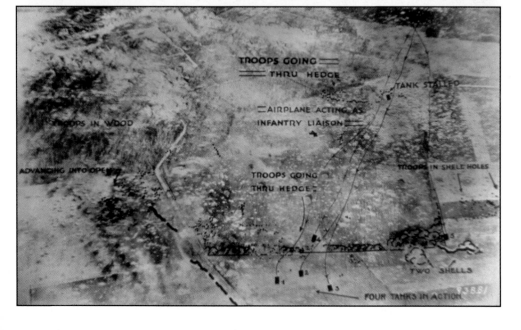

TROOPS GOING
THRU HEDGE

TANK STALLED

AIRPLANE ACTING AS
INFANTRY LIAISON

TROOPS IN WOOD

TROOPS GOING
THRU HEDGE

TROOPS IN SHELL HOLES

ADVANCING INTO OPEN

TWO SHELLS

FOUR TANKS IN ACTION

39 Prisoners taken by the US 105th Infantry, 27th Division, on 27 September 1918, are issued with stretchers at Ronssoy and employed to carry the wounded after the attack on the Hindenburg Line. (USAMHI ASC 28196)

40 Leaving France from Boulogne-sur-Mer. Soldiers of various regiments and nationalities embark for England. (HGG 664)

the four Belfast battalions of 107 Brigade, came through, they found themselves under heavy enfilading fire. Major George Gaffikin of the 9th Royal Irish Rifles (West Belfast) waved his orange sash and cried 'Come on, boys! No surrender!' and the men hurled themselves forward.

The fight for the Schwaben Redoubt was long and vicious. Whole packs of grenades were hurled down dugouts to explode amongst the defenders. The stove-pipes that projected from the shelters were used to post grenades into the living quarters. Captain Eric Bell of the 9th Royal Inniskilling Fusiliers (Tyrone Volunteers), a trench-mortar officer, actually resorted to throwing his mortar bombs at the enemy. He died leading an ad hoc formation of infantry in attack later in the day, and was posthumously awarded the Victoria Cross. The German report recorded that the Russian machine-gun in the Redoubt itself was buried by a direct hit from a British shell and that the flanking machine-guns were also destroyed. The Fasbender Platoon was sent into the front line of the Redoubt, but by mid-morning the position was taken and some 500 prisoners were in British hands. The commanding officer of the 4th Company, 8th Bavarian Reserve Regiment, Captain Schorer, was captured and together with some of his men was marched off towards the British lines. Before he could get there his own artillery killed him. By now the British troops had lost their officers and were also out of touch with their divisional command. A brief foray towards Thiepval found an unmanned trench, which might have enabled them to attack that position from the rear, but they lacked the orders and officers to take the initiative.

What 107 Brigade had been ordered to do, and what they expected to be doing had they not become embroiled in the fight for the Schwaben Redoubt, was to take the second line that ran south from Grandcourt with *Feste Staufen*, which the British called Stuff Redoubt, lying on the line of advance through the Schwaben Redoubt. They pressed on, but fatally ahead of schedule, for they could not communicate with their own artillery to let them know of their progress. At nine o'clock Felix Kircher of the German 26th Field Artillery was warned by a shout that the 'Tommies' were there. He ran from his dugout but, being an artilleryman, had no small arms with which to resist. Surrender seemed to be the only possibility, but just then British shelling began. It fell short, amongst the men it was supposed to support, and they were obliged to fall back.

There were no fighting troops to resist the 107 Brigade, but their own artillery fire stopped their attack. The few who remained could see German troops gathering in Grandcourt ready to counter-attack, and made their way back to their comrades. There, in the newly captured strong-point, the Ulsters found themselves isolated. The attacks on each flank (by 29th Division on the left and 32nd Division on the right) had failed, and these men, who had been the only troops to penetrate to the second German line, had no support against the gathering strength of the enemy.

On the northern side of the Ancre valley an observation post of the German 119th Reserve Infantry Regiment reported to 26th Reserve Division's commander that their stronghold, the Schwaben Redoubt, had been taken by the British. Telephone lines had been destroyed, so it was some time before Lieutenant Scheurlen of 2nd Recruit Company, 180th Infantry was able to bring fire to bear on the British officers studying their maps and deploying their men, forcing them back to the Redoubt. The Germans rallied their forces from their intermediate and second positions to counter-attack. The lack of telephone communication made it necessary for Lieutenant Trainé of the Württemberg Reserve Dragoons to take the orders in person to Lieutenant Colonel Bram, commanding the 8th Bavarian Reserve Regiment. Three groups were to assail the Redoubt from the north- and south-east. The speed of the German reaction was increased when the Corps commander, Lieutenant General von Stein, intervened to order the forces intended for the defence of the second line to mount a counter-attack and recapture the Redoubt.

But it still took time. Lieutenant Colonel Bram did not reach Stuff Redoubt to take over until 2pm. The three attack groups were not in touch with one another nor were they making significant progress in reaching their start positions. Not that the British were better organised. The 49th (West Riding) Division, in reserve, sent two companies of the 1/7th West Yorkshires to support the occupiers of the Redoubt, but they strayed too far left and established themselves in a trench north-west of their objective.

Lieutenant Scheurlen reported on his assault on a forward defence the British had established in front of the Redoubt in what he called the 'Hanseatic Position'. Half of his force managed to get into it on the right, but on the left casualties were heavy and they could not get closer than 100 metres away.

In spite of the partial success here, the attack overall wavered in the face of ferocious resistance from British machine-guns. Lieutenant General Freiherr von Soden sent a peremptory order to the 8th Bavarian Reserve to retake the Schwaben Redoubt and relieve the pressure on the 99th Reserve Infantry. Time crept on. At 7pm the next effort had been stopped and men of the 180th Infantry took their turn. Lieutenant Arnold of 1st Recruit Company wrote that they had been ordered to retake the Redoubt moving off from the

Hanseatic Position they then occupied. As the first wave of the attack made its way across Artillery Hollow it was pinned down by rifle and machine-gun fire. Reinforcements were halted by shelling. The wounded Arnold had to pull back. The Germans found it almost impossible to attack and the British found it impossible to reinforce their hold on the Redoubt. By 10pm the German artillery found their range and an hour later a final assault was launched. Captain Herbert von Wurmb of the 8th Bavarian Reserve Regiment reported that the final retreat of the British took place at 11.30pm. Flares from the German troops on the flank lit up the distinctive shape of British steel helmets and the last of the day's attackers were harried back towards their own lines. He congratulated his comrades on defeating what he claimed was a larger force. The Ulster Division had lost over 700 men in the Redoubt and some 100 made prisoner in this single location.

While the counter-attacks were starting and reserves were being sent to relieve the Ulsters, Thiepval remained in German hands and any attempt to cross no-man's-land from the wood was doomed. Private J. Wilson of the 1/6th West Yorkshires described the experience:

> We went forward in single file, through a gap in what had once been a hedge; only one man could get through at a time. The Germans had a machine-gun trained on the gap and when my turn came I paused. The machine-gun stopped and, thinking his belt had run out, or he had jammed, I moved through, but what I saw when I got to the other side shook me to pieces. There was a trench running parallel with the hedge which was full to the top with the men who had gone before me. They were all either dead or dying.

By midnight the Ulsters were forced to retire to the old German front line, where they were at last relieved by the West Yorkshires. The adversaries were to occupy these same positions for the next three months. The Ulsters had lost some 2,000 dead and 2,700 wounded. 165 were taken prisoner.

Like so many of the regiments of the New Army, those making up the 36th (Ulster) Division consisted of numerous groups of men who had enlisted in the same unit; neighbours and brothers fought side-by-side. From the little town of Bushmills, close by the Giant's Causeway, many of the men joined the 12th Battalion, Royal Irish Rifles, and another Bushmills man, Second Lieutenant Sir Edward MacNaughten, Bart, was seconded to the Battalion from the Black Watch. On 1 July they were on the left flank of the Ulster line, on the river. Twenty-three men from Bushmills died that day, of whom only six have known graves. Alex Craig was twenty-seven. His younger brother, Samuel, was twenty. John McGowan was nineteen, his brother James eighteen; both died, one helping the other. MacNaughten, who was twenty, was killed. Bushmills, with a population not much in excess of 2,500, lost nearly a quarter of all its men killed in the First World War on this one day. Private Robert Quigg won the Victoria Cross on 1 July, and the other decorations won by Bushmills men by 1918 would number two Military Crosses, seven Military Medals, two Distinguished Conduct Medals and one Croix de Guerre.

On 2 July the 36th (Ulster) Division was pulled out of the battle, relieved by the 49th (West Riding) Division. The Ulsters had suffered more than 5,500 casualties, and the Province went into mourning. Throughout Britain towns and villages suffered similarly. Whole village football teams were gone. All the kids in a school class were dead or wounded. The impact was enormous.

The importance of their success in holding the line was made evident by the German decision to make the highest award to the leaders of the counter-attack. The Knight's Cross of the Royal Bavarian Military Max-Joseph Order was bestowed on both Lieutenant Colonel Bram and Captain von Wurmb, for the loss of this position, overlooking the Ancre valley, would have opened the way to Bapaume for the British.

The Northern Flank

At Gommecourt the Third Army had been entrusted with a diversionary attack a mile north of the Fourth Army's left flank. The plan was to convince the Germans that the main assault would take place here, and they reinforced their line accordingly. The British troops, except, of course, for their commanders, also thought that they were part of the main attack. Here the village held by the Germans sits on the north-eastern end of an hourglass-shaped ridge with the British front line running across the narrowest part at right angles. Lieutenant-General Sir Thomas Snow, commanding VII Corps, was left by Allenby to make the detailed plans. Given the allowance of two divisions and no reserves, he decided that they should attack the flanks of the German position with a view to cutting off the village before taking it. The 46th (North Midland) Division would take the northern side and the 56th (London) Division the southern flank. Once again the preliminary bombardment would, it was believed, reduce the enemy positions to rubble before the attack. Once again it did not.

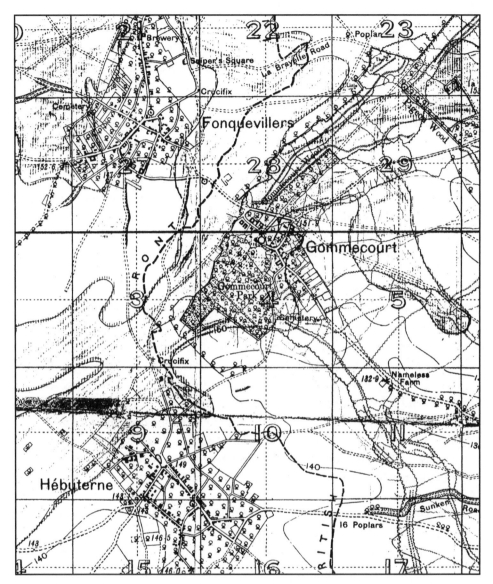

Detail from OS sheet 57D N.E. The hand shading by the owner of the original was added to clarify the 150-metre (492-feet) contour. The 46th Division attacked between the Fonquevillers/ Gommecourt road and La Brayelle Road while the 56th attacked between the southern edge of Gommecourt Park and the sunken road south of Nameless Farm. 'The Z', a salient enfilading no-man's-land, is on La Brayelle Road. The village of Gommecourt itself was fortified to form the Kern Redoubt, but is not evident on this map of 16 May. (TM Accn 453)

At 7.30am, precisely the same time as further south, the troops went over the top. The intention to attack was well known to the Germans. A few days earlier they had captured Private Wheat of the 5th North Staffordshire Regiment, 46th Division and learned a great deal. In the north the North Midland Division had problems. A smoke screen confused the British as much as the enemy and the men milled about trying to get their bearings as the Germans opened fire. The German trenches had been flattened and the wire badly damaged, but no-man's-land had been severely cut up by shellfire. The defending 91st Reserve Infantry Regiment's dugouts had kept them unharmed, and so as the 1/5th and 1/6th South Staffords and 1/5th and 1/6th North Staffords struggled forward towards Gommecourt Wood, they were cut down by rifle fire and hand grenades before they reached the German lines. On the left the Sherwood Foresters did manage to get into the German first and second lines and held out until, by mid-afternoon, they had been all but overcome. The 91st's counter-attacks and the shellfire falling between the lines prevented the supporting battalions even from attempting to reach them. By evening the few survivors filtered back.

To the south the London Division fared rather better. Lieutenant Edward Liveing was in command of No. 5 Platoon in the 1/12th Battalion, London Regiment (The Rangers), ordered to attack in the direction of Nameless Farm. He found it hard to wait for the signal to advance; he wanted to be able to forget the intolerable noise of the bombardment, escape from the confines of the trench and to walk upright in no-man's-land, and if he never made it to the enemy trenches, his fate would have been decided for better or worse. As the time approached, he gave the order to fix bayonets:

> I passed along the word to 'Fix swords'. [Rifle regiments refer to bayonets as 'swords'.]
>
> It was just past 7.30am. The third wave, of which my platoon formed a part, was due to start at 7.30 plus 45 seconds... The corporal got up, so I realised that the second wave was assembling on the top to go over. The ladders had been smashed or used as stretchers long ago. Scrambling out of a battered part of the trench, I arrived on top, looked down my line of men, swung my rifle forward as a signal, and started off at the prearranged walk. A continuous hissing noise all around one, like a railway engine letting off steam, signified that the German machine-gunners had become aware of our advance...
>
> The scene that met my eyes as I stood on the parapet of our trench for that one second is almost indescribable. Just in front the ground was pitted by

shell-holes. More holes opened suddenly every now and then. Here and there a few bodies lay about. Farther away ... lay more. In the smoke one could distinguish the second line advancing. One man after another fell down in a seemingly natural manner, and the wave melted away...

One thing I remember very well about this time, and that was when a hare jumped up and rushed towards and past me through the dry, yellowish grass, its eyes bulging with fear.

The London men, Liveing among them, reached the German front line and entered it. Here he was wounded in the leg and back, and managed to regain his own lines, but his Platoon Observer, Rifleman Dennison, died while helping him to safety. The 12th Battalion had gone into action approximately 850 strong, including twenty-three officers. Eight officers were killed that day and nine wounded. Of the other ranks at least 142 were killed and the regimental history records the total casualties at 567.

The southern flank was defended by the German 170th Infantry Regiment. At 9.30am the British broke into their trenches and they were pushed back to their third trench. They called for support from the 55th Reserve Infantry. Meanwhile the order was given to drive the attackers out and machine-guns were prominent in the action that followed. Lieutenant Koch of Machine Gun Scharfschützen-Trupp 73 later told the tale of two machine-gunners who managed to conceal their weapon under a groundsheet and then sat innocently on it as the British swarmed around and past them. Then, when the attackers began to pull back, they were able to remount the gun and fire on the British as they withdrew, but at the same time they were assaulted from the rear with hand grenades. Distinct lines had become blurred. The confused fighting continued with losses on both sides and as the defenders fell their comrades took their place to resist the tenacious attackers. In front of the British lines a continuous barrage of German shellfire made it impossible to reinforce the initial success. Captain Arthur Agius, 1/3rd London (Royal Fusiliers) wrote:

But what we didn't know was that the Germans had so manoeuvred and organised their line that this part which we weren't to attack was really their strongpoint, and they simply had a clear field of fire on either side and nothing to bother about in front. And the shelling was absolutely appalling. They were simply pouring shells down. We just couldn't get across. We didn't even get as far as the trench we'd dug – well, there was no trench left... We got just about as far as our old front line and then it became quite impossible.

The London Division had penetrated the defences almost to the Kern Redoubt itself, but the North Midland men were repulsed and by the time night fell even the successful attackers, lacking support, and with their left flank in the air, had to withdraw through the ferocious bombardment that had denied them relief. The defending 91st and 55th Infantry had suffered the loss of three officers and 182 men. In front of their positions more than 2,500 London men lay dead.

The Missed Opportunity – the Southern Flank

To some extent the attempt to persuade the Germans that the attack would be in the north was successful. When at 7.27am on 1 July the mine went up under Casino Point, north of Carnoy on the German front line between Mametz and Montauban, surprise was achieved and the French and English advanced together. Alongside the French 39th Division was the British 30th, with the 17th, 18th and 20th King's (Liverpool Regiment) (1st, 2nd and 4th Liverpool Pals) and the 19th Manchesters (4th Manchester Pals) in the front line and, with more of the Manchester Pals, four Regular battalions (2nd Bedfordshire, 2nd Green Howards, 2nd Royal Scots Fusiliers and 2nd Wiltshires) in support. They went forward on a front either side of Machine Gun Wood, directly towards Montauban. Here, for some unknown reason, the German attention to building robust defence works had flagged. The preliminary bombardment had succeeded in destroying much of the wire and the trenches were much damaged. The principal defenders, 6th Bavarian Reserve Infantry Regiment, had been rushed into position here because the British and French shelling had taken a severe toll on the 62nd and 63rd Infantry amongst which they were parcelled out. As a result they were not well settled or deployed when the attack came, and found themselves under the command of Prussian officers.

The first trenches were swiftly overcome. On the left a machine-gun in front of Montauban opened up. Lance Corporal F. Heardman, 17th Manchesters, remembered:

German machine-gun fire was dropping our men by the hundred and when we came to a sunken road we halted in it for cover, although it was wrong to do so. Fortunately our quartermaster sergeant, who was twice the age of most of us and had served his time as a Regular [soldier] ... very quickly did the

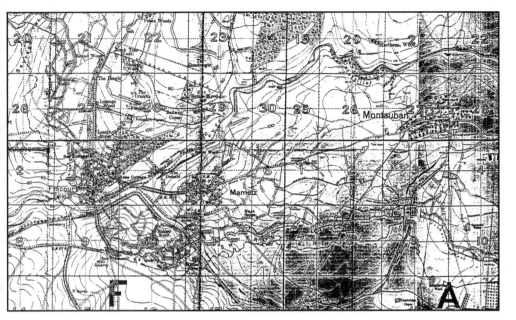

Detail from OS Montauban map, a combination of sheets 57D S.E., 57C S.W., 62D N.E. and 62C N.W., corrected to 2 June 1916. The British front line runs south from La Boiselle and Sausage Valley to turn east before Fricourt. Mansel Copse is in square F11, lower left, and the Halt and Cemetery Shrine are to the north as is Mametz village. Casino Point is the salient in the upper part of square A7 and Machine Gun Wood in A15. Montauban is in square S27 (upper part of the map) and Mametz Wood at S19, north of Caterpillar Valley. Bernafay Wood is at S28. (TM Accn 442.6/8 [3])

necessary rallying and urged us on with his great shouts of what I might call 'cheerful command'.

The enemy gun was eventually silenced by a Manchester Lewis gunner. As the British entered the ruins of Montauban, German troops could be seen in full retreat beyond the village and the artillery was brought to bear on them as they fled. At the far side of the village the British troops looked out over the wide valley and saw nothing but a few swiftly retreating grey-clad enemy. The German memory of events differed somewhat.

Colonel Leibrock commanded the 6th Bavarian Infantry and had reached the dugout housing the Commander of the 62nd Infantry and the Artillery Liaison Officer of 22nd Field Artillery Regiment, south of Bernafay Wood, at about 4am. He learned that the only telephone lines surviving were to the left-hand battalion and to the exchange in Bernafay Wood, which linked to divisional headquarters. Apparently the request to change the site of the dugout and repair the telephone lines had been made in vain. At 8am the Colonel received a message saying that the French had broken into the 'Bayernwald', but he soon learned that it was a British force that threatened his left flank. Two hours later he heard that the assault had succeeded there and in the western part of Montauban.

Believing that this was all the attackers had achieved, Leibrock sent a runner to the telephone exchange to call for support from the divisional reserve in Guillemont – four companies to be sent to Bayernwald. He appears to have been in ignorance of the action where Heardman and the Manchesters had attacked. Officer Deputy Josef Busl of 6th Regiment's 3rd Platoon, 8th Company had led his men to a front-line position south of the narrow-gauge railway the previous day. The trenches were badly damaged and as they laboured to put things in good defensive order a shell drove into yet another dugout. As dawn broke, the shelling became what he termed 'drumfire'. Then the attack came. Busl's men held the frontal assault, but their flanks were soon compromised where shellfire had destroyed their wire. They fought back with hand grenades, but, having lost about two-thirds of their strength, they had to yield.

Colonel Leibrock eventually found that he was surrounded in his bunker. He thought he had succeeded in taking a British soldier prisoner, but the captive told him that the regiment to his right, the 109th Reserve Infantry, had capitulated and that his own unit was digging in. The Colonel saw that the men firing and digging in at his second trench line were not his own soldiers, but British. More were moving into the craters surrounding his dugout. He ordered maps and documents to be burned and, at about 3pm, surrendered.

The going was tougher in front of Mametz, where 7th Division made its attack on the immediate left of the 18th Division. The 9th Devonshire Regiment advanced from Mansel Copse into the shallow valley. Captain D.L. Martin, who led their attack, had studied the ground carefully, even to the extent of making a model of it while on leave. He saw, as Marcel Riser had seen in October 1914, that the shrine at the cemetery in Mametz was a perfect post for a machine-gun, commanding the line of their advance. As the Devons started down the slope, the slaughter Martin had predicted began; he was among those killed. Nonetheless the 7th Division made steady, costly progress as far as the village, and by 3pm they entered it and cleared the last of its defenders. This gave the British 3 miles (5 kilometres) of the German front and with the French success to their right, a 6-mile (10-kilometre) front had fallen to the Allies.

From Maricourt, on the British right, down across the river Somme and as far as Fontaine-lès-Cappy, the French Sixth Army under General Fayolle attacked with General Alfred Micheler's Tenth Army to their right.

Immediately to the right of the British and north of the river was the French Iron Corps, XX Corps, under the command of General Maurice Balfourier. This formation had served at Verdun and now struck a vengeful blow against the Germans. All their objectives were taken with the exception of the village of Curlu on the riverbank east of the high cliff at Vaux. Here, the marshy confusion of the Somme secures the southern flank of the village, and the land falls gently from the west, giving the defenders, 6th Bavarian Reserve Infantry with support from a machine-gun detachment from 63rd Infantry Regiment, an excellent view of their attackers. The artillery bombardment lasted three hours before the first assault took place. The French 37th Infantry Regiment rushed forward to cries of '*Vive la France!*' and ran into withering machine-gun fire from the church, cemetery and cellars of the village. Balfourier declared that he was not going to use manpower to take Curlu and ordered a yet more ferocious artillery assault. Curlu was systematically reduced to ruins. Pierre Corre of the 30th Battalion, Chasseurs Alpins, recalled:

> ... the lovely village was no more than a mass of rubbish, not a wall upright, the cemetery presented a terrible and unforgettable picture; the coffins were empty, the cadavers stripped of their shrouds, the crosses smashed down, the church in ruins, the belfry fallen, and the roads were gone. A deathly silence now rules over this miserable place, torn to pieces by German, French and British artillery.

Two more attacks were mounted, each to be abandoned in the face of stubborn resistance and at 4pm the shelling reached a new intensity with, according to the Germans, super-heavy calibre guns being used. At 6pm Curlu fell to the French.

South of the river the French were profiting from the German belief that nothing was planned for this sector. Here the German 121st Infantry Division was next to the river and on their left the 11th Infantry Division was spread thinly and under observation from eleven French balloons. Every gun position and every trench had been mapped precisely. With ten heavy batteries per kilometre (0.62 miles) of front, the French had knocked out much of the German artillery before they made a move forward. The Germans, on the other hand, were starved of heavy guns in this sector and thus had insufficient counter-battery potential. After the preliminary bombardment the infantry delayed their first move until about 9.30am, reinforcing the perception that no assault was planned, but then the 1st Colonial Corps under General Berdoulat made its move. Only two German batteries were able to offer fire and many of the dugout entrances were blocked by shell damage. In ninety minutes the French took Frise, close to the river, while Dompierre and Bequincourt to the south had fallen to the 3rd Colonial Division. Further south again, the French XXXV Corps occupied Fay, defended by the German 10th Grenadier Regiment. Then they probed forward against the German second line, which had not been subjected to the attention of their artillery yet. In the afternoon General Berdoulat decided to ignore Fayolle's orders that they should proceed only when the preparation was complete.

The Senegalese troops of 3rd Colonial Division, I Colonial Corps succeeded in taking Assevillers in the late afternoon, but were immediately subject to counter-attack by 1st Battalion, 60th Reserve Infantry assisted by elements of 7th Reserve Infantry. The German field guns were effective, unopposed by French artillery. Lieutenant Linder of the 60th was wounded in the arm, but having received first aid rejoined the attack. The Senegalese retreated into the farmyards and barricaded themselves in. The Germans assaulted them one after another. Linder set fire to the gate of one and he and his men broke in. Hard bayonet fighting followed. 'A black soldier', the regimental report states, 'as tall as a tree' thrust at Linder's stomach with his bayonet and the officer tried to parry with his carbine. His arm was shattered by the simultaneous discharge of the Senegalese's rifle and it took a swarm of Linder's comrades to subdue his adversary. Linder lived, but his right arm had to be amputated when gangrene set in.

Closer to the river, the 2nd Colonial Division tried for Herbécourt but was also forced back. Close to the Amiens–St Quentin road the German positions near Fay were overrun by 2pm. Two mines had been blown and the men of the 10th Grenadier Regiment were also suffering from the French gas attack that was coordinated with it. Communications broke down and the defenders fought in isolated groups for as long as they could. Eventually the news reached Major Freiherr von der Goltz in his headquarters in Belloy. The 38th Fusilier Regiment was hurried forward to secure the Second Position south of Assevillers. Lieutenant Jürgens, the adjutant of the 1st Battalion, recalled the clarity of the sky and the brilliant sunshine in which a throng of French observation balloons observed, it seemed, his every move. As he advanced the last of the German balloons fell in flames. Belloy was smashed and stinking with decay. They found Major von der Goltz and got their orders to occupy the Second Position and made their way forward. Numerous other small detachments from 10th Grenadier Regiment and 7th Reserve Infantry Regiment joined with the

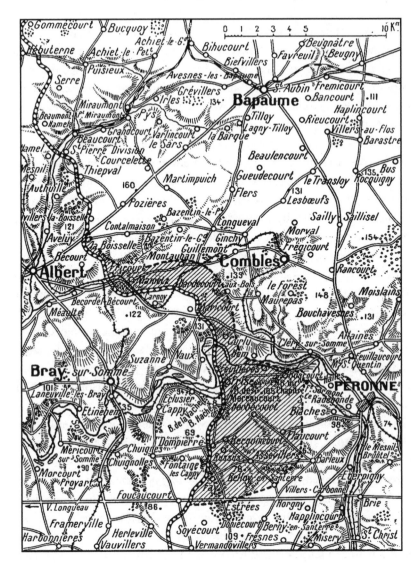

The Somme front, 1–5 July 1916. This map, published in *l'Illustration* magazine in Paris, 7 October 1916, shows the gains of the first few days on the Somme. The shaded area is substantial in the south of the area. *(HGG)*

Fusiliers to man the line and as night came on a defence was established. The French artillery persisted. At 9pm another gas attack. At 10.30pm the heavy guns once more. On 1 July the French had dealt their invaders a heavy blow.

To the rear of the British, Haig's beloved cavalry waited for the breakthrough. The local corps commander, Lieutenant-General Walter Congreve, VC, XIII Corps, hurried to telephone a report of the promising situation at Montauban to Rawlinson. The answer was to stand firm on the original objectives. In his diary Rawlinson airily noted 'There is, of course, no hope of getting the cavalry through today.' The cavalry were ordered to retire at 3pm, just when the opportunity they waited for presented itself – the Manchesters were enjoying the view to the open country north of Montauban and the French were waiting for their allies to exploit their success.

As darkness fell and the artillery fire subsided, a new noise emerged from the bedlam – the cries and groans of the hundreds of wounded lying in no-man's-land. Throughout the day gallant attempts to rescue stricken comrades had been made, though most ended with the rescuers themselves falling to enemy fire. The slightest movement by a wounded soldier drew fresh fire from the German trenches and the living either took shelter in shell-holes, kept absolutely still or died. Where the Germans no longer felt under threat from the British, informal truces were arranged, as at Gommecourt, and the Germans themselves helped carry casualties back to the British lines while darkness lasted. Elsewhere, any attempt to succour the wounded caused a fresh burst of machine-gun fire. The advanced dressing stations were overwhelmed with the wounded, and the arrangements to move the casualties to the rear by train proved to be entirely insufficient. Unable to spare the time to evaluate the seriousness of the injuries, medical staff added to the overload by sending both the seriously and lightly wounded back regardless.

The outcome of the day's operations was terrible beyond anyone's advance predictions. Apart from the south, practically no ground had been gained. Even to determine the numbers lost was impossible at first. The roll calls gave figures of 8,170 killed, 35,888 wounded and 17,758 missing. As days and weeks passed stragglers came in, men lying in the mud and shell-holes were discovered miraculously alive, and investigations showed that men logged as missing had, in fact been killed, while a few had been taken prisoner. The final British count was 19,240 killed or dead from wounds, 35,493 wounded, 2,152 missing and 585 taken prisoner. A total of 57,470. The figures for German losses are not precisely calculable, but some 2,200 had been taken prisoner, and approximately 6,000 were killed or wounded.

Never, before or since, has the British Army suffered like this.

Chapter 4

The Somme 1916: Experiment and Attrition, July to November

The Second Day

With the dawning of a new day the British leaders appeared dazed. While their plans had gone awry on a scale they could scarcely have comprehended, the information they actually had led them to underestimate the true scale of the setback north of the Bapaume road, and to fail to see what opportunities awaited them south of it. Haig was in favour of exploiting the gains south of La Boiselle to outflank the stubborn defences to the north, but Rawlinson still made Thiepval his objective; instead of attempting to come to grips with failure, he pressed on as if the setback was negligible. Haig's diary records, on Sunday 2 July:

> The news about 8 am was not altogether good. We held Montauban in spite of a counter-attack delivered at dawn. This was good, but the Enemy was still in Fricourt, La Boisselle, Thiepval. It was also said that we had 2 battalions cut off in the 'Schwaben Redoubt' ... and that VIII Corps (Hunter-Weston) had 2 battalions cut off in the village of Serre...
>
> After church ... saw Sir H Rawlinson. I directed him to devote all his energies to capturing Fricourt ... then advance on Enemy's second line. I questioned him as to his views of an advance from Montauban and his right, instead of from Thiepval and left. He did not seem to favour the scheme...

Haig received a report of casualties that Sunday – over 40,000 to date. He observed:

> This cannot be considered severe in view of the numbers engaged, and the length of front attacked …

General von Falkenhayn was displeased by the performance on the German left, close to the Somme, where Second Army's XVII Corps had been allowed to withdraw to consolidate their line in the face of French success. The army's Chief of Staff, Major General Grünert, was relieved of his duties and General von Below, no doubt after an uncomfortable interview with his superior at headquarters in St Quentin, issued an order for determined counter-attacks to regain lost ground as soon as reinforcements were to hand. In the meantime everything possible was to be done to hold the line. 'The enemy must be made to pick his way forward over corpses.' This was, of course, exactly what Rawlinson would have been delighted to hear – it was the reaction he aimed to provoke.

In one or two places small groups of men still clung onto pitiful gains. The German front-line trench between the massive crater of Lochnagar, south of La Boisselle, and the village of La Boisselle itself, was still in the hands of the British, but they had to be reinforced if the position was not to be lost. A colonel from the 19th (Western) Division joined a tiny group of the Tyneside Scottish and had their signaller, Private Tom Easton, bring his semaphore flags. Standing in front of the old German line, Easton relayed four letters of the alphabet at intervals as the officer read them out. At each signal a line of troops of the Wiltshire Regiment appeared as if from nowhere and advanced against the remaining German lines, and as they did so the torrent of machine-gun fire and shelling rose once more.

Men of the Wiltshire's 6th Battalion and of the 9th Royal Welch Fusiliers scrambled up the hillside to the edge of Lochnagar crater and plunged over the rim. Those who hesitated were shot down. They managed to gain the far edge and there they held on as evening fell and fresh waves of their comrades beat against the defences of the village. By 9pm they had secured the western half of the village. At 3am the next morning the 10th Worcestershire Regiment were thrown into the battle, 810 men, of whom only 448 were to return from the line. The village was a maze of fortified positions in buildings, trenches and dugouts through which they fought as the darkness faded. During the day German counter-attacks were held off but it was not until 5 July that La Boisselle was finally secure.

The neighbouring village of Orvillers, just to the north overlooking Mash Valley, now had to be taken before any thought could be given to the first day's objective, the Pozières Ridge. The next major attack was almost trumped by an unexpected German advance from the village. It was not only thrown back, but also on 7 July the 12th (Eastern) Division clawed their way into all three lines of the German trenches. Their losses were so great that they could not hold, and they had to withdraw to the first line, converting it to the British front line. It took a fortnight to seize Orvillers. The German determination to hold on consumed many of their finest troops: 9th Grenadier Regiment, the Fusilier Guards and Lehr Infantry Regiment fought and held, counter-attacked and were driven back and were eroded by constant artillery fire. The policy of counter-attack had a heavy price.

With the fall of Mametz and Montauban on 1 July, German positions at Fricourt had been left exposed to attack both from the south and from the direction of La Boisselle. The German defence depended on surviving elements of the 111th Reserve Infantry and the hastily deployed 186th Infantry regiments. Reserve Lieutenant Ballheimer of 12th Company, 186th Infantry, wrote of his experience of the confusion that gripped headquarters. Captain Kade was able to regroup the 12th Company near Mametz Wood and as they made their way forward they, by chance, made contact with their 11th Company again. The trenches were all cut up, their objectives ill-defined and their coordination with other units tenuous. They were attempting to relieve the 111th Reserve Infantry. By 7.30am they had made contact with some of them but not others, and at the same time were trying to organise the defence of an almost obliterated trench. At 9am they saw British troops advancing through Mametz Wood (perhaps Bottom Wood mistakenly identified) to their left. They drove them off with machine-gun fire, but soon they came again. It seems probable that the British 17th Division was their adversary, with the 7th Lincolnshire, 8th South Staffordshire and 10th Sherwood Forester Regiments carrying out the assault. Both attackers and defenders were hurling grenades, but the German supply of both these and machine-gun ammunition was sparse. They were then fired on from the rear. Alarm flares brought no support from their artillery. Finally their attackers rushed them and they were forced to surrender. Both to the left and right the British had made up the shortfalls of the previous day around Fricourt. The virtually undefended Bernafay Wood was occupied, but Mametz Wood was left alone. The Germans, therefore, were pushed back but could make their new line in front of Contalmaison, through Mametz Wood to Trones Wood.

South of the Somme the French remained active. On 3 July Flaucourt, east of Herbécourt, was taken at midday. General Foch ordered Fayolle to make the position on the Flaucourt plateau secure in order to give artillery support to the XX Corps on the north bank of the river and to create a south-facing front on the Estrées to Villers–Carbonnel road, with a view to possible further advance there. However, the Germans were striving with the 5th Division, which until now had been held up in St Quentin by air raids, to establish their line from Biaches, on the left bank of the Somme, south-west of Péronne, southwards through Barleux and on to Belloy-en-Santerre. On 4 July the 9th and 41st Companies of the Régiment de Marche of the Foreign Legion, assaulted Belloy. One of those killed was the American poet, Alan Seeger, who had written home in a letter of 22 May 1915:

> If it must be, let it come in the heat of action. Why flinch? It is by far the noblest form in which death can come. It is in a sense, almost a privilege …

His famous poem 'I Have a Rendezvous with Death' conveys the same idealism; an outlook that would, by the end of the war, have become unfashionable in the extreme.

Maurice Le Poitevin wrote:

> In front of Estrées new shelling, this time on the flank, luckily. Once again, and even more so, I feel as if I'm being crushed… Gallon, my old pal, leader of the band, and who kept near me, was bringing a jug of water and gave a cry, he'd got a hit in the spine. On the slope opposite six or eight stretcher-bearers shouted in pain, hit by another shell. On the road where the bearers set down to apply dressings, a casualty and his stretcher-bearer were blown to bits. And we just had to pluck up the guts to keep going, plugging wounds in the blood and skull-busting inferno.

By the evening of 5 July the French Sixth Army occupied the old German first line from Hardecourt-aux-Bois to Hem north of the river and their third line from Biaches to Estrées south of it; an advance of 4 miles (6.5 kilometres) with eleven villages retaken.

North of Contalmaison on the top of the ridge is Pozières. The failure to exploit the success in this sector on the first day allowed the Germans to reinforce this southern flank with its broad open fields and blocks of dense woodland. On 9 July the 13th Rifle Brigade moved up from La Boisselle to attack from the west with the fortified communication trenches from Contalmaison to Pozières as their objective, while the 23rd Division went for the village itself and the Welshmen of the 38th Division threw themselves against Mametz Wood.

The plan was changed at the last minute and the attack by the 13th Rifles was cancelled, together with the supporting bombardment. But the message, sent by runner, did not reach the riflemen. Sergeant Jack Cross of C Company told his men: 'Don't stick together, don't bunch. Keep apart. If you bunch up they'll pick you off like rabbits.' He continued:

> The whistle went and away they went... There was a gap in the wire and the platoon in front of us converged on it and into the gap. They went down, just like that! I should think every man was mortally wounded.

Rifleman George Murrell, B Company, said:

> There was no artillery barrage and so every sniper and machine-gunner had a marvellous target as we advanced in short rushes. I was so laden that I had difficulty in keeping up and I must have made a good target at times.

Both he and his brother were hit but the battalion pressed on and took the German line. Then the tardy message arrived to say the attack had been cancelled; there would be no second wave to relieve them. The survivors started to withdraw to their starting point, but the activity was misinterpreted by the 23rd as reinforcements approaching for a German counter-attack, and shelling was called down. The slaughter was terrible.

The first attack on Mametz Wood on 7 July was a pincer operation, the 38th (Welsh) Division coming from the east and the 17th Division from the west. It failed. Captain Wyn Griffith of 17th Royal Welch Fusiliers was at the headquarters of 115th Brigade and bitterly regretted his lack of attention on a course he had attended on artillery cooperation back in April. Now he found all telephone communication with supporting batteries cut just as the attack went in. Two days later the Welsh gathered once more and early the next morning mounted a frontal assault on the south of the wood. This time the artillery fired too early and on the wrong targets. Runners dashed about carrying messages with frequently fatal results; Griffith's brother was killed on such a mission. Once in among the trees and trenches, the Royal Welch Fusiliers fought a long, bloody hand-to-hand battle with the Germans. On the night of 11 July the enemy was forced to withdraw. The need for a close relationship and skilled teamwork between infantry and artillery was a lesson expensively learned.

Immediate counter-attack being the policy, the German 1st Battalion, 91st Reserve Infantry was withdrawn from the Gommecourt sector and mounted their attempt on Mametz Wood the next day. The artillery preparation had been trivial and, as 2nd and 4th Companies made their way across from Bazentin Wood, the Welsh Division shot them down with the same methodical thoroughness as the Germans employed on 1 July.

Robert Graves, 2nd Battalion, Royal Welch Fusiliers, did not arrive at Mametz Wood until 15 July, but he wrote of the activities of his friend, Siegfried Sassoon, an officer with the 1st Battalion, which had been in the action against Fricourt and then in the advance on the wood. Sassoon had been given a Military Cross for bringing in a wounded man under heavy fire and had also earned the nickname of 'Mad Jack'. The attack on the wood was delayed because Sassoon had, single-handedly, driven the defenders out of a fortified position in front of the wood, but had then become distracted by a book of poems and settled down to read. On his return he had failed to give a report and was rebuked for his behaviour, his colonel pointing out that he would have been awarded a medal if he had returned promptly and reported correctly. Graves later went into Mametz Wood itself:

> … to find German overcoats to use as blankets. Mametz Wood was full of Prussian Guards Reserve, big men, and of Royal Welch and South Wales Borderers of the new-army battalions, little men. There was not a single tree in the wood unbroken… There had been bayonet fighting in the wood. There was a man of the South Wales Borderers and one of the Lehr regiment who had succeeded in bayoneting each other simultaneously.

Philip Gosse was a doctor serving with the Royal Army Medical Corps. They arrived at Fricourt on 9 July to prepare to deal with the casualties of the forthcoming attack. They pitched their tents and made arrangements for the rush of wounded they expected. The heavy howitzers alongside them kept up their fire through the night and Gosse thought of the men in the mud and shallow trenches ready to attack the next day:

> Presently the wounded began to pour in, some on stretchers, others more lightly wounded, walking. Each officer at the dressing-station had a bell-tent, where he examined and treated each case in turn. Hundreds of wounded men were soon gathered in the open space, some sitting, others lying on the ground… Before long the whole place looked like a shambles, with wounded and bandaged men lying everywhere…

Gosse also wrote:

> But even at shattered Fricourt there was something pleasing. In the vault of what had once been a house a pair of swallows had their nest, and all day long kept flying in and out through a dark opening in the ground. They must have built their nest, laid their eggs, and hatched their young during an almost continuous hail of shot and shell.

Forward to High Wood

Mametz Wood, or the patch of torn ground and shattered trees that had once been a wood, had eventually fallen to the British, but progress was staggeringly expensive in casualties. Improved methods grew, in part, from the problems of supply; the artillery were getting short of ammunition. After consultation of the corps commanders by Rawlinson, it was decided an attack was to be mounted on 14 July, on a front north of Montauban between Mametz Wood and Trônes Wood. Thirteen battalions, including only one regular battalion, would take part. The plan had been discussed in detail by Haig, Rawlinson and their staff. Haig was worried that a dawn attack meant trying to control the movement of a large mass of troops at night. The need for action was reinforced by consideration of the situation of the French at Verdun and south of the Somme, where the assault of Barleux had cost so much. On 13 July Haig recorded the final plan, and the use of cavalry.

> The [cavalry] divisions were not to go forward until we had got through the enemy's fortifications, except a few squadrons to take 'High Wood'. For this he had the 2nd Indian Cavalry Division under his orders. As soon as he judged the position favourable he had the 1st and 3rd Cavalry Divisions available. I also stated his objectives as,
> 1. Occupy position Longueval-Bazantin le Petit, and consolidate it.
> 2. Take High Wood, and establish right flank at Ginchy and Guillemont.
> 3. At same time (if possible, as there are ample troops) extend left and take Pozières Ridge and village of Martinpuich …

He does not mention the refusal of the French to give more than artillery support. Fayolle had dismissed the operation as an attack by amateurs conceived

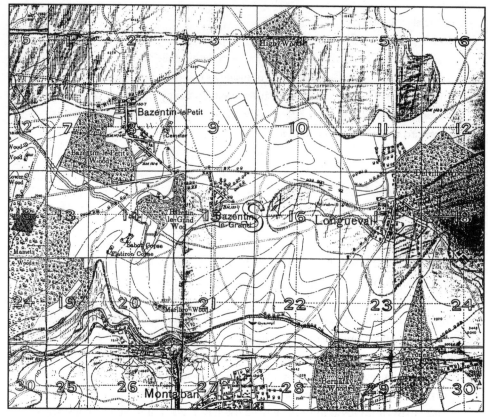

Detail from OS sheet 57D N.E. (for terrain information only). Much of the high ground above 150 metres (493 feet) has been crudely shaded in some time before 1 July 1916. High Wood is at S4, Delville Wood at S12 and 18 with Longueval at S17 and Bazentin-le-Petit at S8. Mametz Wood is at S13/19 and Trônes Wood S29. (TM Accn 463)

by amateurs. Perhaps the losses his men had sustained gave rise to this bitter remark. Lieutenant Bardon of 4th Company, 67th Territorial Infantry, wrote to his friend Emile Neslin:

> 67th Regiment took part in three major offensives up to 16 July, lost a great part of our strength. We began with 260 men per company. There are now about 90 or 100.

The Germans, meanwhile, were feeling the pressure. The offensive by General Brusilov on the Russian front had compelled von Falkenhayn to send fifteen divisions to the east and the fighting at Verdun still consumed vast effort. He had come to the conclusion that the scope of the action on the Somme was now too great for a single army and commander to control, and von Below's First Army sector was reduced to the region north of the river Somme. To the south, a new formation, including the Second Army, was created under the command of General Max von Gallwitz: Army Group Gallwitz. There was some confusion over who was the senior, and it seems likely that von Below was intended to remain in overall command, but technically von Gallwitz, ten years younger, outranked him and First Army was part of his Army Group. It did not make for smooth relations. Crown Prince Rupprecht noted in his diary on 17 July:

> General von Below is justifiably sickened by this slight. The guilt for the reverses which his Army has suffered lies with the Army High Command, not him. They ignored his reports and took no account of his requests for reserves. When, at last, reserves did arrive, it was too late. They arrived in dribs and drabs and had to be deployed immediately to plug gaps. As a result there has been such a mixing of formations, that nobody knows what is happening.

Von Below divided his sector into three, each to be defended by an army corps. From the north, von Stein was responsible as far as the Ancre, von Arnim from the Ancre to Longueval and von Glosser from there to the river. This reorganisation was, coincidentally, to take effect from 9am on 14 July.

The bombardment, in the early hours of the morning, lasted only five minutes, just long enough to send the Germans scampering for their dugouts. The British XV Corps troops, from the 7th and 21st Divisions with 3rd Division on their right, went over the top immediately, having moved up to within 300–500 yards (275–457 metres) of the German front line in the night. The tactics were dazzlingly successful. Bazentin-le-Grand and Bazentin-le-Petit were taken in a matter of hours and the village of Longueval on the edge of Delville Wood soon after. The classic attack-at-dawn approach had, by and large, worked perfectly. Wilfred Cook was a stretcher-bearer with 1st Northumberland Fusiliers and he described the activity of the artillery:

> Caterpillar Valley was a scene fit for any film epic. Guns stood out in the open, even 9-inch howitzers with huge wheels like traction engines. The crews worked ceaselessly loading and firing, paying no heed to the hail of shells seeking them out and bursting all around. The horse driven ammunition columns rode up at full gallop, discharging their load and turning about to bring more still from the rear.

As a stretcher-bearer, Cook took no part in the fighting, but he was no less exposed to danger and he also had an excellent opportunity to observe his comrades in action. He was much impressed by the Stokes mortar:

> The Stokes gun … was the best reply we had to the German trench mortar. A simple thing invented by a man called Stokes, it was merely a kind of stove pipe some 4 feet [1.2 metres] long on a portable stand. The shell operated when dropped into the muzzle by its own propellant on one end of the shell and exploded on impact. The effect was devastating on open ground… It had the great advantage of being operated by our own crews at will and they became expert with it.

There was, however, a check to progress west of Longueval where the wire was uncut. The German view gives a slightly different angle. Their troops were a motley mix of units and their trenches already badly damaged. Reserve Lieutenant W. Steuerwald of 91st Reserve Infantry tells a story of efforts to reinforce their line during 13 July, hampered by heavy and accurate British artillery fire. The attack of 14 July was expected. The intense shelling reduced the 77th Reserve Infantry's 8th Company to its commanding officer and his runner. German counter-battery fire was absent.

> … around 3.00 am 2nd Company observed strong forces on the edge of Mametz Wood. The company was stood to … The enemy advanced in strong waves …three waves of attackers were beaten off… Fresh masses pressed forward and there was heavy hand to hand fighting. It was possible to hold the left flank of the position until about 4.00 am, but then strong enemy forces had broken through to the left.

1st and 4th Companies were overrun. 2nd Company fought on until 6am and then, out of ammunition, surrendered. The 3rd Company lasted until 8.30am and the shared command post of the 91st and the 3rd Battalion of the 16th Bavarian Infantry fell at 2pm. The 16th had, by the end of the day, been reduced to a handful of men: nine officers and 688 other ranks.

With a position established at Bazentin-le-Petit by 9am, the British peered forward from the little ridge that overlooked the broad, shallow valley that separated them from High Wood. Nothing could be seen except the miracle of standing crops. Clearly High Wood was unoccupied. While shellfire and smoke obscured Longueval to their right, and on their left the advance to Pozières was stalled, here was a huge gap in the German defences. Immediate permission was asked to send the reserves forward. It was denied. This was, in the view of headquarters, the long-awaited opening for the cavalry. They could move fast and might even break out beyond towards Bapaume. So, the 7th Division waited. The Indian Cavalry had been moving forward from a position south of Albert since 8am, but had to cross ground torn to shreds by the fighting of the previous fortnight. By noon they had scarcely reached the original front line. Meanwhile the Germans were moving into High Wood.

The 33rd Division were preparing to move up from Fricourt and ahead of them one of their artillery's forward observation officers, Lieutenant F. W. Beadle, was cautiously working his way forward through the maze of trenches to familiarise himself with the ground, revolver in hand. Just before 7pm he turned a corner in the communication trench to find himself facing a German soldier whom he shot as the enemy tried to bring his rifle to bear. Raising himself to peer over the parapet, he saw the 20th Deccan Horse and the 7th Dragoon Guards making their long-awaited charge. He described the scene:

> It was an incredible sight, an unbelievable sight, they galloped up with their lances and with pennants flying, up the slope to High Wood and straight into it. Of course they were falling all the way... They simply galloped on ... horses and men dropping on the ground, with no hope against the machine-guns... It was an absolute rout. A magnificent sight. Tragic.

Fortunately the cost to the cavalry appeared to be more severe than it actually was, although ten men were killed and ninety-one wounded.

General Haig was pleased with the attack; he had been doubtful of the ability of unseasoned troops to make a night-time approach and attack successfully. Late in the morning his private secretary, Sir Philip Sassoon, MP, was told to send Lady Haig a telegram saying they hoped to get the cavalry through. Haig notes that the cavalry set off at 7.40am,

> ... but the ground was very slippery: it was very difficult to get forward. [Brigadier] General [Henry] MacAndrew commanding the division had two falls. So High Wood was shelled and the infantry pushed on to take it. Fierce fighting continued all day. Enemy retook Bazentin-le-Petit, but it was retaken by the XV Division [in fact XV Corps] ...

The cavalry secured a line from High Wood to Longueval, but the ground between the wood and Bazentin-le-Petit was unoccupied and the 33rd Division, 1/9th Highland Light Infantry and 1st Queen's Royal Regiment, were hurriedly pushed into the gap, entrenching themselves through the night, under fire, to establish a line inside the wood from which to attack the next day. As dawn broke they were withdrawn to dig yet again outside the wood. Headquarters had decided on an attack towards Martinpuich to the north, neglecting all reports that the Germans were still holding at least the north-western half of High Wood.

From a point almost halfway between Martinpuich and Bazentin-le-Petit, protecting the former on the south-eastern flank, then curving south-east to cut through the edge of High Wood before running just south of east in front of Flers, was a powerful German line of defence, the Switch Line (see the map on p.137). The planned attack towards Martinpuich exposed the 33rd to enfilading fire from the wood itself and the commanding officer, 100th Brigade, Brigadier General Harry Baird could only obey his orders by attacking the wood at the same time. The situation had all the makings of disaster, and the actuality confirmed Baird's assessment. This attack was just the first to fail in the next two months. Late that night, the 7th Division troops holding part of High Wood, the 7th Dragoon Guards and the 20th Deccan Horse holding a line south-east of the wood, and the 100th Brigade of 33rd Division on the western side, were all withdrawn.

Delville Wood

Although Longueval had been taken by the 9th (Scottish) Division on 14 July, the wood that sheltered it from winter's easterly winds remained in German hands, and until it was seized no action could be taken against the Switch Line beyond. The task of taking Delville Wood was given to the 3,150 men of the South African Brigade, one of the three brigades that comprised the 9th Division.

A ferocious artillery battle started at dawn on 15 July, and five days of vicious hand-to-hand fighting followed. A terrifying hazard was the danger of being buried alive by bursting shells. Lord Moran, who was to become Winston Churchill's physician in later years, but was then, as Charles Wilson, an officer in the Royal Army Medical Corps, gave a moving account of the panic-stricken efforts he and his companions made to rescue victims of such a fate, scrabbling with bare hands for fear of injuring the men whose muffled cries could be heard from beneath the torn earth while themselves risking the same awful death from continued shelling.

For five days the South Africans attempted to carry out their orders to take the wood at all costs. The cost was immense: 758 survived, and when the brigade was relieved on 20 July, only 147 men were left in the line. The dead outnumbered the wounded by four to one. More than a month would pass before the job was done. The 18th Division was sent to take over on 19 July, relieving the Scots, clearing the southern edge of the wood, and allowing the scant remnants of the South African Brigade to withdraw the following day. The wood soaked up men. On 22 July XV Corps attempted to push the Germans out. They failed. The 2nd and 5th Divisions crept forward against dogged resistance at the end of the month, but still the Germans held on, having lost nearly 9,500 men so far.

Lieutenant Bardon of the French 67th Territorial Infantry had been enjoying the quiet of a rest period and the reconstitution of his unit. In a letter to Emile Neslin dated 21 July he wrote:

> ... 18th, by train, for a day. On the 19th at 6.30 am, we disembarked on the Somme and marched 22 km [13.6 miles] to arrive at our camp. We got there at 19 hours in the evening and I felt like a vegetable. Happy to be out of the sound of the guns – a lovely, sunny evening. But we are soon to be in action. Leave is suspended. I've now been 23 ½ months in the field. We move on at 23 hours ...

The Fight for Pozières

The long, hard climb from La Boisselle to the summit of the ridge was attempted throughout July. On 21 July the Australians came to the Somme. The Australian and New Zealand Army Corps, the ANZACs, had proved themselves to be outstandingly tough and courageous in the fruitless campaign at Gallipoli, as well as refreshingly free from the servile deference to rank that was normal in the British Army. They had already had a taste of the Western Front since coming to France. A few days earlier the 5th Australian Division had floundered with incredible but unproductive courage in the mud bath of Fromelles, west of Lille, where an ill-conceived operation intended to divert German support from the Somme achieved none of its objectives. They had attacked alongside the under-strength 61st Division, an inexperienced formation which did little to help. The losses were severe. For the 1st Australian Division further south, the well-drained countryside of Picardy was not as hopeless underfoot as the flatlands further north, but the Germans were quite as well entrenched.

General Haig visited the Reserve Army headquarters on 20 July:

> I also saw General [Hubert] Gough at Toutencourt... The Australians went in [to the line] last night opposite Pozières... He proposes to attack Pozières with them on 22nd early, 1.30 am. I told him to go into all the details carefully, as 1st Australian Division had not been engaged [in France] before, and possibly overlooked the difficulties of this kind of fighting.

Haig went back to Toutencourt the next day and the next, to make sure the Australians were fully briefed and appropriately tasked.

At 12.30am on 23 July the 1st Australian Division went for Pozières from south of the Albert to Bapaume road, while the British 48th Division attacked from Orvillers-la-Boisselle up Mash Valley towards the left flank. To the Australians' right an assault towards High Wood and the Switch Line by the British 1st, 19th and 51st Divisions, and against Delville Wood and Guillemont to the east by 5th, 3rd and 30th Divisions, were also attempted, but failed. The Australians were inside Pozières within the hour and, finding that the 48th Division's attack was lagging, poured over the main road to storm the Gibraltar strong-point. Only 200 yards (182.8 metres) away was the windmill that marked the summit of the ridge. By the end of the day the 17th Royal Warwickshire Regiment had managed to join the Australians to the north-west of the village but the top of the ridge with its two lines of massive trenches, OG1 and OG2, still lay before them. In the early morning of 24 July they began to clear the village of German resistance and a position beyond the cemetery was secured north of the village. A German counter-attack at 8.30am was shelled into retreat. The 2nd Australian Division relieved their compatriots that night and continued the action over the next four days. Private Fred Russell, 22nd Battalion, 6th Victoria Brigade, 2nd Australian Division, recalled that night:

> ... we had to take over from where the 1st Division were to carry on the fighting and go as far as we could. The place by this time was one shambles of destruction ... where I was with the CO of the battalion, was in a fort called Gibralter. It was a German concrete dugout with a six-foot [1.8-metre] tower

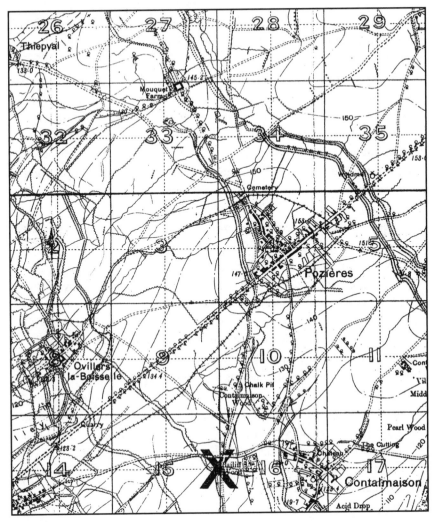

Detail from OS map area of Martinpuich, part of 57D S.E. and 57C S.W., corrected to 6 July. The railway ran diagonally across square X3, north of Pozières and across square 5. The Gibraltar strongpoint dominated, from the north, the road junction in the lower left of X4. 145 Brigade started from the curved trench in lower X3 and the Australians from a trench close to the 130m contour in X10. The windmill is in square [R]35 and Mouquet Farm in square [R]33. (TM Accn 8291)

above the ground... We weren't in there ten minutes when a nine-inch [230-millimetre] shell landed on top of it... the compression was terrific. All night long we were calling for stretcher-bearers... We took an awful lot of casualties that night, even before the boys went over.

The 2nd Division's 5th Brigade was not relieved until 6 August. Their attacks had brought them no closer to the windmill and the ANZACs had lost 3,500 men.

The Germans had not found the defence easy. Corporal Klussman of 5th Company, 77th Reserve Infantry, had been huddled in a dugout with his comrades, all trying to calm themselves by smoking. The bombardment buried the commander of 7th Company three times, but each time his men managed to dig him out.

Geoffrey Malins went up from the chalk pit near Contalmaison Wood to film the scene.

> The enemy must have been putting 9-inch and 12-inch stuff in there, for they were sending up huge clouds of smoke and débris... From the chalk-pit to Pozières was no great distance. The ground was littered with every description of equipment, just as it had been left by the flying Huns, and dead bodies were everywhere... The place was desolate in the extreme. The village was absolutely non-existent. There was not a vestige of buildings remaining, with one exception, and that was a place called by the Germans 'Gibraltar', a reinforced concrete emplacement he had used for machine-guns. The few trees that had survived the terrible blasting were just stumps, no more.

At the end of the month an effort was made to straighten up the line nearer the Somme, where to the south the French had pushed forward to Biaches but, on the right bank, north of Biaches, Cléry-sur-Somme remained in German hands and the line followed the river west to Hem, and then ran just west of due north, towards Longueval.

Emile Naslin wrote home:

> On the evening of the Anglo-French offensive I did 45km [28 miles] by bicycle then 20km [12.4 miles] by lorry to take leave from my post with several friends in a town near the front. Barrage was a problem en route. We had to dodge shells and undergo the spying aircraft surveillance. In the evening, in beautiful sunshine, the ground trembled, tormented by our heavy guns. Day and night the sky is lit up... I guarantee victory will be the outcome.

Roger Charlet had been back at the front for a week. He wrote home in cheerful mood, sure of a German retreat:

Since visit to Amiens we have travelled a good distance and we are now actually at the front, before our town of P......[Péronne]. Tonight we move on – we are pushing the enemy out of his lines.

On 30 July at 4.45am the 30th Division's 89th Brigade, on the left flank of the French XX Corps, attacked from trenches south of Trônes Wood. The 2nd Bedfordshire Regiment and the French 153rd Infantry took Maltz Horn Farm and further south, near the river, the French 41st Division gained Monacu Farm and Hem Wood. There was also a French advance on a limited frontage south-west of Maurepas, in the centre, but from Longueval to the river, that was all. The 1st, 3rd and 4th Liverpool Pals (17th, 19th and 20th King's), the 1st, 2nd and 3rd Manchester Pals (16th, 17th and 18th Manchesters), with other battalions, attempted to take Guillemont and Ginchy. Mist shrouded the fields. The Germans had crept forward to avoid the shelling, hidden from view, and resumed their trench positions as, at 4.45am, the British advanced. Still neither side could see the other, but the Germans were able to machine-gun at random into the fog with terrible effect. Further south, beyond the Amiens to St Quentin road, the French Tenth Army took the German salient around Soyécourt – a modest advance. It had been an expensive, and virtually unproductive, joint effort.

After a month of battle, the British first day's objective, the Pozières Ridge, was still in enemy hands. The British and Empire forces had taken 165,000 casualties, including 40,000 dead. Disquiet was at last being felt in England, where the hospitals were thronged with the wounded. General Sir William Robertson, Chief of the Imperial General Staff, wrote to Haig to tell him that: 'The powers-that-be are beginning to get a little uneasy... [wondering] whether a loss of say 300,000 men will lead to really great results, because, if not, we ought to be content with something less than we are doing now.' Haig responded: 'In another six weeks the enemy should be hard put to find men. The maintenance of a steady offensive pressure will result eventually in his complete overthrow.' Clearly the vision of a breakthrough had been abandoned, and equally clearly the underestimation of German strength and courage persisted. Foch pointed out that the fundamental purpose of the Somme battle had been and remained to support the British action to the north; the action south of the river was secondary.

The Hard End of Summer

The beautiful summer weather continued, sunny and warm. The flies prospered. They were everywhere, tormenting troops on the move, settling on troops in the trenches. The maggots waxed fat on the profusion of flesh scattered over the fields of Picardy. The rats thrived. The battle went on remorselessly.

On 31 July Haig received General Trenchard's report on the Flying Corps. July had been a costly month for the service; nearly 100 machines and their aircrew had been lost. For the next few weeks the domination of the British De Havilland D.H.2 and the French Nieuport XI would persist, but Trenchard said that on 30 July more German aircraft had been seen than on any previous day in this battle, although only 20 had crossed the British line. On the same day the British had made 500 flights. There was a good deal of uncertainty in the information available to the commanders. Haig wrote:

> It is now impossible to say how many [air] fights take place in a day. So many of our machines fight 4 or 5 Germans in one flight: also it is impossible to know how many hostile machines our men really do bring down, because there is no time for our victorious airmen to watch a machine crash to earth before another enemy is upon him and has to be engaged!

The loss of trained pilots was a matter that worried both sides. The need to save weight delayed the employment of the well-known parachutes, which had first been demonstrated in 1797. Balloonists made regular use of them when attacked by enemy fighters. The first time a fighter pilot used one to save his life was on 27 June when the German Lieutenant Steinbrecher of *Jasta 46*, in an Albatros DVa, was shot down by Sopwith Camels over the Somme front.

The realisation that infantry tactics were unsuited to the challenge was slow in coming. Reliance on artillery support alone persisted, although as early as 3 August the commander of XIV Corps, Lieutenant-General Cavan, had issued a memorandum to his divisional commanders suggesting changes. He advocated the close cover of 18-pounders firing shrapnel in the advance, and the immediate digging of communication trenches across no-man's-land to give cover for reinforcements to positions taken. He further ordered that assaulting troops should be spared carrying any but absolutely necessary kit; only fifty rounds of ammunition, a half-dozen bombs (grenades), haversack, water bottle, rifle and bayonet 'have been found to meet all requirements'. This approach was slow in gaining wider acceptance.

The Australian pressure on the Pozières windmill continued, no doubt to the satisfaction of those who believed in steady offensive pressure. Finally, on 4 August, they prevailed. To their left the ridge stretched away, past Mouquet Farm, which still held out against the Allies, to Thiepval, still secure in German control.

On 1 August Roger Charlet scribbled a note home:

'Au grand galop,' I write to you ... thanks for your parcel. Hope you are well. I, at the moment, am in good health. In the line, under one of those pretty, enjoyable bombardments of 210cm, etc.!

On 8 August another joint action with the French was mounted on the right flank where the Germans still held Guillemont and Ginchy. The artillery had been pounding at the defences ever since. The Germans were giving at least as good as they got. The new attack fared no better than the last, this time stopped literally dead by the blanket of shellfire that enveloped no-man's-land. A few men got into Guillemont itself for a while, and a trivial length of enemy trench was taken, but the 1/5th and the 1/8th King's (Liverpool Irish) had been cut to ribbons.

All up and down the line the artillery, both Allied and German, maintained an almost continuous fire. It is close to impossible to imagine what that was like. It wore down the gunners and threatened both body and mind of the targeted troops. Gunner George Worsley shelled Guillemont:

There were gun lines everywhere – a continuous row of them. There was no end to them – and all of them were firing almost non-stop, right round the clock... What really began to get to me was the sound of our own guns. The sound waves were going over your head all the time, like a tuning fork being struck on your steel helmet. A terrible sound – ping, ping, ping, ping – this terrible vibration day and night... You couldn't get away from it.

The French trench newspaper *La Saucisse* carried an account of being shelled.

There can be no doubt about it, this is a bombardment, a real one, one of those artillery preparations that precede attacks... Soon the noise becomes hellish; several batteries thundering out together. Impossible to make out anything. Shells fall without interruption. He feels his head is bursting, that his sanity is wavering. This is torture and he can see no end to it. He is suddenly afraid of being buried alive... What has happened to his friends? Have they gone? Are they dead? Is he the only one left alive in his hole? It's too stupid to stay there, waiting for death! Oh! To see the danger face to face! To fight back!!! To act!! The deluge continues... And the man remains in his hole, powerless, waiting, hoping for a miracle.

On 13 August the 10th Durham Light Infantry took up the task at Delville Wood. Corporal Edward Parker recalled:

At Longueval we came out into the open and found the crumpled bricks of a shattered village, still littered with bodies long dead. The village pond, once green, was now a vivid red and the corpses we stepped over were mainly those of the South Africans whose faces were blackened by three weeks of hot sunshine. At the edge of the wood we came into full view of the watchful enemy and therefore advanced by short rushes, each of which drew a long burst of machine-gun fire, and the soon to-be-dreaded point-blank stab of screaming whizz-bangs. One section remained motionless in line sprawled on the ground never to move again, and in my mind's eye one man, Allen, is kneeling still where the gunners caught him...

Their trenches were shallow scrapes and afforded little cover. Parker's platoon sergeant was hit in the stomach and died as the young man tried to stuff his entrails back. The next day, when bringing up the rations, they were caught again by shelling and two of their party disappeared from sight, the remainder running, shuddering over ground that gave under their feet, the 'soft springy place beneath which our comrades were so freshly buried.'

Bombing patrols at night were an entirely different experience:

We walked into the front line and first visited the latrine, where a man's booted leg projecting from the bench served as a hanger for our equipment. No-man's-land in the wood was a complete surprise. After the incessant strafing of the trenches, here was a sanctuary of quiet, filled with the dense blackness of deep shell holes and uncanny shapes of tortured trees. At every step we paused, listening intently, for with so much cover, surprise would be easy.

A swelling on his foot kept Parker out of the line for a few days, and by the time he was fit again, 25 August, he was told the last trench in Delville Wood had been cleared. He met his victorious battalion with envy at missing 'the best show yet' and was amazed to find that the booty acquired included, instead of the chlorinated water the British troops put up with, mineral water bottled for the Germans in one of the French villages nearby. The best show yet had cost the 10th Durhams six officers and 203 men killed or wounded.

Parker was too optimistic. Perhaps the Durhams had taken their objectives, but there were still Germans in that wood. Even after the hard fighting of the first week of September, the trench on the eastern flank of Delville Wood was in enemy hands. It would take something remarkable to shift them.

On 14 August it started to rain. A general attack on an 11-mile (18-kilometre) front was planned for 18 August, and it rained for those four days. The trenches filled with water and the tortured earth became a morass in which men and horses could hardly move. In the north, on the edge of the little valley south of Thiepval, a toe-hold had been gained on the top of the ridge at Leipzig Redoubt. The Australians were still in front of Mouquet Farm and away to the south of the Albert to Bapaume road the Switch Line defied the British. They had not got beyond Delville Wood and Guillemont was yet to be taken. Gains at all these points were the objective.

On 1 July the artillery had laid a lifting barrage; that is, when the attack went in the guns increased their range by a substantial distance to shell the second line of enemy trenches. This left the front line relatively safe for defenders to man their parapets and shoot down the attackers. Now a new technique was to be used, the creeping barrage. The guns were to increase their range every few minutes by a small distance to lay down a moving curtain of fire ahead of their infantry. Precise timing and good communications were vital if the gunners were to avoid killing their comrades. A pause in the shelling was to be a signal for the start of the advance, but with German shelling of stunning density taking place at the same time, the pause went unnoticed. Wireless communications were now being attempted, but were clumsy, unreliable and had to use immobile signalling posts. Death by friendly fire was common.

The problem of communication had not been neglected. Captain A.P. Corcoran wrote about it in *Popular Science Monthly* in 1917. Early in the war, he stated, a radio set on a lorry or truck was used, a 1½ kilowatt Marconi. The vulnerability of telephone lines was evident, and wireless, or radio, telegraphy was seen as a possible solution. It was still cumbersome, needing two 8-feet (2.4-metre) poles 80 feet (24.4 metres) apart and a ground mat on which the apparatus was placed and made earth contact. 'Fairly loud' signals could be heard some 3–5 miles (1.8–3 kilometres) away. Eventually this was all mounted in a box that a man could carry on his back, together with his aerial and ground-mat, so as to advance alongside the attacking troops. The messages from the newly captured trench were sent by Morse code and the introduction of the system was limited by the need to train key operators, a process that took three months or more.

Amongst the German commanders dissatisfaction with von Falkenhayn was reaching its height. Colonel Bauer of the Operations Section of the General Staff said:

> From week to week … things became more desperate. Falkenhayn, formerly unruffled and superior, was visibly losing his calm and security…

Crown Prince Rupprecht confided to his diary during July:

> The dissatisfaction with Falkenhayn's performance is increasing everywhere… General von Bissing [Governor General of Belgium] asked me to give him my thoughts about Falkenhayn. I mentioned his disastrous intervention before the Battle of Ypres, his responsibility for last year's defeat at Arras, the crazy offensive at Verdun and the current defeat of the Second Army.

Just after Romania entered the war on the Allied side and invaded Hungarian Transylvania, he wrote, on 29 August:

> At 5.15 [pm] a telegram arrived, announcing that General-feldmarschall von Hindenburg has been appointed Chief of the General Staff and General [Erich] Ludendorff as first Quartermaster General! At long last!

The Allies' gains of 18 August were tiny. The position at the Leipzig Redoubt was improved by the capture of a couple of trenches to give the British a position overlooking Thiepval, and the Australians had inched forward towards Mouquet Farm, but the 7th Rifle Brigade took heavy casualties in front of High Wood, and the gains by the British at Guillemont and the French at Maurepas were trivial. The exhausted French XX Corps was relieved by the 1st under General Marie Louis Adolphe Guillaumat, a long-serving soldier in his fifties who brought fresh vigour to the Sixth Army. Haig was, nonetheless, satisfied, particularly with the modest success near Thiepval which had demonstrated the effectiveness of the creeping barrage.

On 24 August the French 2nd Battalion, 1st Regiment, was sent to take the village of Maurepas, between Curlu and Combles. The fighting was hard and it was not until the morning of the following day that they succeeded. As one unit moved on up in the wake of the retreating Germans, they observed a series of dugout entrances along the side of the road. Then they came to a meeting of roads. Bits of masonry and the odd brick lay about. The officer commanding called to an infantryman who was passing, 'Where is Maurepas?' 'Here,' came the reply. 'You are in Maurepas.'

On 3 September, they tried again where the armies stood shoulder-to-shoulder. The joint effort of the French and British up the valley to the right of Guillemont towards Leuze Wood (known to the British as Lousy Wood) was unsupported by artillery; a German counter-attack on the French flank called for all their fire-power. The first assault was cut down, but the next attack by 1st Duke of Cornwall's Light Infantry and 12th Gloucesters (Bristol) fared better, and by afternoon Guillemont was in British hands. Among the defenders of what, to the Germans, had become an iconic symbol of resistance, was Reserve Lieutenant Wetje of 2nd Company, 73rd Fusiliers:

> After dawn, the artillery fire increased, peaking at about 8.00 am. Enemy airmen flew low over us, machine-gunning the position and giving their hooter signals. One entrance to the dugout was crushed. The artillery fire continued relentlessly... At about 1.00 pm the second entrance ... was crushed...

They struggled to open it up again, and the first man out shouted that the British had arrived. There was a rush to get out, but as each man emerged he was shot down, blocking the entrance again. Pulling the body aside just opened the way for grenades to come in. They now struggled to surrender.

Private Tebbe, 6th Company, 164th Infantry, had been in similar circumstances:

> Terribly cramped, the wounded huddled together as deep as possible, helpless before the hand grenades. The wounded British soldier [whom they had brought in early in the day] who was down below in the dugout, became our saviour. He shouted up to his comrades, climbed the steps... Protectively, he stood in front of the Germans who had earlier treated him in a knightly manner...

Two days later, on 5 September, Leuze Wood fell at last, and four days after that battalions from 16th (Irish) Division seized Ginchy on the ridge beyond, just to the north of Guillemont. Among those who died there was Tom Kettle of the Royal Dublin Fusiliers, an Irish nationalist, poet and Professor of National Economics in Dublin. In a letter written the previous day, he declared his wish, if he survived, to work for peace. 'I have seen war, and faced modern artillery, and know what an outrage it is against simple men.' A comrade emptied Kettle's pockets of his papers and possessions to return them to his wife. Within seconds this kindness was set at nothing as a shell blew the man to pieces.

To the east of Ginchy, on the Morval road, the Germans had constructed a massive strong-point, the Quadrilateral. It lay north of Leuze Wood, now in British hands, and north-west of Bouleaux Wood which was still held by the Germans. A major effort was planned for 15 September to push north from the ruins of Delville Wood, to the edge of which the Germans clung, to take High Wood and the Switch Line at last, but the Quadrilateral position threatened the flank of the intended advance. On the night of 9/10 September the Guards Division moved up to take over Ginchy, Leuze Wood and the intervening positions, while in the centre the New Zealanders were entering the line for the first time on the Somme between Longueval and High Wood, and away to the left, near Pozières, the Canadian Corps relieved 1 Australian Corps.

On 13 September a message from GHQ was issued to all troops exhorting them to even greater efforts in the coming attack. It suggested a new and previously untried weapon would be deployed, and promised a situation in which 'risks may be taken with advantage which would be unwise if the circumstances were less favourable to us.'

Rumours circulated among the troops. Many had seen the huge shapes shrouded by tarpaulins and many were aware that these were not the mobile water tanks they were said to be. But what the tanks really were and what they could do was not known. Could they be the answer to this slow slaughter?

The First Tanks in Battle

Early in the war it had become apparent that the trench systems, protected with barbed wire, supported by pre-ranged artillery and armed with machine-guns, were almost impregnable to infantry and to cavalry. Colonel Ernest Swinton summed up the requirements for a device to overcome trenches, rather than a machine to reintroduce mobile warfare. The bullet-proof vehicle had to be 'capable of destroying machine-guns, of crossing country and trenches, of breaking through entanglements and of climbing earthworks.' The inspiration was found in the many and curious machines that had been developed for agricultural use, where the track-laying vehicle had proved its ability to deal with broken ground. The army wanted nothing to do with the silly idea and in the early days the development was pressed ahead by the Royal Naval Air Service! The first example, *Little Willie*, was built in 1915. It was high in the body, and mounted on conventional caterpillar tracks low in profile. An improved version, *Mother*, soon followed, designed by Lieutenant W.G. Wilson and William Tritton of Foster's, the Leicestershire company contracted to produce tracked vehicles for the army. A rhomboid profile lowered the overall height, and the tracks ran right round the rhombus, giving improved performance in trench-crossing and dealing with embankments and shell-holes.

The vehicles were very primitive, even by the standards achieved later in the war. Weighing 28 tons, they were powered by unreliable engines of only 105 horsepower and could manage a snail-like 0.5 miles per hour (0.85 kilometres per hour) off the road, consuming a gallon of petrol in the process. Their armour was light, sufficient to withstand small-arms fire but easily penetrated by shell-fire. The impact of machine-gun bullets on the armour caused flakes to peel off, sending metal fragments, 'splash', flying around inside. Crews were issued with bizarre leather helmets with goggles and chain mail visors for protection. Few bothered to wear these uncomfortable and restricting head-pieces, and veterans could be recognised by the black powdering of tiny scars on their faces. The noise and fumes inside were indescribable.

The first orders were placed with Messrs. Foster & Co., Lincoln, and the Metropolitan Carriage, Wagon and Finance Co., Birmingham. Two models of the Mark I tank were made. The 'male' was armed with two 6-pounder naval guns in pod-like sponsons, fitted on each side. The 'female' had twin Vickers machine-guns. To protect it from grenades, the tank had a chicken-wire shield mounted on top; a device soon abandoned as it caused more problems than it solved.

Navigation and steering were difficult. Two brakemen controlled a track apiece, and the officer in command used compass bearings and time elapsed to attempt to work out his position. Vision was poor, and on more than one occasion the tanks opened fire on their own troops. Radio communication was not developed until late in the war, and the first tanks could only send messages by using the infantry's systems, where telephone lines were intact and not cut by the tank tracks, or by carrier pigeon. When radio was first introduced it could be used only when the tank was stationary. In spite of all these shortcomings, the new weapons had a significant impact.

Haig had wanted at least 100 tanks for 1 July, and by 15 September still had only forty-nine at his disposal. There were doubts that, in such small numbers, they should be used at all, but the cost of the battle so far had been fearful and an answer to the puzzle of how to take a trench line had to be found.

The artillery barrage was to leave unshelled lanes open for the tanks' advance and the infantry were to follow close behind. The tanks were to be used to overcome strong-points, working in subsections of two or three machines, and the plan was to have them move some five minutes in advance of the infantry to avoid drawing down shellfire on the men in the open.

On 11 September the secret weapons began their move into the line. Seventeen of them failed before they got there. Seven could not even set out. But the twenty-five that did make it had a wonderful effect. Geoffrey Malins had been sent back from London especially for the occasion, though what he was to film was kept a secret.

It was 4.30... The trenches were full of life. Men were pouring in to take up their positions. Boche ... was evidently nervous about something, for on several occasions he sent up star-shells, in batches of six, which lighted up the whole ridge like day, and until they were down again I stood stock still... All at once it seemed as though the sky had lightened... 'What's that, sir?' said the man at my side... For a moment I could discern nothing. Then, gradually out of the early morning mist a huge, dark, shapeless object evolved...

What in the world was it? For the life of me I could not take my eyes off it. The thing – I really don't know how else to describe it – ambled forward, with slow, jerky, uncertain movements... At one moment its nose disappeared, then with a slide and an upward glide it climbed to the other side of a deep shell crater which lay in its path...

It waddled, it ambled, it jolted, it rolled, it – well it did everything in turn and nothing wrong... It came to a crater. Down went its nose; a slight dip, and a clinging, crawling motion, and it came up merrily on the other side. And all the time as it slowly advanced, it breathed and belched forth tongues of flame; its nostrils seemed to breathe death and destruction, and the Huns, terrified by its appearance, were mown down like corn falling to the reaper's sickle.

Malins was in front of Martinpuich with the 7/8th King's Own Scottish Borderers, 10th Cameronians (Scottish Rifles) and 11th Argyll and Sutherland Highlanders, battalions from two brigades (45 and 46 Brigades) of 15th (Scottish) Division. With the tank advance leading the way, they took the village. Reserve Lieutenant Hermann Kohl of the 17th Bavarian Infantry was there:

During the early hours of 15 September, a forest of guns opened up in a ceaseless rolling thunder of fire... A sea of iron crashed down on all the front and support

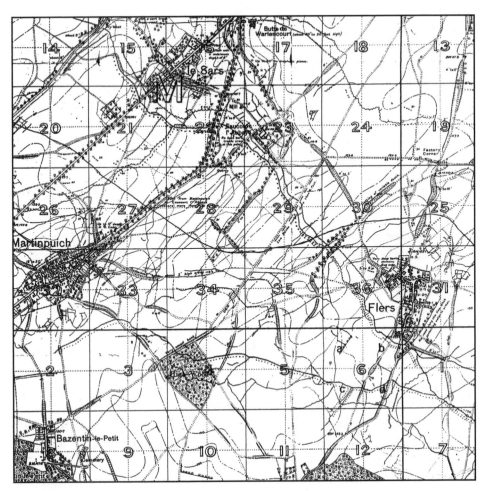

Detail from OS sheet 57C S.W. corrected to 3 September 1916. The original map is annotated: 'Donor: W. Vickers, MM, RE. The line running through square M 20, 27, 28, 29, 30 and N25 was marked in pencil the night after the attack and gives an idea of the ground gained and the bulge around Flers demonstrates the advantage gained by the surprise use of tanks.' Switch Trench runs from square 2, across the edge of High Wood and on through square 6. (TM Accn 2458)

lines of the area…From the direction of High Wood … the British flood overwhelms them, consumes them and passes on. Wave upon wave. An extraordinary number of men and there, between them, spewing death, unearthly monsters; the first British tanks… Our artillery does not fire a single round.

On the eastern flank the only tank to make it to the start line in Delville Wood was D1. With bombers (grenade-throwers) of the 6th King's Own Yorkshire

Light Infantry it made its way round the eastern end of the wood to attack Hop Trench and Ale Alley. Lance-Corporal Lee Lovell followed behind it:

> The tank waddled on with its guns blazing and we could see Jerry popping up and down, not knowing what to do, whether to stay or run. We Bombers were sheltering behind the tank peering round and anxious to let Jerry have our bombs. But we had no need of them. The Jerries waited until our tank was only a few yards away and then fled – or hoped to! The tank just shot them down and the machine-guns, the post itself, the dead and the wounded who hadn't been able to run, just disappeared. The tank went right over them.

The trenches, which had for so long secured the German positions on the edge of Delville Wood were gone. The tank itself then suffered a direct hit from a German shell and was destroyed. To the right things did not go so well. On the 14th Division's right was the Guards Division, with 6th Division on their right attacking towards the Quadrilateral. In that attack the 9th Norfolks were strafed in their jump-off trench by a tank which lost its bearings while 1 and 2 Guards Brigades never got the ten tanks that were meant to spearhead their attack; of the five that made it to the start line, all became unserviceable or lost direction. In the confusion the 2nd Grenadiers and the 2nd and 3rd Coldstream got separated. In spite of their vulnerability and the loss of two-thirds of their men, they managed to take the Triangle strong-point, some 500 yards (457 metres) north of the Quadrilateral, before noon. On this day Raymond Asquith of the 3rd Grenadier Guards, son of Britain's Prime Minister, was mortally wounded.

In front of Delville Wood a single tank, D3, led the way forward, smashing through the enemy wire in textbook style. Lieutenant H.G. Head was in command of D3 and had made his way to the edge of the wood:

> At the very edge of the wood we had to turn at right angles and pass along the front of the wood and wait for dawn. The fellow following me unfortunately got into the wood too far and got his tracks suspended on the stump of a tree. The stumps were not more than four feet [1.2 metres] high ... we manoeuvred into such a position to tow him out, which we did just before dawn ... at half past six ... we made our way slowly towards Flers. On the outskirts of Flers, unfortunately, the tank got hit and that was the end of me for the day.

Switch Trench was taken, and the infantry – the 8th Rifle Brigade and 8th King's Royal Rifle Corps – swept forward to the next trench line, though their supporting tank had been knocked out by then. On 14th Division's left 41st Division attacked towards Flers; on their left the troops of the New Zealand Division, from their positions north-west of Delville Wood, pushed forward and captured the section of the Switch Line facing them, then pressed on and took the German positions west and north-west of Flers, and were thus able to consolidate a position on the crest of the ridge. Lieutenant A.E. Arnold of D Company, Heavy Section, Machine Gun Corps, as the tank formation's 'cover' name had it, was in command of *Dracula*. He found the ground dry, but peppered with shell-holes which slowed his progress. He saw his companion tank hit and catch fire, the crew escaping by the back door. 'This was not encouraging,' he remarked. As they approached the German trench line he attempted to open fire with his Hotchkiss machine-gun, but it would not fire. They straddled the trench and the Vickers machine-guns were able to open fire and clear the enemy from the trench. They paused, and Arnold discovered that his gun had been hit by a shell splinter, which had rendered it unserviceable, so he mounted the spare weapon:

> ... we were advancing in the direction of Flers. The bombardment had slackened right off. Opposition was slight and the New Zealanders ... were advancing and taking prisoner any remaining Germans. We soon covered the mile or so the Flers and on my right I saw the tank proceeding up the road into Flers. The New Zealanders immediately set about consolidating the position and took possession of a sunken road which leads out of the village to the north-east. I sent off a pigeon with a message ... to Corps HQ. It was now about 8 am ...

The machines of Lieutenants Huffam and Cort, D9 and D14, became jammed when trying to cross a trench during their approach to the start line. They were dug out by a Chinese labour battalion that afternoon. The tank effort in High Wood, on the New Zealanders' left, was a failure, as the terrain was impossible for the new machines. But with success on either flank – for 50th Division took Hook trench west of the wood – it became possible, though horribly expensive in men, for the 47th (1/2 London) Division (made up of Territorials) to push the Germans out of their lines, and by the middle of the day High Wood was, at last, in British hands. Away to the west of 15th Division at Martinpuich, and north of the Albert to Bapaume road, the 2nd and 3rd Canadian Divisions headed for Courcelette. They outran their tank support and took the village.

The Royal Flying Corps were intensely active that day. Seventy enemy artillery batteries were attacked and nineteen German aircraft shot down. Two-seater aircraft flew patrols to spot targets and fall of shot for the artillery, and in support of the troops on the ground the British pilots machine-gunned enemy trenches and forming-up points, as well as any reinforcements they spotted heading for the hard-pressed German positions.

The advance was, by the standards of this static war, remarkable, but the casualties had still been heavy and the majority of the tanks were now either stuck, destroyed or had broken down. The Germans rushed reinforcements forward and the attack petered out. The hoped-for breakthrough never came and the waiting cavalry were once again sent back to their quarters.

That the day was a success is undoubted, but Winston Churchill, a prime mover of the development of the tank, complained 'My poor "land battleships" have been let off prematurely and on a petty scale.' However, it is certain that, at the state of technical development then attained, five times the number would not have done much better; they were too slow and too unreliable. What they had achieved was of immense value. Not only had they taken part in an advance of over 2,000 yards (1,828 metres), but they had dealt a profound blow to the enemy's morale and given the British Army the invaluable gift of hope in battle conditions of unprecedented horror.

Situation Normal

Some 2.5 miles (4 kilometres) to the rear, behind Montauban, the 10th Durham Light Infantry, one of the 14th (Light) Division's reserve battalions, were coming up into the line, eager to see this new weapon, the tank. Their brigade, 43, was to relieve 42 Brigade, now holding a line running east from the northern outskirts of Flers. Their first task was to move munitions up to Delville Wood. Stokes mortar bombs were carried up on 14 September, six of them by each man, which took ten hours. No sooner were they back at Pommiers Redoubt, between Mametz and Montauban, than they were turned out again, this time to carry 'toffee apples'; mortar shells which weighed 60 pounds. That done, the rest that they expected was denied to them; another journey with yet more munitions had to be made before they could sleep. On the afternoon of 15 September they made their way forward through Delville Wood itself, curious at suffering no casualties. Climbing to the ridge through German shellfire they took shelter in the craters and admired the view the enemy had enjoyed of every movement in the wood they had just left. They lay under shellfire until night, when they went forward to relieve the 9th Rifle Brigade. They were surprised at the distance they had to go before they found them. In the morning they were to attack towards Gueudecourt, less than a mile north-east of Flers, as part of a general assault by II, Canadian, III, XV and XIV Corps to capitalise on the previous day's successes.

The Durhams were miners. Scornful of the Rifle Brigade's trench-making, they set to at once to make proper trenches. Lance-Corporal Edward Parker, a southerner himself, held that the Durhams dug for pleasure. He spent the night in a forward observation post, looking out for a counter-attack, and was recalled to a deep, secure trench for breakfast. Mail was, to his surprise, being distributed and Parker got a parcel of chocolate bars. He realised that he had been twenty years old for the past three days.

At dawn the 10th Durhams went over the top, at first running forward unmolested, then through heavier and yet heavier rifle and machine-gun fire. The line thinned as they went. Their forward rushes became shorter and shorter. Eventually Parker found himself on the forward slope of a small ridge above a shallow valley that rose suddenly towards the village of Gueudecourt. Only one other man was in sight, and as he turned his head in response to Parker's call, blood spouted through his hair and down his features. Parker, alone, lay still, daydreaming until the firing died down, then hurled himself into a shell hole. To his pleasure he found one of his companions, 'poor old Stone, the deaf man' already there. And there they stayed. They saw only one other British soldier that day, their Commanding Officer's Runner, who told them that the battalion was scuppered. Parker saw plenty of Germans:

In the afternoon a whole company of Jägers rushed forward about one or two hundred yards to our right front. I kicked Stone and began firing rapidly over the top of the crater. By the time he had joined me, the dark green figures ... began to falter, falling fast under our enfilading fire... We kept up the fire until all movement ceased and our ammunition was exhausted. When we looked at the bottom of the shell hole, there were two or three hundred empty cartridge cases under our feet... We began to realize that we had wiped out the whole company. It seemed strange that no one on the British side joined in. Clearly we were alone.

As evening drew near it became clear no one knew they were there. A heavy British barrage fell around them, threatening to finish them off and sending them burrowing into the sides of their crater for shelter. When darkness fell they made their way to the summit of the ridge and found two or three other survivors with whom they dug a trench and scavenged ammunition, grenades and food from the corpses that lay along the skyline. There they readied themselves for a dawn counter-attack. Footsteps alerted them. Out of the darkness emerged their CO and the adjutant to rebuke them for being too far forward. They crept back to join a party of about forty, and dug in again. When dawn came up Parker was out in no-man's-land looking for wounded to bring in and had to retreat quickly to rejoin his fellows and tramp back towards Delville Wood. On reaching Pommiers Redoubt once more they found food for the 500 men of the battalion who had set out. There were fifty of them to eat it. Back at Maricourt a new captain paraded them for rifle inspection. They were severely criticised for having dirty rifles. During their four days in the front line they never saw a tank.

When, some time later, Parker was recommended for a commission, the colonel did not know who he was; indeed, he denied ever having seen him.

Despite some small gains, the attacks on 16 September had achieved little along the whole sector of assault. For the next eight days operations were mainly confined to small, local actions, night patrols and consolidating positions won on the 15th and subsequently. Some ground was gained from the Germans, and the enemy's counter-attacks beaten off.

On 15 September Haig noted in his diary:

Certainly some of the Tanks have done marvels! And have enabled our attack to progress at a surprisingly fast pace... the French attacks against Rancourt and Frégicourt failed. I don't think there was much vigour in them.

What Haig omits is the event which must have had an influence on what the Germans could offer by way of resistance on the 15th: the massive effort the French put in on 12 September. The whole of the French Fourth Army, north of the Somme and to the British right, thrust forward to continue the assault it had begun nine days before. Cléry-sur-Somme had already been taken and now the French crossed the Bapaume to Péronne road and the 41st Division seized Bouchavesnes, fighting from house to house. But by then Fayolle's I and VII Corps had lost some 17,000 men on this front and the reinforcement by the V Corps did not suffice to maintain momentum. Nonetheless Foch promised to support the British attack of 15 September with a powerful artillery action; a promise he kept.

Captain Roger Charlet, 87th Infantry, wrote to his priest, M. Canaple, on 15 September. His hopes of getting home on leave had been, he regretted, dashed because a new attack was planned:

Yesterday my section had six wounded ... but I remain... I have no taste for anything, no hope, and all is suffering to the end! Our Corps is very thin, and it isn't finished. Farewell, dear Monsieur Canaple.

He died that day near Belloy-en-Santerre, twenty-four years old. The brigade citation said of him that he excelled as a soldier and was an excellent machine-gun commander, with a steady courage under all circumstances. He stood to his post under heavy bombardment and there was killed.

Widening the Front

The dramatic advance of 15 September, falling short though it did of the longed-for breakthrough, created a salient limited to the west by Thiepval and on the east, where the British and French armies met, by Morval and Combles. Beyond these villages the French had a good chance of getting to Péronne if the British could sort out the eastern flank of this salient.

On 24 September René Gain, of the French 61st Regiment of Artillery, wrote to his brother Camille:

It's my second day on this front ... my corner is not too 'marmité' [bombarded with heavy shells]. I'm close to the divisional ambulance and see lots of wounded, even dead, men; just in front of my dugout there is a cemetery. The surroundings are less than pleasing, but what can you hope for? It's war. My little dugout is satisfactory, as long as no marmites fall on it.

We are right on the line of advance. All along the old trenches there are plenty of enemy dead – the flies have no rest. The shelling must have been ferocious. Nothing fell nearer to me than 500m. I saw an aircraft in flames. I'm frightened when under shelter, but not when I'm busy.

On 25 September the east was the target. Malins was told an attack was planned for midday on the 25th, XIV Corps to push east and north-east of Guillemont against Morval and Lesboeufs; at the same time XV Corps and III Corps, and, a day later, Canadian Corps were to attack in support. South of the Somme the French Tenth Army was to attack Barleux and Villers-Carbonnel. The day before, Malins had gone over to film the build-up. That night he was with a battery of 18-pounders firing through the gloom and also experienced heavy German shelling:

On several occasions I really thought my last minute had come. The noise was deafening, the glare and flash although beautiful was sickening. Our guns were pouring out a withering fire, and the ground quivered and shook, threatening to tumble the temporary shelter round my ears. One shell, which came very near, burst and the concussion slightly blew in the side of the shelter; it also seemed momentarily to stun me; I crouched down as close to earth as possible. I will admit that I felt a bit 'windy', my body shaking as if with ague; a horrible buzzing sensation was in my head, dizziness was coming over me.

He clambered into the open and took shelter in an old trench, clutching his head and shaking with pain and tension, fighting to regain control. The battery officers thought him blown to bits, and cheered at finding him still alive, offered tea.

With the coming day, Malins looked for Guillemont. He could not see it; there was no way of telling where the fields had finished and the village had begun. It no longer existed. Shortly before the attack was to go in, the British artillery opened up once more with a bombardment that even the experienced Malins found astounding. Then, accompanied by tanks, the attack began. The fighting continued through the afternoon, and both Lesboeufs and Morval were taken.

The northern end of the line attacked on 1 July was just where it had been. South of Thiepval a hold had been secured on the tip of the Thiepval ridge at Leipzig Redoubt, but north from there no progress had been made in nearly three months. The dry summer had given way to a wet autumn and the weather could only be expected to worsen. It was vital to push the Germans off the ridge, to take the Schwaben Redoubt and its satellites, Stuff and Zollern Redoubts. The Battle of Thiepval Ridge began on 26 September, and involved, from the left, II Corps and the Canadian Corps, with III, XV and XIV Corps also pushing forwards from their positions at the south-eastern end of the British lines. In II Corps' sector, 18th (Eastern) Division captured Thiepval on 27 September and 11th Division on its right had taken Mouquet Farm and occupied the Zollern Redoubt by the evening of the 26th. Away to the right in XV Corps' area 64 Brigade from 21st Division managed to enter Gird Trench in two places on the 26th, but there was 1,500 yards (1,370 metres) of solidly defended trench between them. A tank was summoned for the next morning and at 6.30am, accompanied by bombers (soldiers with hand grenades), moved south-east along the trench, over the wire, firing as it went. The report of XV Corps states:

No difficulty was experienced. The enemy surrendered freely as the tank moved down the trench... By 8.30 the whole length of the trench had been cleared and the 15th Durham Light Infantry moved over the open and took over the captured trench... What would have proved a very difficult operation, involving probably heavy losses, was taken with the greatest ease entirely owing to the assistance rendered by the tank.

The Germans had been trapped. Many were killed, and 370 of them made prisoner. British casualties in this particular operation came to five. In the afternoon, after a squadron from the Cavalry Corps had reconnoitred Gueudecourt, 21st Division infantry occupied the village. By the time operations ceased on 30 September, the British front line to Combles had been pushed forward, in places by more than a mile (1.6 kilometres).

Once Thiepval had fallen, the Germans had not been able to hold Mouquet Farm. It had been taken by the Canadians on 16 September, but a German counter-attack subsequently drove them out. Now battalions from 11th Division's 34 Brigade retook it, and held it. When Malins went to film it a few days later, a machine-gun officer showed him around, taking him down the dank stairs beneath the wreckage of the old farm and into the bunkers 40 and 50 feet (12–15 metres) below. The smell of rotting bodies filled the damp air; a whole gallery had been blown in together with its occupants. Off the galleries were countless rooms hollowed from the chalk, a complex like a rabbit warren. The officer showed Malins the gouged wall where the bullets from a machine-gun had zipped through the dark as the attackers broke in and the photographer tried to imagine the scene as the fight continued underground. When they emerged, Malins found himself 100 yards (90 metres) from his entry-point.

Come October, the rain fell once more; solid and continuous. What had been mud became deep mire. The poet John Masefield described it as being like a stagnant river, unable to retain footprints, almost up to his knees. That, of course, was on the roads. In the trenches the mud rose thigh-high. The shell-holes filled to make deadly pools where once there had been shelter. Every movement became an effort. As October wore on the cold weather arrived. The surface of the mud froze, catching at the feet that broke through it. The fighting continued. The capture of the Thiepval Ridge had been completed on 30 September, and from 1–18 October the British fought the Battle of Transloy Ridge, and from 5–11 November the Battle of the Ancre Heights. 47th (1/2 London) Division captured Eaucourt l'Abbaye, between Flers and Le Sars, on 1 October, and Le Sars fell to 23rd Division on 7 October. On 9 October the 10th Cheshire Regiment stormed Stuff Redoubt and held it against two German counter-attacks. The Schwaben Redoubt finally fell to an assault by the 4/5th Black

Watch and the 1/1st Cambridgeshire Regiment, assisted by the XVII King's Royal Rifle Corps (British Empire League) from II Corps' 39th Division. The generals wondered how much more could or should be achieved before winter. Rawlinson, the Fourth Army commander, wrote:

> The bad weather which has forced us to slow down has given the Boche a breather. His artillery is better organised, and his infantry is fighting with greater tenacity, but deserters continue to come in; and, the more we bombard, the more prisoners and deserters we shall get. I should like therefore to be more or less aggressive all the winter, but we must not take the edge off next year.

The ensuing winter would surprise him. The events of November were already in hand.

The Battle of the Ancre

In April 1917 John Masefield walked over the high ground to the east of Serre, between Beaucourt-sur-Ancre and Hébuterne. Looking west, he could see how well the Germans were placed to repel the British attacks of the previous July and November. He wrote home to say that most of the British front line was open to his gaze and just how easy it had been for the Germans to call down shellfire on troops massing for an attack was clear to him.

At the start of November 1916 the British lines were still in the same place and the Germans still faced them both from these hillsides north of the Ancre and from the hills to the south, where St-Pierre-Divion and Grandcourt were in their hands. The French, on the other hand, had used the last three weeks of October to attempt to extend their hold on the Bapaume to Péronne road with the British alongside, in what they called the Battle of Transloy Ridge. South of the river Somme French XXXII Corps efforts had been frustrated by German counter-attacks when the 70th Infantry Division had retaken La Maisonette on 29 October. On 1 November the German 39th Infantry Division planned to attack the French near Sailly Saillisel, north of Bouchavesnes, but the conditions were terrible: cold, muddy, wet and with incessant shellfire. The scheme included aerial support, but the outcome was not a success. Flight Lieutenant Johannes Fischer of 8th Air Wing took off shortly before 7am to bomb and strafe the French, but cloud closed in and, despite flying around for three quarters of an hour, could not go into action. They made their way back to their aerodrome, sighting a French Caudron biplane as they went. The next day the weather was much improved and they flew to spot for the artillery and take photographs for the map-makers and again flew back. As they did so one of their comrades came gliding steeply in to the airfield. The pilot had to be lifted out; in a dogfight he had been shot through the back.

On 5 November 126th Infantry's 1st Battalion was engaged. They managed to hold where 1st Company's trenches were relatively intact, but the 2nd and 3rd Company positions were severely damaged. As Captain Tobias remarked:

> The surprise attack by the French was met only by the wounded, those buried alive and those deafened by hours of drumfire. It broke through…

By the end of the day the French had broken through north of Rancourt and entered St Pierre Vaast Wood.

To the north-west the British were overlooked by the Germans on the Ancre, where they still held Beaucourt and Grandcourt, and, on the lower ground, Beaumont-Hamel to the west and St-Pierre-Division to the south. The time had come for the British to straighten up their line by taking these villages and removing the salient. The rainy weather of the first week of the month gave way to dry, bright, crisp late-autumn days, and the ground started to dry out to some extent. Haig had given General Gough, whose 5th (formerly Reserve) Army now manned this sector, discretion to cancel the attack if conditions became unfavourable, but there was no need to do so.

The Germans had re-entrenched since the summer. The Hawthorn Redoubt, blown up with a mine on 1 July, had been rebuilt, and the British had tunnelled under it once again to repeat the destruction when the attack went in. Crown Prince Rupprecht noted in his diary entry of 2 November:

> General von Below stated that he was expecting an attack along the Gommecourt-Ancre sector, because the enemy had smashed all the trenches along this line… It is striking that the enemy is digging in vigorously on the high ground near Courcelette, Martinpuich and to the west of Delville Wood. This could well indicate that the enemy only intends to carry out an offensive with limited objectives … considering spending the winter in these positions…

On 8 November General Haig met Lieutenant-General Lord Cavan, who commanded XIV Corps:

We had a good hour's talk. I told him that the main position of defence would be the main Thiepval ridge – Flers – Les Boeufs. As our advanced or first position there would be the front line we were now holding. This must be made very strong...

The communications are still very bad. In fact we are fighting under the same conditions as in October 1914, i.e. with rifle and machine-guns only, because bombs and mortar ammunition cannot be carried forward as the roads are so bad.

Four days earlier Haig had noted Cavan's observation on the conditions:

No one who has not visited the front trenches can really know the state of exhaustion to which the men are reduced. The conditions are far worse than in the First Battle of Ypres, and my General Officers and Staff Officers agree that they are the worst they have seen, owing to the enormous carry of all munitions, food, water and ammunition.

The misery of standing knee-deep in mud appears to have been of minor interest.

In front of Serre the 3rd Division was in readiness, with XIII Corps' 31st Division on its left and 2nd Division on its right. V Corps' 51st (Highland) Division faced Beaumont-Hamel and the 63rd (Royal Naval) Division were just to the south at Hamel. The Royal Naval Division had been formed of men excess to the requirements of the seaborne force and caused the dyed-in-the-wool army commanders a good deal of grief by persisting in naval attitudes to rank and discipline (although one of its three brigades was made up entirely of army battalions, and its Pioneer battalion was also army). The fact that they were an excellent fighting force in spite of their lack of spit and polish maybe made matters worse in senior soldiers' eyes. Attached to them for the attack was the 13th Rifle Brigade, so that the division at the time actually consisted of six Royal Navy, two Royal Marine and six Army battalions.

The morning of 13 November was foggy and the attack went in while it was still dark. At Serre the valley was heavy with mud. Many men got stuck waist-deep and were sitting targets for the defenders. The attack by the 3rd Division was a total failure, and that night 31st Division, on the extreme left, was ordered back from the German front line north of Serre, which it had taken in the morning. At Beaumont-Hamel, however, the Highlanders found the German front line empty; the Germans were still in their bunkers assuming this was just the routine morning shelling. Sergeant William Stevenson of 6th Argyle and Sutherland Highlanders recalled:

> They put us in the tunnel the night before and in the morning they blew the top off it and the infantry went straight over. The machine-gunners and trench-mortar parties [the new organisational structure] were the last to get out …we got right into the German trenches – and there was nobody there! They were all still in their dugouts …

What was to become a river of prisoners started to trickle back to the cages awaiting them behind British lines. On Hawthorn Ridge and the spur that ran towards the Ancre the fog confused the attackers as much as the defenders. The Royal Naval Division's leading battalions, Hood and Hawke, overran the German line without pausing to mop up. The defenders emerged from their shelters to open up on them from behind. The attack faltered. A 26-year-old New Zealander, Lieutenant-Colonel Bernard Freyberg, pulled the scattered formation together and renewed the attack. The Royal Naval Division now held the ridge above the valley that ran down from Beaumont-Hamel to the Ancre, and here hundreds of German troops were trapped. The flow of prisoners to the rear became a flood. On the Highland Division's left, 2nd Division overran Beaumont Trench and linked up with the Highlanders on the northern outskirts of Beaumont-Hamel.

The Highlanders were in full control of Beaumont-Hamel by mid-afternoon, and the deep dugouts in Y Ravine were also in their hands. On the other side of the river St-Pierre-Divion also fell, to troops from II Corps' 39th Division, who took all their objectives that day. The dugouts had been cleared one by one, each yielding its crop of prisoners or corpses. On the north bank, the next day saw Beaucourt fall to the Royal Naval Division, this time its Army battalions leading the assault. Here Freyberg again distinguished himself, though at the cost of a near-fatal wound. He was awarded the Victoria Cross, having already won the DSO at Gallipoli in 1915. That day, too, I ANZAC, away to the right near Gueudecourt made a series of largely unsuccessful attacks, while other units of II and V Corps attempted to drive forward from positions they had won on 13 November, with some local successes. The pressure was maintained by the II Corps for the next three days.

Behind Beaumont-Hamel, on the forward edge of the plateau that runs away to the east, two massive German lines, Frankfort and Munich trenches, still threatened the newly won positions. On 15 November battalions of the 37th,

51st and 2nd Divisions attacked but were driven off. Lance-Corporal William Mullen of the 8th East Lancashire Regiment remembered the approach:

> ... getting out of the trenches we tramped across a great many fields that were nothing but a mass of shell holes, and the mud was almost up to our waists and water over our knees in most places... It was bitterly cold and fritz was knocking sparks off us with shrapnel. Many men dropped exhausted through struggling to get through the mud.

The attack took place at 8.30am, in fog. Mullen again:

> Then the order came to fix bayonets and prepare to attack. Men fixed their bayonets. I loaded my Lewis gun... We had not gone more than 100 yards [90 metres] when the Germans spotted us coming. As soon as they saw us they jumped out of the trench, planted their machine-gun on top and simply poured lead into us with a coolness and skill that any machine-gunner might envy. Our lads were dropping like skittles, but we still kept going and hung onto the enemy like glue. Most of the Germans retired into the second line as out lads got among them...

They held on until evening. Mullen survived being hit in the head by shrapnel – his helmet saved his life, but he was seriously wounded. The assault had failed and the fortunate ones regained their own lines. The 8th East Lancashire and the 10th Loyal North Lancashire alongside them lost eighteen officers and 350 men that day.

The task of taking Frankfort and Munich trenches was now given to the 16th Highland Light Infantry. On 18 November the twenty-one officers and 650 men went forward. They succeeded in entering Munich Trench and a small party even got into Frankfort Trench beyond, but the main force was ejected from the first objective by a massive counter-attack. The forward troops were cut off by 21 November and remained so, for attempts to fight through to get them out failed. The Germans also failed to shift them for the next four days, by which time the ninety originally cut off had been reduced to thirty, and half of those wounded and unable to fight. The survivors were taken prisoner. It was the last action of the First Battle of the Somme.

Chapter 5

The Somme 1917: A False Quiet

In mid-September 1916 it had been dawning on the Germans that they were not going to hold the French and British on the Somme and the Ancre. They had already lost their forward positions on the southern end of the front, and when Thiepval fell, the area south of the Ancre had now to be defended on the level – the advantage of the terrain was no longer with them. Their losses at Verdun were also severe, so the holding of a large salient in front of Bapaume and Péronne no longer served their purpose. What was needed was a new line to the east which could be fortified thoroughly and which was positioned where the natural characteristics of the countryside favoured defence. Then the Allies could start to wear themselves out all over again.

First Quartermaster General Ludendorff outlined the strategy in his memoirs:

Our [i.e. his and Field Marshal Hindenburg's] conclusion was no sudden one, but had gradually grown upon us since we took over our posts at the end of August 1916. Accordingly, the construction had begun as early as September of powerful rear positions in the West; the Siegfried Line, running from Arras, west of Cambrai, St. Quentin, La Fère, Vailly-sur-Aisne to get rid of the great Albert-Roye-south-west of Noyon-Soissons-Vailly-sur-Aisne salient, in which the Somme fighting had made a large indentation; and south of Verdun the Michael Line, in front of the Etain–Gorz line, to straighten out the salient of St Mihiel. These strategic positions had the advantage of shortening the front and economizing men, and their occupation according to plan was prepared. Whether we should retire on them, and how the positions would be used, was not of course decided in September, 1916; the important thing then was to get them built. This made comprehensive measures necessary and I made heavy demands for labour from home.

The cost of resisting the British and French on the Somme had been immense. More than 300 counter-attacks had been mounted, and more than half a million casualties had been sustained, inflicting enormous damage on the experienced troops. Further fighting would reveal the loss of quality that marked the generality of the German Army in the second half of the war. Allied losses were of the same order of magnitude: British 415,000 and French 195,000. But the men of Kitchener's Army, the patriotic amateurs of 1915, were now battle-hardened professionals and yet more men were becoming available.

The British spoke of the new German defences as the Hindenburg Line, a result of misinterpretation of intelligence gained from a prisoner. It was, in fact, a series of fortified lines rather more complex than Ludendorff recalled. They started in the north round Lille with the Wotan Position which ran south towards a point west of Cambrai, where a branch snaked back up towards Arras and Vimy, and the principal line ran south in the form of the Siegfried Line to St Quentin. This section made use of the empty channel of the unfinished Canal du Nord and the existing St Quentin Canal. The line continued with further positions north of the Aisne on the Chemin des Dames and, east of there, eventually to Metz. If the works the Allies faced in July on the Somme were daunting, these were yet more formidable.

The prosecution of the war as a whole was also on Ludendorff's mind. The largest uncertainty related to the position of the Americans. If their resources were concentrated on the war in Europe, defeat was inevitable. But even without that concentration, the supplies reaching England and France were significant and the temptation to unleash the German submarine fleet against merchant shipping was immense. Meanwhile the Allied blockade of Germany was hurting badly. Hopes of a diplomatic solution were entertained and Ambassador Count Bernstorff should, it was suggested, approach the American President, Woodrow Wilson, to intervene. The alternative was to start sinking all ships supplying Germany's enemies and accept that the United States would enter the war alongside France and Britain; it would then be a race to secure victory in Europe before the United States could exert overwhelming force. Eventually this risk was accepted and unrestricted submarine warfare commenced on 31 January 1917. The United States of America declared war on Germany on 6 April 1917.

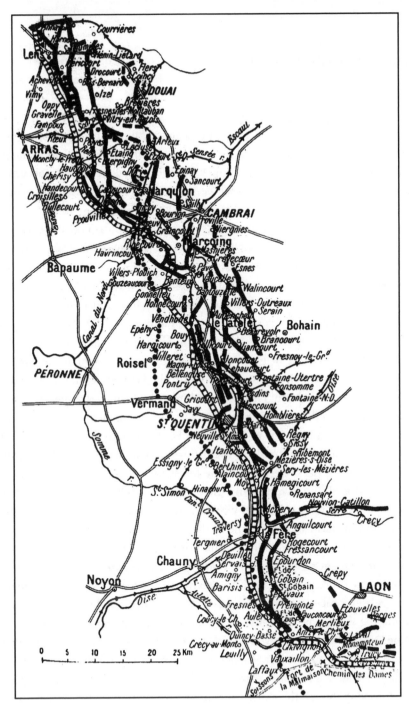

A map, based on the information held by the French, of the part of the 'Hindenburg'
Line between Lens and the Chemin des Dames, as it became when fully developed. It
can be seen to be a complex of defence positions. *From* l'Illustration, *14 September 1918.*
(HGG)

Operation Alberich

The complicated manoeuvre of moving two armies back from contact with the Allies to new positions was named Operation Alberich and comprised not only the movement of men and munitions, but also the destruction of currently occupied positions, and of roads, canals, houses and farms on the way. Water supplies, springs and sewage disposal works would be blown up. Moreover, the French inhabitants would be removed. It would create a desert.

In December 1916, at Douilly, a little village north of Ham on a tributary of the river Somme, Madame Demarolle witnessed the operation. On Christmas Eve the crib in the church was destroyed and the brass ornaments taken, and the next day, Christmas Day itself, the bells were taken away. Over the next few days the rest of the church property was removed, Mme Demarolle's house was searched, and the last of the mattresses were requisitioned for the farm where the wounded were being treated. On 4 January 1917 the demolitions began. Trees were felled on the St Quentin road and the walls of the kitchen gardens were knocked down. On 6 January the Germans searched her house again and took all the domestic linen. There was nothing left. The next day she noted that it was fifteen months since Fernand had been deported; she does not mention her relationship to him. On 16 January Mr Furcy came to fit a wood-burning stove and an electricity supply in the bathroom. The reason for this becomes clear a couple of days later; part of the house was taken over by soldiers and she was reduced to two rooms and the bathroom/kitchen as accommodation. There were fifty-three soldiers at work, laying mines. The wounded were evacuated from the farm and were gone by the end of the month. Early in February her grain store was plundered and she, with Emile and Amilia (possibly her children), were ordered to leave her house, taking refuge in the Daissaint household. On 11 February the garden was destroyed, the nearby villages of Cuivilly and Toule evacuated and thirty-eight of Douilly's menfolk departed. The order to quit the village entirely came on 13 February and at 7am the next morning Mme Demarolle ate the remaining fifty Eucharist wafers, gathered up the sacred vessels and set off, arriving at Maubeuge at midnight on 20 February. This bleak story is set out in her sparse diary as a series of facts without emotional gloss, heartbreaking though the experiences must have been.

Among the British, the interpretation of the German Operation Alberich – the withdrawal from the positions they held at the end of 1916 – was at first quite wrong. Malins stated with complete conviction that 'the enemy is falling back, not for strategic reasons … but because he is forced to by the superiority of our troops and our dominating gun-power.' In February 1917 the first stage of the withdrawal took the Germans back towards Bapaume and Le Transloy.

The advancing soldiers were, as usual, on the hunt for souvenirs. The spiked German helmet was a prized find, but many of those left behind were booby-trapped. A tempting jar of spirits lifted up could detonate a bomb.

The nineteen-year-old Edwin Vaughan, recently commissioned and serving with the 8th Royal Warwickshire Regiment, arrived in France in January 1917. His journal tells of a quiet, casual existence in the rear, visiting cathedrals, eating good meals and playing practical jokes. In time this juvenile frivolity would wear off, but it does show how distant from the reality of war an area only a few miles to the rear could be. His first experience of the front line was in the trenches previously held by the French south of the river, between Herbécourt and Biaches. They were still there two months later, their tedious existence punctuated by the occasional bout of shelling or sniping by the Germans. A German aircraft attacked one of the British observation balloons:

He made one circle, one dive and then sped back to his lines. A wreath of smoke appeared and then the balloon burst into flames. We saw the two observers climb out of the basket and drop; their parachutes opened and very slowly they commenced to descend. But there was no wind to carry them away and after a few agonizing seconds the balloon collapsed and falling directly upon them bore them to the ground in its flaming folds...

On 13 March they had the unpleasant experience of being shelled by their own side. Vaughan tried to rescue the men buried in the neighbouring dugout, but found only fragments of them remained. Three days later, beyond Herbécourt, he was leading a road-mending party when a slightly wounded private of the 4th Gloucestershire Regiment met them and announced that the enemy had gone:

We thought, they was very quiet, so we showed ourselves a little bit at first, and nothing happened. Then we sent a feller out just before dark: he walked slowly across, waitin' for a shot to be fired, but none came. He went on over their first line, over their second, and then when he reached the third line we all went over. There wasn't a Jerry anywhere except a few stiffs. They've gone clean back over the canal. And the trenches they had! Why, Sir! We was living in *muck* to them!

Vaughan asked, if the enemy had gone, how he came to be wounded.

The trenches were left full of booby-traps. All I did was to pick up a Hun's helmet from the floor of the trench, and a bomb went off underneath. Lucky for me, Sir, that it was buried, and I only got it slightly. Ye'll perhaps know Mr Harcourt of the 6th Warwicks, Sir? Well he's bought it … he went down a dugout, but as soon as he put his hand on the hand rail, the bottom two steps blew up, and took both his legs off. He died before they could get him away.

Vaughan spent the night of 17 March near Biaches, just west of Péronne, and during the following day they moved north-west to cross the canal on a bridge hastily erected by the Royal Engineers to reach Halle. By 11pm they were in the main street of Péronne. They had seen the glow of fires in the town as they approached, and buildings in the square were burning as they sought shelter for the night. The next day the fires were still burning, and the young man saw the extent of the destruction the departing Germans had wrought. One of those departing was Dr Hugo Natt of 118th Infantry Regiment. On 11 March, he said, many places in Péronne had been blown up and several houses had burned out. The next day, he reported that the Town Hall was still on fire. He was clearly fascinated: 'spellbinding' he called the sight. Some houses had been blown up, leaving only a wall or two standing. On 13 March the telephone system was being dismantled in preparation for the retreat starting that evening.

Ten days later the Warwickshires were on the move again, to the north-east. The scorched-earth policy was evident everywhere. Vaughan wrote in respectful horror:

In their retreat the Germans have been very thorough, and mines have been exploded at every crossroads…on hillsides and in cuttings, so that transport is quite impossible. The engineers are finding it quicker to make new roads than to fill up the craters. In addition to this trees have been felled across the roads in hundreds of places, and most of the wells have been blown in or poisoned – in some cases dead horses and mules have been thrown in.

On 18 March Dr Natt was at Vendelles, north of Vermand and more than halfway to St Quentin. He summed up the situation thus:

The Division has already occupied the Siegfried Line, and our line is the fighting front… To the left and right of the street fire and smoke. Only a few houses are to be left standing, apart from these the village is a smoking ruin. The entire evacuation district looks the same: all fruit tress felled, together with all other large trees, all river crossings, railway lines, highways blown up, all houses destroyed. It is said 500 villages have been obliterated... The water system has been systematically destroyed and polluted with faecal matter. The enemy's planned offensive has been rendered pointless ...

By the end of March the Germans were established behind their new lines and the British dug in facing them. There they were to stay for a year, mounting raids, shelling and being shelled, resisting the occasional German foray and waiting the next development.

The Lessons of the First Battle of the Somme

The men of both sides were eager to draw conclusions from the experience of the great battle of 1916. Their interests were very different. Ludendorff's memoirs state:

> The course of the Somme battle had also supplied important lessons with respect to the construction and plan of our lines. The very deep underground forts in the front trenches had to be replaced by shallower constructions. Concrete 'pill-boxes', which, however, unfortunately took a long time to build, had acquired an increasing value. The conspicuous lines of trenches, which appeared as sharp lines on every aerial photograph, supplied far too good a target for the enemy artillery. The whole system of defence had to be made broader and looser and better adapted to the ground. The large, thick barriers of wire, pleasant as they were when there was little doing, were no longer a protection. They withered under the enemy barrage. Light strands of wire, difficult to see, were much more useful. Forward infantry positions with a wide field of fire were easily seen by the enemy... could be destroyed ... difficult to protect by our own artillery. Positions further back with a narrower field of fire and more under the protection of our own guns were retained. They were of special service in big actions.

He also gave careful attention to his artillery. The Verdun and Somme battles had seen not only guns lost to the Allies, but also the high rate of fire had simply worn out many of them. Further, he wanted more long-range heavy guns; of howitzers he had enough. For anti-tank work the 06 field gun would be satisfactory if enough could be manufactured. As to shells, he favoured sensitive fuses to make a shell explode immediately on contact, spreading shell fragments wide, instead of shrapnel. Gas shells were to replace cylinder release, and smoke shells were being made. For the infantry, a new, light machine-gun was being introduced, each company to have four of them. Motor transport had priority as horses were becoming harder to acquire, but he thought it premature to think of making tanks. In short, the entire concentration was on the perfecting of defence.

The Allies, on the other hand, were thinking about how to succeed in attack. During the course of the great battle on the Somme, previously held concepts of the build-up for, and conduct of, an assault – long and careful preparation, the accumulation of supplies and material of war, detailed reconnaissance, using rested and well-fed troops, careful coordination and so forth – were often forgotten under the pressure of events. Failure was reinforced with further failure – troops were thrown hastily into poorly planned operations on small frontages and lines of supply were allowed to become over-stretched. Not that critical thought was absent. Lieutenant-General Claud Jacob of X Corps, for example, proposed attacking with a single line close behind a creeping barrage in the grounds that the inevitable counter-barrage would hit succeeding waves of attackers. His commanding officer, Gough, accepted this inasmuch as he advocated speed of movement in the second and third waves to avoid the defensive shelling. As early as July 1916 *SS 119: Preliminary Notes on the Tactical Lessons of Recent Operations* appeared. In addition such matters as signposting and taping routes, direction keeping and signalling evolved during the battle. German tactics were examined and the wastefulness of knee-jerk counter-attacks was recognised. The significant product of all the thinking was published in the winter of 1916–17.

In December 1916 *SS 135: Instructions for the Training of Divisions for Offensive Action* was issued. The principal conclusion was that the creeping barrage was essential to success, with the attackers close behind it. The infantry are not reduced to mere moppers-up, but are to carry out detailed operations making use of the modern weapons now available to them. The tank had still to be incorporated into general attacking concepts. This manual was followed by *SS 143: Instructions for the Training of Platoons for Offensive Action*. This set out a revolutionary new structure for the platoon. It was to have four specialist sections reporting to a small command unit to make it a self-contained fighting formation.

The specialist sections consisted of, first: two bombers with three supporting men, second: a Lewis gun with nine supporters carrying thirty ammunition drums, third: nine riflemen, a sniper and a scout, and fourth: four rifle-grenade men with nine supporting troops. The array of long- and short-distance grenade strength, machine-gun power and flexible rifle fire-power made for a versatile formation that was able to deploy that force needed to meet a wide variety of circumstances; an independent tactical unit. The method of attack called for the riflemen and bombers in front, to the left and right respectively, followed at some 15 yards (13.7 metres) interval by the rifle-grenade and Lewis gun sections, with the command group in the centre. On contact with the enemy the rifle group would engage with covering fire from rifle grenades and machine-gun while the bombers would take the objective in the flank.

The Great Attacks of 1917

While, after the German withdrawal to the new defence lines, the Somme would be relatively peaceful for the year, the war was prosecuted with vigour elsewhere and new lessons were learned and more sophisticated tactics developed. The plans for 1917 were founded on the confidence of the new Commander-in-Chief of the French Army, General Robert Nivelle, that a knockout blow could be delivered to the Germans. While the British would hold enemy reserves in the north with attacks around Arras, the French were then to assault and to break through on the Chemin des Dames between Soissons and Reims, north of the valley of the river Aisne.

Nivelle had faith in the power of the artillery and believed that it could be used, as on the Somme, first to destroy defensive works and, second, to provide cover for the advance. These were rational views, but needed to be tempered by practical considerations in their application.

The British action around Arras was on two fronts. To the north the land rose along Vimy Ridge, overlooking the flat, open plains on which the battles of Loos and Neuve Chapelle had been fought earlier in the war. The German fortifications on the ridge formed the westward arm of the Wotan Position, of which the other, eastward, part was known to the British as the Drocourt–Quéant Switch Line. The Canadian Corps, part of General Sir Henry Horne's First Army under the command of Lieutenant-General Sir Julian Byng, was to take Vimy Ridge. To achieve all of this, 2,879 guns, one for every 9 yards

(8.25 metres) of front, had been assembled with 2,687,000 shells – missiles of greatly improved quality compared to those used on the Somme. In front of Arras the complex of underground caves and tunnels created over the centuries in building the city were augmented and used to move troops forward under cover. At Vimy Ridge tunnels were dug for the same purpose, generously large and lit with electricity. As only forty tanks were available, in part Mark I veterans of the Somme and in part Mark II training tanks without proper armour, surprise could form no part of the plan and a massive bombardment prepared the way. Moreover, the small tank force was shared out in little groups all along the front of attack.

The bombardment of Vimy Ridge began on 20 March and increased in intensity over the days that followed. The Germans called it 'the week of suffering'. At 5.30am on 9 April the Canadian attack went in, and met with considerable success. The weather was terrible; a blinding snowstorm onto ground already soaked with rain. The tanks were useless in such conditions, but, emerging from their tunnels, the men moved fast. At the southern end of the line the attackers surprised the Germans while they were still in their bunkers, but at the highest point of Vimy Ridge (now crowned with the Canadian Memorial) the German resistance lasted all day. It was broken the next morning by the Manitoba and Calgary Battalions. The Canadians suffered some 11,000 casualties, 3,598 of them killed. The taking of Vimy Ridge was one of the outstanding operations of the entire war.

Field Marshal Haig, who had been promoted to this rank in January, noted in his diary on 13 April:

> I was greatly pleased at the way the wire had been quite destroyed. This shows how effective our new instantaneous fuse (No. 106) for destroying wire is with the large heavy shells and no craters are formed. Beyond the defence wire no shell holes, showing how good our shooting was!
>
> On the way I looked at our heavy artillery which were all ready to leave their emplacements... It is fairly easy work moving these great heavy guns nowadays by means of tractors. The real difficulty is getting the large amount of shells forward. Luckily our railways are following the advance well.

Further south the river Scarpe runs between Arras and Douai, and to the north and south of it the British XVII Corps, part of Allenby's Third Army, attacked after the customary bombardment which blended into a creeping barrage, supported by about forty tanks. The advance of some 3.5 miles

(5.6 kilometres) yielded a bag of more than 5,000 prisoners, but brought the British up against the next arm of the Wotan Position. The tanks bogged down in the snow and mud, and German reserves were coming up. The main action was over, but lesser, though no less lethal, actions stuttered southwards along the line. In mid-June Edwin Vaughan remarked that another attack had taken place at Bullecourt: '... For half an hour we stood admiring the spectacle, and pitying the poor blighters who were in the thick of it.' It is interesting to note that, apart from noticing the shelling, he had not the least idea of what was going on.

The assault of Bullecourt was undertaken by the Fifth Army, commanded by General Gough, using the Australian 4th Division, I ANZAC Corps and 62nd (West Riding) Division on their flank. The objective was covered by the Hindenburg Line, by now protected with substantial barbed wire barriers and freshly completed trenches of formidable proportions. The original plan was to undertake the assault on 11 April, but that led to a danger of the front to the north having an open flank until Gough's men could fill it, and it was therefore with relief that he learned that Major William Watson's No.11 Company, D Battalion, Heavy Section Machine Gun Corps (as the future Tank Corps was then entitled) could carry out an attack on 10 April, substituting the surprise of their concentrated action for the tell-tale of preliminary barrage. It would be necessary to make a night approach because the Royal Flying Corps could not provide air cover to bring the tanks up the previous day. The Australians lay out overnight in the snowstorm. The snow affected the tanks as well, preventing their arrival at the intended start time of 4.30am. The attack was cancelled, but no one told the West Riding men. They suffered severely as they attempted to attack in support of the now-abandoned operation. It was fortunate that more snow covered the Australian withdrawal, but all units were angry with each other, failing to understand that staff communications overall had not dealt with the problem posed by the weather. The next attack, on the originally planned date of 11 April, reverted to standard procedure; preliminary barrage followed by tank and infantry advancing together. The tanks made excellent targets against the snow, and the Germans were entirely prepared for the attack. The coordination of artillery with the advance was poor, the lack of shells with the new fuses in this sector left wire uncut and as tank after tank was immobilised, most of them by shellfire, the assault disintegrated. The Australian confidence in the relevance of tanks was seriously undermined as their losses mounted. In the days that followed, further attacks and German counter-attacks increased the damage to both sides. Bullecourt would go down in Australian history as inflicting their worst losses on the Western Front. In the first battle they lost 3,300 men and in the second 7,500. The 62nd (West Riding) Division lost 4,200 men and the 7th Division 2,700. Sadly the disputes attempting to attribute fault echoed on to undermine mutual British and Australian confidence for some time.

The German defence had been in the hands of the 27th (Royal Württemberg) Division. The divisional report on the battle noted:

> On reaching or passing our trenches the majority of tanks turn to the right or left, to assist the infantry in the mopping up of trenches. Odd tanks go ahead to enable the infantry to breach our lines.
>
> Ordinary wire entanglements are easily overcome by the tanks. Where there are high, dense and broad entanglements, such as those in front of the Hindenburg Line, the wire is apt to get entangled with the tracks of the tanks. On 11 April one tank was hopelessly stuck in our wire entanglement. Deep trenches, even eight feet wide, seem to be a serious obstacle to tanks.

This account bears witness to the involvement of the tanks, later wrongly accused of failing to engage at all in the fight.

The French attack was to be launched against German positions on the Chemin des Dames, the road running along the ridge to the north of the river Aisne between Soissons and Berry-au-Bac. The eastern end of this ridge had been held since the first battle here in September 1914 and the front then ran down into the valley at Condé before climbing once more to Laffaux. While the new 'Siegfried Stellung', the Hindenburg Line, ended further west, the positions here had also been thoroughly fortified. The French plan was to storm the crest above their front line, break through the enemy line and advance past Laon onto the wide plains to the north to link with the British coming from Arras and another French advance along the river Oise. Success would depend on surprise, overwhelming force and speed. A major obstacle was that the plan was soon far from secret, for Nivelle himself had chatted away about his ideas during a visit to London in January, documents had been captured by the Germans and their spies sent numerous, detailed reports of the preparations. Surprise would be now be impossible to achieve.

The French Reserve Army Group under General Alfred Micheler was ordered to undertake the operation with 1,200,000 men (fifty-six divisions including twenty-six in reserve), 128 tanks and 5,544 guns of which 1,466 were heavy artillery. General Charles Mangin's Sixth Army (seventeen infantry and one cavalry division) was to attack on the left and General Mazel's Fifth Army (sixteen infantry and one cavalry divisions), the right. Having carried the German lines, each would turn outwards to allow General Dûchene's Tenth Army (twelve infantry and three cavalry divisions) to break through the centre. The requirements of the assault were that the first 3,000 yards (2,750 metres) of wooded hillside should be crossed in three hours, the next 3,000 yards (on the reverse slope and thus out of sight of artillery support) in the same time and the final 2,000 yards (1,828 metres) at the same pace; eight hours of advance, three-eighths of it unsupported by guns.

The Germans had adopted the defence-in-depth concept in detail. The front line, overlooking the French start line in the valley below, was lightly held. The next section, the intermediate zone, was peppered with machine-gun positions and the artillery were scattered artfully to the rear. There were twenty-one German divisions in the defence zone with another fifteen, ready to counter-attack, held behind them.

The attack began at 0600 hours on 16 April. At first the men moved quickly, but then it began to rain, with occasional flurries of snow thrown in. The artillery barrage moved forward inexorably, according to schedule, whether the infantry were keeping up or not. The machine-gun posts took their toll. The creeping barrage moved steadily onwards at 100 metres a minute, come what may. The French exhibited extraordinary courage on this day and the next, but after the swift advance of the first day nothing more was gained and on 20 April the effort ceased. The losses had been huge. The Germans had expended 163,000 men in holding the line and the French suffered 187,000 casualties in failing to breach it. The French heavy tanks, Schneiders fitted with 75-millimetre (3-inch) guns, had made some inroads but most of them bogged down, broke down or were hit by German shellfire. Worst of all, some French units began to refuse orders.

Although the diversionary attack by the British had served its function in distracting German reserves and, indeed, had made significant gains, the French troops had been asked to do the impossible on the Chemin des Dames. On 29 April a unit at Châlons sur Marne declined orders. Other units followed. This was mutiny, at least to the extent of refusing to obey further orders to attack; more worrying, however, numbers of them began to desert. That the French troops were as vigorous as ever in defence concealed the crisis from the Germans. On 15 May Nivelle was sacked and Pétain, taking over as Commander-in-Chief, was given the task of restoring not merely order, but spirit, to the shattered forces of France. General Ferdinand Foch took over as

Chief of the General Staff, the post to which Pétain had been appointed on 29 April. On 27 May the growing number of desertions became outright mutiny, and Pétain acted swiftly to stop the rot: some 23,000 French soldiers were found guilty of mutiny by courts martial, and 400 were sentenced to death, of whom fifty were shot, the remainder being sent to penal colonies. Pétain also acted to improve his troops' lot, instituting longer periods of rest, more frequent leave and better rations. It was clear, however, that while the French Army would defend its positions, it would not, for the time being, make any major contribution to an offensive. Any such plans would have to fall to the British and Dominion forces on the Western Front.

Haig was now faced with having to use British forces to carry the whole burden of action. Events in Russia that would lead to the Revolution and a Russian surrender were already in train, and the possibility of German divisions being switched from the Eastern Front to France and Flanders was very real. Attacks on Allied shipping by German submarines operating from their bases in Belgium were causing serious damage to supplies and morale, although, because of a number of sinkings of US ships, they also had the effect of bringing America into the war on 6 April. A major attack in the north, in Flanders, was to be undertaken.

Ypres had remained in Allied hands since 1914. On 7 June 1917, at 3.10am, a line of huge mines was detonated beneath German positions on the Messines Ridge and the British and ANZAC troops from General Sir Herbert Plumer's Second Army advanced. One day sufficed for them to achieve their objectives, for, like Vimy Ridge, the operation had been well planned, prepared and executed. The mines had so shocked the defenders of the ridge that many were reduced to passive helplessness. The tank and infantry assault was well supported by the artillery. The objective was sensibly limited so that the advancing troops remained supported and were able to entrench to resist counter-attacks.

The six weeks following the success on the Messines Ridge were filled with activity. In the warm, sunny weather the roads behind the British front line were filled with men, munitions, stores and equipment gathering for the next great onslaught. Field Marshal Haig was planning to strike into Belgium to seize the ports and put a stop to their use by German U-boats, as well as to inflict further heavy losses upon his enemies. It was an operation aimed at making a breakthrough and exploiting the space beyond the trench lines, not, Haig thought, an action suited to the steady, meticulous Plumer, architect of the recent success, but more to the flair and panache of General Sir Hubert Gough, commander of the Fifth Army.

The Germans observed the build-up of forces from the air and from their posts on the Passchendaele Ridge. They attempted to disrupt the activity with an attack at Nieuport on 10 July, fighting in the shifting terrain of the sand dunes. They shelled the British with a new and foul type of gas, dichlorodiethyl sulphide – called mustard gas because of its effects. It was almost odourless and, heavier than air, lay in hollows. It was soluble in water, which meant you could wash it off, but also that it lingered in puddles and in the water at the bottom of shell holes in which a man might shelter from shellfire. The victims suffered burning and irritation of the skin or, if it was inhaled, the lungs and digestive tract. In extreme cases vomiting and death followed. On 12 July the Germans used gas shells on the salient, killing eighty-seven of the 2,500 injured. Another 14,726 were gassed in the next three weeks and about 500 of them died. The British opened a bombardment on 17 July that would last until the battle began at the end of the month, hurling 4,283,500 shells, about 100,000 of which contained chloropicrin gas, a more sophisticated form of chlorine gas, at their enemies.

The Fifth Army was to strike between Zillebeke and Boesinghe, a front that included the rising ground of the ridge along the Menin Road to the Gheluvelt plateau in the south and the succession of undulations divided by a herringbone web of streams rising to Passchendaele in the north. To the left General François Anthoine's French First Army would secure the flank, while Plumer's Second Army was to perform the same function to the south. If the attack was successful a flanking operation was to be mounted, landing the 1st Division south-west of Ostend from specially built landing craft and with tank support.

As July drew to a close the fine weather came to an end. On 31 July, the day of the attack, more than three-quarters of an inch (21 millimetres) of rain fell. The Germans, expecting the assault the next day, pulled their troops back from the front line opposite Boesinghe on 27 July and the French and the Guards Division moved quickly forward to occupy the ground and to bridge the canal now in their rear. On 0350 on 31 July a creeping barrage moved ahead of the advancing troops. On the left the Guards had reached the Steenbeek stream by 0930 and to their right the 38th (Welsh) and 51st (Highland) Divisions also achieved their objectives, although with rather more difficulty than the Guards. The 39th Division was making for Kitchener's Wood, supported by tanks of 19 Company, the Tank Corps. Only one tank reached its objective, the Alberta strong-point, and neutralised it; the others, when off the roads, bogged down in the shell-torn, rain-sodden soil.

To the south, along the Menin Road and towards Shrewsbury Forest, much smaller progress was made, but the first day did give cause for satisfaction. The rain, however, persisted. In the next two weeks 3½ inches (90 millimetres) of rain reduced the earth to soup. The Germans mounted repeated, desperate and, for both sides, costly counter-attacks. The British attacks made negligible progress and the cost was high. The prospect of a breakthrough drowned in the morass of the Ypres Salient. On 18 August the tanks were used in a carefully crafted operation against a line of troublesome blockhouses: The Cockroft, Maison du Hibou, Triangle Farm and Vancouver. As it became light, without a preliminary bombardment and covered by a creeping barrage, tanks and infantry moved in concert, the machines following the scarcely discernable routes of the roads. By 0700 hours all the objectives had been taken, the tanks suppressing fire from the blockhouses and the infantry moving to occupy them. The total casualties among the attackers were fifteen British wounded. Correctly used, tanks worked.

On 25 August Haig, under continuing pressure to maintain the fight here and avoid a German attack on the still-vulnerable French army, transferred the responsibility for the battle to General Plumer. He, true to form, adopted a policy of setting limited objectives, basing each operation on detailed planning and ensuring that his infantry always had artillery support. Bite and hold. It was three weeks before he was ready to renew the attack and during that time the weather cleared. At 0540 hours on 20 September the battle of the Menin road ridge began. The ANZACS took Glencorse Wood and advanced as far as the edge of Polygon Wood. Having nudged forward, Plumer paused to prepare the next effort. On 26 September the fight continued and Polygon Wood fell to the Australians and the line both north and south of it was, over a couple of days, moved forward.

On 2 October the rain set in again, and it continued for most of that month. Men could hardly move; indeed, some drowned in mud. What was worse was that the guns could not be moved. On 4 October the Germans were planning to counter-attack, but Plumer's men were also on the point of moving without a preliminary bombardment. When the British artillery laid down its creeping barrage the massed Germans were caught in the fire and the Australians swept through them up to the ridge at Broodseinde while, to their left, the Gordon Highlanders and the Border Regiment also made their objectives and further north again, Poelcapelle was taken. The terrible weather halted progress. The British had established themselves close to Poelcapelle in the north and the Australians were on the ridge at Broodseinde, but left and right of the ANZACS the line sagged west in pools of mud. A massive effort on 12 October gained nothing of significance and left the surviving men exhausted. Plumer paused.

On 26 October the battle was taken up by the Canadian Corps and, after costly fighting, some Canadians actually entered the village on 30 October, only to be pushed back by German counter-attacks. Passchendaele finally fell to them on 6 November.

The likely total figures for all casualties (killed, wounded, missing or made prisoner) are 244,897 British (including Dominion and Empire forces), 8,525 French and approximately 230,000 German. The horror of the conditions obscured the lessons of the few successes. Preliminary artillery bombardment and the close contact of the infantry with their creeping barrage had, when mud had not wrecked performance, worked well. Tanks used on appropriate terrain had succeeded. That does not mean that the battle overall was a success; simply that certain tactical approaches could be seen to work.

The German Experience

On the Western Front the emphasis for the German armies was on defensive systems and tactics. On the Eastern Front matters were different. The Tsar of Russia had abdicated on 15 March but the new government's Minister of War, Alexander Kerensky stood by a previous agreement with the Allies to undertake an offensive in Galicia, a region now divided between modern Poland and Ukraine, under the command of General Alexei Brusilov. The 'Liberation Offensive' was launched on 1 July and scored a significant success, but the Russian logistic support was unable to sustain it.

The counter-offensive came on 19 July in what is now southern Poland, north-west of Krakow. East of Zloczow nine German divisions, eight of which had been brought from the Western Front, smashed through the Russian Eleventh Army behind a hurricane bombardment designed by Lieutenant Colonel Georg Bruchmüller. The advance had swept forward to Czernowitz by 3 August and only halted because the Germans themselves also lacked the logistical means to sustain it.

The Germans were not content with what they had achieved so far, and the fact that Riga on the Baltic Sea was still in Russian hands worried them. The place was held by General Vladislav N. Klembovski's Twelfth Army, virtually the last operational unit the Russians possessed. On 20 August they shortened their line by evacuating some positions south-west of the city and sent away the sick. The German Eighth Army under General Oskar von Hutier made ready to take Riga. The plan was to avoid a direct assault in favour of crossing the river Duna further east and circling west to envelop the place. Two factors were to contribute to success: the use of new tactics by the infantry, and new fire and control systems by the artillery.

The infantry attack using numerous small groups in place of long lines of troops was not, as we have seen, a brand new concept. It had been proposed by the French Captain André Laffargue in 1915 and developed by German Captain Willy Rohr that same year. The British manual published after the first Somme battle, *Instructions for the Training of Platoons for Offensive Action* adopted a new organisation of infantry to accommodate the tactics. Hutier's 120 divisions trained for ten days in these tactics some 75 miles (120 kilometres) behind their front lines. What was new was the scale on which they were used and their combination with new artillery methods. The artillery consisted of 615 guns, of which 251 were heavy, and 544 trench mortars with supplies of 650,000 rounds of ammunition. The additional guns did not fire in order to register on their targets, but used the first phase of the actual bombardment to register on selected points before switching to their actual targets. The artillery fired a carefully planned mix of explosive and gas shells, precisely targeted to achieve neutralisation of enemy artillery with gas and destruction of defensive positions with explosives. Finally, the artillery preparation was short – a mere five hours. All of this was orchestrated by Bruchmüller.

At 0400 hours on 1 September the artillery barrage began on Russian batteries and after two hours some of them shifted onto infantry positions. In a final phase only few guns persisted in gassing Russian artillery positions while most saturated front-line positions with shellfire. At 0910 hours the infantry pushed forward across the river accompanied by observers whose telephone lines unreeled behind them. The creeping barrage moved forward to a predetermined point and stood there until a green flare indicated it should move forward once more; the troops were not outrun by the barrage. Once the second defence line had fallen, covering fire first protected the bridge-builders, then the movement forward over the river of German artillery and finally provided the preparation for renewed advance. By noon the Russian Twelfth Army was starting to break. By evening six German divisions had crossed the Duna. On the afternoon of 3 September they were in Riga at a cost of 4,200 casualties. Russian losses were 25,000 men, of whom 9,000 were prisoners and 1,000 gas victims.

Artillery fire of this new sophistication was also used in Italy. After the fall of Riga the Germans were able to send troops from the Russian front to stiffen the forces of their Austrian allies. On 24 October, in the early hours, German Lieutenant-General Richard von Berendt's artillery barrage began. The Battle of Caporetto had started. Gas shells poured down on Italian positions for two and a half hours. Then there was a pause. The rain started to fall, light at first, then with increasing force on lower ground while snow fell on the heights. As dawn came the bombardment was renewed with high explosive and then with trench mortars; an unprecedented weight of gunnery that smashed Italian defences and cut communications. The Italian artillery did not, in gas and confusion, reply. Then two huge mines, on the Monte Rosso and the Monte Mrzli, blew up and the Fourteenth Army swept forward. In less than two hours the Italian IV Corps's front had been broken by von Krauss's Austrian corps. Just north of Tolmino, von Stein's German troops hit the Italian line; it was destroyed and the Germans thronged over the river Isonzo. Part of Stein's force attacked north of the Colovrat Ridge, aiming for Monte Matajur, where the young Lieutenant Erwin Rommel would distinguish himself by leading the successful assault by the Württemberg Mountain Battalion on 26 October. The rest of Stein's men headed north-west and had taken the village of Caporetto by 1600 hours. In the following days a massive retreat took the Italians back to the river Piave with the loss of some 320,000 men, of whom more than a quarter of a million were made prisoner. The new German use of artillery and infantry had scored a mighty success, both in Russia and in Italy.

The Tanks at Cambrai

The progress of the war, as the autumn of 1917 advanced, was depressing from the point of view of the Allies. The campaign in the Ypres Salient was grinding on at terrible cost, the Russians, embroiled in revolution, were no longer reliable allies and the Italians had suspended offensive action. It seemed an excellent time to revive a plan that had been put forward earlier in the year for a tank raid south of Cambrai.

The terrain near Cambrai, firm chalk-based country, was much better suited to tanks and the sector was lightly defended. Colonels Ernest Swinton and J.F.C. Fuller argued for massed formations of tanks on suitable terrain and the idea was finally accepted by General Sir Julian Byng of Third Army. He took the concept as far as breaking through the Hindenburg Line between the unfinished Canal du Nord on the west and the Canal du St Quentin on the east in the area south-west of Cambrai, capturing that town and Bourlon Wood, which gave an overview of the German-held country beyond, and, what was more, to exploit that with a breakthrough in the direction of Valenciennes.

Byng placed his IV Corps on the left with the 36th (Ulster), 51st (Highland) and 62nd (West Riding) Divisions, 1st Cavalry Division and 1st Tank Brigade. III Corps, on the right, had 6th, 20th, 12th and 29th Divisions and the 2nd and 3rd Tank Brigades. There were nine tank battalions in all with 378 tanks while another fifty-four machines were held in reserve. Most were equipped with fascines, great bundles of wood carried on their roofs to be dropped into enemy trenches and permit the machines to cross. Some tanks were equipped as wire cutters and others as mobile radio stations or supply vehicles.

A second, and less remarked on, aspect of the planned attack was the use of artillery as arranged by Brigadier General H.H. Tudor. He decided there should be no preliminary bombardment, thus gaining both surprise and unbroken ground, and that predicted fire should replace registration. Registration was a system of experimental firing at the intended target to work out the difference between the laying of a gun according to theoretical calculation and actual experience. Predictive firing meant testing the gun elsewhere to establish its deviation from its theoretical performance. It would then be possible to open fire accurately on a target located on a map.

At 0620 hours on 20 November the artillery opened fire and the tanks moved forward. The infantry followed, closely in all cases except for the 51st (Highland) Division. Their commander, General G.M. Harper, thought the tanks would attract German artillery fire and thus put his men in peril. They were ordered to hang back. The bombardment was fairly effective, but the British predicted fire had failed to take account of variations in the quality of the ammunition or of muzzle velocity variations for each individual gun. Surprise was, however, complete. The tanks worked in groups of three with the advance tank crushing the enemy wire, then turning left and opening fire on the first trench while the next tank came on to drop its fascine into it before crossing and opening fire on the second trench. The third tank then dropped its fascine and covered for the first tank to come through and bridge the third and last trench of the line; then off they went to knock out the strong-points to the rear. On the right, III Corps reached all of its objectives that day, getting as far as the St Quentin Canal south of Crèvecoeur and supporting crossings at Masnières and Marcoing. On the extreme left the 62nd (West Riding) Division struck north as far as the Bapaume to Cambrai road. Between these two, progress was held up. The unsupported tanks climbed rising ground south of Flesquières and came under fire from field guns of the German 54th Reserve Division. Outranged, and with no covering rifle or machine-gun fire from the 51st (Highland) Division to distract the gunners ahead, the tanks were knocked out one after the other. The delay allowed the covering barrage to move on and left the Highlanders without support from the guns. It was not until the next day that the 51st took Flesquières and pressed on to Fontaine Notre Dame on the flank of Bourlon Wood. Haig wrote in his diary on 22 November:

> On the ridge about Flesquières were a dozen or more Tanks which were knocked out by artillery fire. It seems the Tanks topped the ridge and began to descend... all the personnel of a German battery ... fled. One officer however was able to collect a few men and with them worked a gun and from his concealed position knocked out Tank after Tank ... This incident shows the importance of infantry operating with Tanks at times acting as skirmishers to clear away hostile guns and reconnoitre.

The planned cavalry breakout could not take place as they had been too far in the rear on the first day and the Germans acted quickly to close the gap smashed in their line. The Germans had seven divisions at Cambrai by 26 November and pressure was mounting. On 30 November, the Germans counter-attacked not only in force, but using the penetration tactics developed on the Eastern Front at Riga and proven in Italy at Caporetto. The barrage began at 0800 with a high proportion of gas shell and the masses that had been rushed into the sector, an additional thirteen divisions in four days, allowed an eleven-division assault. The assault forced the abandonment of Bourlon Wood by 4 December and, after counter-attacks by the Guards Brigade to regain Gouzeaucourt on 30 November and 1 December, the eastern flank stabilised with the Germans having gained just about as much ground here as the British had in the north. The American 11th Engineers were building a railway yard at Gouzeaucourt at the time of the German attack and, as they were unarmed, made a swift retreat until they could obtain weapons from the British and join the defence. Some made do with picks and shovels. Of the men captured, most managed to escape when the Guards counter-attacked.

The inability of the British to follow up their initial success was the result of excessive commitments elsewhere and the breakthrough plan had been too ambitious to begin with. The tanks had performed well, but their endurance was not great and many of them simply broke down. The tank losses totalled 179; of these seventy-one had broken down and forty-three had become stuck or had been ditched. British casualties were 44,207 of whom some 9,000 were taken prisoner.

The Germans lost 41,000 of whom 11,000 were made prisoners. The Americans sustained eighteen casualties to add to the two that their unit had suffered on 5 September when two men became the first Americans wounded at the front.

What had been shown, despite the disappointing outcome, was that, subject to mechanical reliability, the tanks were capable of overrunning the strongest positions the Germans could create. Contact with the covering barrage had been lost, however, and the coordination of all arms of the fighting machine remained the weakest point of British tactics.

Lengthening the British Line

On 17 December 1917 General Pétain and Field Marshal Haig met and decided that, in accordance with the will of their political masters, the British would take over the front as far south as the river Oise by the end of January 1918. This meant taking over 25 miles (40 kilometres) of the former French line from St Quentin to a point halfway to Soissons at Barisis, south of the Oise; an increase of frontage of almost 30 per cent without a similar increase of manpower. Ten days earlier British GHQ had come to the conclusion that the Germans would launch an offensive in the west no later than March. At the same time the new British Prime Minister, David Lloyd George, was resisting Haig's demands for more troops. Given the awful toll of the Third Battle of Ypres there he was not without a reason, but the outcome was a shortage of men to defend the extended line; of the 38,225 officers and 607,403 men trained and ready in England, fewer than 200,000 were released. Nor could either the French or the English look to America to plug the gap. Although the first detachment of the American Expeditionary Force had landed, 14,000 strong, at St Nazaire the previous June and more had arrived since then, they were still not fully trained and ready to enter the line. On the other side the Germans and the Russians were now in negotiation to end the war on that front, so the prospect of German reinforcements arriving in the west was very real. The British reorganised, reducing the strength of a division from twelve battalions to nine, thus releasing 150 battalions for allocation to other units. The effect on morale and the destruction of established relationships was marked.

The British were now giving serious attention to defence. The new concept was defence in depth – a zone some 12 miles (19 kilometres) deep. The front line was to be lightly held, giving a Forward Zone of barbed wire and machine-gun nests covering the front trench and dominated just to the rear by redoubts, positions of all-round defence. Behind that was an area occupied by artillery that could be withdrawn if threatened with being overrun. Then came the Battle Zone, an area between 1 and 2 miles (1.5 to 3 kilometres) deep, peppered with machine-gun positions, in which an enemy would be shattered by artillery and cut down by machine-guns. The Rear Zone was, in effect, a second battle zone to be brought into use in the event of the first one being overcome. On paper it was all very fine. The problem was that it did not exist on the ground in January 1918, having only been formulated and propagated by GHQ on 14 December 1917.

The German Concept of Attack

Ludendorff had been planning an attack since the middle of 1917. He wrote in praise of his troops, but recognised that continual defence was not the way to seize victory, and it was vital to gain success before the full force of the Americans was brought to bear in Europe. He later wrote of the tactics and organisation in the infantry he had introduced:

> The light machine-gun and the rifleman formed the infantry group, which hang together in trouble and danger and the life and death struggle. Its fire power was further increased by quick-firing weapons of all kinds and various sorts of rifle grenades.
>
> To the heavy machine-gun, with its longer range and greater effect, fell the task of facilitating the approach of the groups to the enemy's position by keeping the latter under fire. Of course, it had to accompany the advance of the infantry. Therefore, although itself 'infantry', it had already become a sort of 'companion' or auxiliary arm to the infantry.
>
> The second auxiliary arm, of special use at short ranges against targets offering more than usual resistance, was the light trench mortar…
>
> Of course massed artillery prepared the attack. It could, however, only do so in a general way, and left untouched too many of the enemy's strong points, which had to be dealt with in detail at the shortest ranges. In each division, therefore, field guns were withdrawn from their units for short-range work, and were attached to battalions or regiments as infantry guns.
>
> In addition, each division had a company of medium trench mortars which were also to be made as mobile as possible and allotted to battalions as required.

Finally, there were the flame projectors, which could be brought into action at the shortest ranges against an enemy in blockhouses, dug-outs and cellars.

We had no tanks. They were merely an offensive weapon, and our attacks succeeded without them.

At a meeting in Mons on 11 November 1917 the German High Command entertained a range of attack plans and from these 'Michael', the attack at the southern end of the British line, between Arras and the French, was eventually selected to be the first of them. The tactics would be based on Captain Hermann Dreyer's paper, *The Attack in Positional Warfare*, published on 26 January 1918, which summarised their most recent thinking. The approach was to use small, specialist units to penetrate the enemy line and bypass strong-points, allowing the follow-up troops to complete their envelopment and destruction. The leading units relied on light machine-guns and grenades, while the more conventional troops that followed brought with them mobile trench-mortars and horse-drawn field guns, as Ludendorff described in detail. Battalion organisation now generally consisted of four rifle companies with five light machine-guns and two light mortars, a machine-gun company with twelve Maxims, and a mortar platoon with four *Minenwerfer*. The way would be opened for them by a 'fire-waltz' as designed by Colonel Georg Bruchmüller. The components of the bombardment were a mix of shells – high explosive, smoke, tear-gas and poison gas – on front-line positions and suppressive artillery fire on enemy artillery.

To avoid ranging shots revealing German knowledge of British positions, a variant of the British method used before the Battle of Cambrai was developed for the artillery by Captain Erich Pulkowsky. The guns were characterised individually by test firing them well away from the line to determine the precise performance of each weapon. Each one could then, taking account of meteorological conditions, be targeted on a specific point identified on a map. Total surprise and comprehensive confusion of the defenders was the desired result. In addition registration of guns took place during the bombardment to range guns onto the targets they were given for later phases of the gunnery assault.

As the winter of 1917–18 softened to spring the race was on, with the British furiously constructing their defence and the Germans gathering for attack. The Somme had been comparatively quiet for almost a year while other fronts learnt lessons in warfare, bought in blood. The Somme was to be riven once again.

Chapter 6

The Somme 1918: Operation Michael

The dividing line between The Hon. Sir Julian Byng's Third Army and Sir Hubert Gough's Fifth Army positions was at Gouzeaucourt on the road between Péronne and Cambrai. North of that, the front bulged north-east in the Flesquières Salient, the area pushed forward in the Battle of Cambrai of the previous November. Here it was held by Lieutenant-General Sir Edward Fanshawe's V Corps (from south to north, 47th, 63rd Royal Naval and 17th Divisions). To their north was IV Corps under Lieutenant-General Sir George Harper with the 51st Highland and 6th Divisions. Then came VI Corps, Lieutenant-General Sir Aylmer Haldane with 59th, 34th and 3rd Divisions and finally, in front of Arras, XVII Corps of Lieutenant-General Sir Charles Fergusson with 15th and 4th Divisions.

The southern flank of the salient, a section of the line centered on Epéhy east and north-east of Péronne, was held by the northernmost formation of the Fifth Army, Lieutenant-General Sir Walter Congreve, VC, with his VII Corps (north to south, 9th (Scottish), 21st and 16th (Irish) Divisions). On their way to Péronne, the river Somme and its associated canal come from St Quentin in a great loop curving as far south as Ham and the junction with the Crozat Canal, which heads up from the south-east. The two canals make a triangular area with the front line between St Quentin and La Fère, while the river runs north through marshy flats cut into the broad, high, rolling countryside which lay behind the British lines. The area east and south of Péronne was held by Lieutenant-General Sir Herbert Watts with XIX Corps (66th and 24th Divisions) about as far as the Roman road that runs due west to Amiens. From there to a point south of the Somme Canal and south of St Quentin was Lieutenant-General Sir Ivor Maxse's XVIII Corps (61st, 30th and 36th (Ulster) Divisions) and facing the line down to the Oise river was Sir Richard Butler's III Corps with 14th, 18th and 58th Divisions. The Cavalry Corps, three divisions including the Canadian Cavalry Brigade, did not operate as a single unit but was divided up for use where necessary and in the event provided an invaluable emergency mounted infantry support. Four divisions would be added from the reserves to the Third Army and three to the Fifth in the first few days of the coming battle.

There were intimations of the start of the 'Kaiserschlacht', the Kaiser's Battle, of which Operation Michael was just the first part. In spite of the secrecy with which the Germans amassed their forces, aerial observation told the British something was going on. The major concern was to defend what was vital, that is, the Channel ports and their protecting positions at Arras and Vimy and their more southerly flank towards Péronne, where a good deal of energy and manpower was expended in the construction of defenses that, in the event, would prove irrelevant.

Field Marshal Haig wrote in his later report, and with all the benefits of hindsight:

> In the northern portion of the British area lie the northern Channel ports of Dunkirk, Calais and Boulogne, the security of which necessitated the maintenance of sufficient troops in the neighborhood. Little or no ground could be given up on this front, and therefore the necessary reserves must be kept in close proximity.
>
> Although, as a rule, the state of the ground would preclude a general offensive in this sector early in the year, the weather had been exceptionally dry...
>
> In the southern portion of the British area south-east of Arras, in contrast to the central and northern portions, ground could be given up under great pressure without serious consequences, the forward area of this sector consisting chiefly of a wide expanse of territory devastated by the enemy last spring in his withdrawal.

Opposite the British the Germans deployed their Seventeenth Army in the north, facing Arras, with eighteen divisions and 2,236 guns under General Otto von Below. The Second Army, twenty divisions and 1,789 guns under General Georg von der Marwitz, was north of St Quentin and the Eighteenth Army, twenty-seven divisions, 2,448 guns and nine tanks under General Oskar von Hutier faced St Quentin and the river Oise. The twelve, cut-back divisions of Gough's Fifth Army thus faced all of the German Eighteenth Army, itself equal to the whole BEF on this front, as well as part of the Second Army. The German policy was summed up in the orders sent to General von der Marwitz:

> The aims must be achieved in an uninterrupted attack movement, a schedule has therefore not been prepared. The quicker the aim is achieved, the greater will be the initial success: the wiping out of substantial British forces and the overrunning of enemy trench systems.

On 20 March, near Fayet, just north of St Quentin, a raiding party consisting of A and C companies, 2/6th Royal Warwickshire Regiment, XVIII Corps, took prisoners from the German 28th Division who revealed that the attack was scheduled for the next day and that the bombardment would begin at 0440 hours – and could they be taken to the rear of the British lines with all speed, please? No general alarm was given.

The Second Battle of the Somme

The German bombardment was carried out in five phases and employed both light and heavy guns and both gas and high explosive shells in a precisely organised system. The shelling of a primary target covered the business of registering some guns on the subsequent target.

The use of gas was cunningly arranged. Each was used for a specific purpose. Mustard gas immobilises by causing blisters on the skin and in the lungs and it also causes blindness, usually temporary. It penetrates and persists in clothing and hair, but can be washed off, which is a sound reason for being clean-shaven and crop-headed and it thus put an end to Edwardian flowing locks and stylish whiskers. It is soluble in water and thus lingers anywhere damp or wet, so it is useful for shielding the flanks of an attack and for putting enemy gunners out of action. Gas masks were now standard issue in both armies, and they were proof against poison gas such as chlorine, but not arsine (diphenylchloroarsine), which was a powder, and able to filter past the mask. The mask itself, short of gluing to the skin, did not make a precise fit to the face, even close-shaven ones. Arsine causes sneezing, retching and vomiting and thus encourages the victims to remove their gas mask, and thus expose themselves to a poison gas. Arsine shells were marked with a blue cross, chlorine with green, and the cocktail

---

Eighteenth Army Artillery Preparation: The Fire-waltz

Phase	Time	Duration	Purpose
1	0440	120 min.	Overall, with gas and high explosive.
1a	0530	10 min.	All mortars and lighter guns on infantry positions.
2	0640	10 min.	As Phase 1 except for registration by close support batteries on second line targets.
3	0650	10 min.	As Phase 2, but registration on rear of front line.
4	0700	10 min.	As Phase 3, but registration on intermediate position targets.
5	0710	70 min.	Counter-battery and heavy guns fire on artillery and redoubts.
5a	0740	15 min.	Front line shelled by close support howitzers.
5b	0740	15 min.	Redoubts shelled by howitzers.
5c	0740	15 min.	Field guns shell intermediate zone with gas.
6	0820	75 min.	As Phase 5, but different targets.
7	0935	5 min.	All guns, saturation fire on front line.

---

of both was named *Buntkreuz*, and was multi-coloured. This was the weapon visited upon the British.

The British had no choice. Peering into the foggy dawn, they could see little. The Royal Artillery did what it could to respond to the bombardment, but the fog, and the mix of gas and impact of high explosive did its work to great effect. The Forward Zone was largely destroyed, men killed and wounded, dugouts caved in and trenches smashed. Deeply buried telephone lines were severed and roads, railways and airfields heavily damaged. At 0940 hours the creeping barrage began and the masked German infantry moved forward.

The German Seventeenth Army pushed forward against the Flesquières Salient, advancing along the valley of the Hirondelle river, west of Cambrai. Here was the British IV and VI Corps boundary. Bullecourt was threatened and by the end of the day the 59th and 6th Divisions had been pushed out of the Forward Zone and to the very rear of the Battle Zone, as had the right wing of the 51st (Highland) Division. The plan was to nip out the salient from north and south, so the defenders of the objective were excused direct assault and suffered simply the gas. To the south, where VII Corps of the Fifth Army were positioned, the South African Infantry Brigade of 9th (Scottish) Division were eventually reduced to clinging on to Gauche Wood, but they did so with such

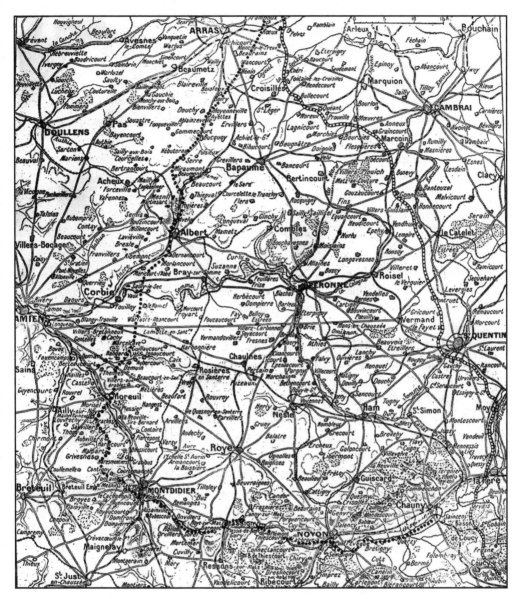

The Second Battle of the Somme. The German line on 21 March 1918 is on the right and the dotted line to the left shows the front at the end of the battle. *From l'Illustration, 6 April 1918. (HGG)*

tenacity that the Germans did not take it until midday. Of the 130 men of the 2nd South African Battalion, forty came away.

To their south, 21st Division were holding positions from Chapel Hill to the village of Epéhy on the right. The 1st Lincolns held the hill stubbornly and were reinforced by the 4th South Africans from 9th Division. In the centre, Vaucelette Farm was fiercely attacked but the 12/13th Northumberland Fusiliers held out until about noon when mortar fire from their rear overcame them. The fog, however, chose this moment to lift, exposing the attackers to fire from Chapel Hill and from the three Leicestershire Regiment battalions of 110th Brigade in the redoubt at Epéhy. The redoubt concept worked perfectly; the Germans, who were coming forward in parade ground style, depending on being invisible, were shot down. The 110th Brigade was ordered by Major-General D.G.M. Campbell, commanding 21st Division, to pull most of its men out of the forward line an hour before dawn and now, from the fastness of the redoubt, the ill-organised Germans were easy targets for their Lewis guns. They were lucky; nowhere else was the fog so willing to disperse and other redoubts were surrounded before they could see to defend themselves. On the 110th Brigade's right flank, matters were not going so well. The 16th (Irish) Division could not hold the attackers and penetration was threatening to outflank the Leicesters, but both Chapel Hill and Epéhy remained in British hands at nightfall.

The 16th Division held positions looking down towards Bony, where the Americans would attack in the coming September, and Le Catelet, where the St Quentin Canal tunnel has its northern exit. Here the wisdom shown by Major-General Campbell was lacking, or rather, Major-General Sir Charles Hull was overruled by Lieutenant-General Sir Walter Congreve who feared an attack in great strength might emerge from the canal tunnel, an obvious place to hide troops and store ammunition. When General Gough visited, Major K.S. Mason, the Divisional Machine Gun Officer, overheard Hull try to make his point once again. Mason recalled:

> General Gough would not agree to this and said, 'I wouldn't dream of such a thing. The Germans are not going to break my line.' I saw quite a lot of General Gough during his visit and came to the conclusion that he was a very arrogant, conceited and pompous man.

The outcome was a terrible loss of men in the Forward Zone and only one position, the redoubt at Malassise Farm, managed to offer serious resistance.

The 2nd Royal Munster Fusiliers held out until about 11am. The 39th Division, in reserve, was brought forward to plug the gap.

Gunner Maurice Burton, 342nd Battery, Royal Garrison Artillery, was recently arrived in France, and amazed by the events of the day. He later wrote of the lack of information and the struggle to hitch the guns up to the trucks to get away:

March 21: The opening day of the massive German offensive. We were in reserve positions, waiting to meet the Big Push. The day dawned fine. A mist covered the low ground everywhere. A thunderous barrage broke out in the distance towards which our gun barrels pointed. As the sun rose above the horizon the first walking wounded began to stream over the ridge, coming through our gun positions and disappearing to the rear.

During the morning the stream continued. Rumours ran rife. How rumours spread over a battlefield is a mystery but they do. The Guards Brigade had broken though at Armentières to the north of us, it was whispered. The French were advancing in the south. Everywhere was success for the Allied armies.

Every wounded man that went by asked us what was happening. We passed on to them the good news we had been receiving. Yet the stream of wounded continued. Towards midday all sound of gunfire ceased. The stream of wounded petered out. I was in my machine-gun post, a sandbagged pit to the left of the battery and, as I recall it now, I was happily oblivious of what might be happening elsewhere, keeping watch on the sky which was singularly free of aircraft.

Then in the afternoon, our own guns opened up, firing as fast as the gun teams could load them, firing though open sights, which meant that the barrels of the guns were down to the horizontal instead of, as is normal with howitzers, near the vertical. Our shells were bursting on a slope opposite us and we could see the lines of German infantrymen advancing, coming down the slope, sun glinting on their bayonets and their spectacles.

Apparently our barrage was effective as first one battery then another on either side of us fell silent and we were aware they were pulling out and falling back. Finally ours were the only guns firing and even they fell silent about mid-afternoon... There were no infantry in sight. Friendly or hostile, no planes flew overhead. There was no sound of rifle, machine-gun or mortar fire, no bursting shells. It was not until later that we learned the enemy had broken through on either side of us and had surrounded us until a counter-attack by the Highland Light Infantry had opened the road behind us. So it remained until night fell when all hands were mustered to load the convoy of lorries drawn up on the road running beyond our left flank.

Everything was carried on our backs or shoulders including several hundred rounds of hundred-pound shells. All was done in silence and smoking was forbidden.

Then came the turn of the guns. Each had to be manhandled up a slope, all hands to each of the guns in turn. Each gun was fastened to its four-wheel drive lorry to be towed away. Presumably, by the time we came to pull the fourth gun up the slope we were beginning to tire, for the procession moved slowly.

One of our sergeants, a schoolmaster by profession, took charge. 'Now boys', he bellowed, 'Left- r-r-right, left-r-r-right, left-r-r-right,' he called, rolling his r's. It was as if he were marching a class of boys back into school after morning break. I know I inwardly cursed him and I expect everyone else did for giving our position away; but we got the gun onto the road and hooked to its lorry with no more than a few rounds of machine-gun fire aimed at us, fortunately at random, the bullets buzzing over our heads.

Piecing the story together afterwards it became clear we were surrounded on three sides by the enemy.

The convoy of lorries got on the move just before dawn when the enemy laid down a barrage on the road we had just left. It passed through a village a little further on, just as this was being heavily bombarded, or so I was told. I heard nothing of it for I was fast asleep on my feet, standing in one of the lorries.

While the retreat was under way on the northern part of the front, it was by no means a breakthrough by the Germans. On III Corps front, from St Quentin southwards, it was a different story. In the persistent fog the Germans moved forward against men dazed and disorientated by relentless shellfire. The redoubts, deprived of vision, could not function as intended even where the defence works had reached near-completion. In July 1918 the French Fourth Army published a captured document, a memorandum dated 1 May by Captain Schmidt, Chief of Staff of the German 28th Infantry Division, and this was translated and issued by the AEF in August. 'The Battle in the Intermediate Zone' gives an insight into the experience of Operation Michael and its tactical effectiveness. The nature of positional battle, character-ised by large masses of men following a rolling barrage, was contrasted with this new idea of battle. In 'intermediate zone' fighting, artillery preparation has ceased to have effect and the defending machine-gun nests open fire and counter-attacks commence. The artillery has to be mobile and flexible in engaging new targets from temporary positions. Where resistance is low, the attackers must penetrate. Outflanking is preferred to confrontation, although the latter may be needed to allow the former to take place and render the defensive position untenable. The attackers must take care to secure their own flanks. The document continues:

> The battalion thus becomes a mixed body of troops composed of companies of infantry and machine-guns, light trench mortars and accompanying artillery. This has demonstrated its effectiveness. It permits the battalion commander to fulfil the duties which fall to his lot in the intermediate zone without outside aid.

The 28th Division advanced westwards from the St Quentin sector to attack towards the Forest of Holnon, south of the road leading west to Vermand and Amiens:

The British positions in the forest threatened the advance of the 28th and the way they were dealt with is reported in detail in the document as an example for others to follow.

As the infantry approached the objective the artillery laid down a barrage on the southern edge of the forest. There were also batteries accompanying the attack, including divisional artillery. They moved as quickly as they could to 'Hill 123.7, situated about 2km southwest' of the forest. On the right wing of the infantry 118th Regiment engaged and the machine-gun company with them set up their weapons to enfilade the southern edge of the forest. A group from the 14th Field Artillery had its first battery advance to within firing range and then 'neutralise' the British machine-guns. With this covering fire, and that of the infantry, taking place, the rest of the artillery bypassed the forest. Meanwhile, on their right flank, 3rd Infantry Division could be seen progressing through the forest by the flashes of their grenades, so 233 Mountain Machine Gun Section laid down enfilading fire to assist them. The British had, the report mentions, 'obstinately defended by fire and by hostile counter-attacks.'

On the 28th's left, the 50th Infantry Division were faced with Manchester Hill Redoubt, which stood north of the road to Savy and straddled the side-road to Francilly-Selency. Here the 16th Manchesters, originally the 1st Manchester Pals, had been told by their commanding officer, Lieutenant-Colonel Wilfrith Elstob, 'Here we fight and here we die.' Their position was soon surrounded by the Germans, which left them with eight officers, 160 men, and three radio signallers of the 11th South Lancashire Regiment. It was not until the afternoon that the Germans bothered to attack them. The 158th Infantry, supported by field artillery, took ninety minutes to reduce the strong-point, killing Colonel Elstob in the process.

The Canal de la Somme runs south-west from St Quentin to St Simon where, then with the name 'Crozat Canal', it turns south-east while the Canal de la Somme curves northwards to Péronne. This sector of the British line, the triangle with these two canals to the rear, was held by the 36th (Ulster) Division of Maxse's XVIII Corps in the north and III Corps to their right. It was attacked by three divisions of the German XVII Corps. Here the fog prevented the redoubts doing their job as the Germans isolated them and rushed westwards. Three of the Ulster's front line posts held out until after midday while the Germans steadily made their way westwards.

Near Castres, one of the redoubts, Boadicea, held by the 2nd Royal Inniskilling Fusiliers, was bypassed with the 2nd Battalion, 463rd Infantry Regiment left to guard it until artillery had been assembled to support an assault. Before they launched their attack a group of men approached their company commander and, explaining that they all spoke excellent English, asked if they could try to persuade the defenders that their position was hopeless and that they should surrender. Permission was given and, under a flag of truce, the envoys made their cautious approach. Shortly thereafter Lieutenant-Colonel Lord Farnham led his ten officers and 241 men out of the redoubt and into captivity. On the other side of the railway line the smaller fortification, Race Course Redoubt, was held by the 15th Royal Irish Rifles. They held out until 6pm, when their commanding officer, 2nd Lieutenant Edmund de Wind, was killed.

Herbert Sulzbach of the 63rd (Frankfurt) Field Artillery rejoiced in the day's events:

21 March: The artillery fire begins at 4.40am and at 9.40 … came the infantry assault and the creeping barrage. Meanwhile I'm sitting on a limber and can hardly collect my impressions of today. I'd like to write volumes about this day; it really must be the greatest in the history of the world. So the impossible thing has been achieved; the break-through has succeeded! The last night of the four years of static warfare passed …

As evening drew in the German 238th Division had advanced as far as Seraucourt-le-Grand, almost on the banks of the Canal de la Somme as it led north-east towards St Quentin. The British 14th Division, III Corps, had been forced out of its battle zone and had needed reinforcement by 5th Dismounted Brigade. General Gough took the decision to pull out of the triangle, making the canals his front.

Ludendorff was not entirely satisfied with the day's gains. He summarised the position thus:

> The 17th Army, which had the strongest enemy in front of it, only reached his [the British] second line; the barrage had gone far ahead; the infantry had lost touch with it. They remained in this position, lying down, with no artillery support.
>
> In the 2nd Army's attack, the co-operation between the infantry and the artillery was better. The infantry penetrated into the enemy's second position.
>
> With the 18th Army everything proceeded as intended. It was making good progress.

The cost of the first day's fighting had been heavy for both sides. The British had sustained 38,500 casualties, of which number 21,000 were made prisoner. The German losses came to about 40,000, of whom 10,851 were killed. The overall sum exceeded that of 1 July 1916.

General Gough met the French Third Army commander, General Georges Humbert on the morning of 22 March. To his dismay, the Frenchman accurately described his Third Army as existing in name only; he had no troops under his command, Pétain's apprehension of a huge attack in the Champagne region having sent all possible forces to that front. Nor was Haig's chief-of-staff much comfort. Lieutenant-General Sir Herbert Lawrence gave his opinion that the Germans would not follow up their success that day and declined to send Gough the two divisions he asked for. However, the French fears included the possibility of danger to Paris, and they were to prove quicker in reinforcing this sector than Haig was.

Rodolphe Rey was a lawyer, now working as a correspondent for the newspaper *Dépêche Algérienne*. His draft despatches were submitted to the Third Army censor, and must be read in that light. This is from an article he entitled 'How H[umbert]'s Army Closed the Route to Paris' – he used only initials to identify the commanders:

> On 21 March at 9 o'clock in the evening the Germans reached Pargniers and H[umbert]'s army was altered. The [V] Corps, [General Pellé] was given the

mission of assisting the English right in holding the Crozat Canal. The troop movements began next day at noon.

At the same time on 23 March General H[umbert] took command of the French troops which were arriving and the English troops between Barisis and the west of St Simon. It was necessary to relieve the English forces between the Oise and a line north through St Simon to Montdidier through Roye.

Meanwhile Gough had sent his 2nd Cavalry Division to reinforce Butler's III Corps on the Crozat Canal. The 1st Bavarian Division attempted to cross the canal at Jussy, halfway between St Simon and the Oise, but the bridge had been blown the night before and they failed. Further south, at Tergnier, they succeeded in establishing a bridgehead by the end of the day. Butler's position was jeopardised by XVIII Corps when Maxse formed the opinion that his right flank was compromised and so ordered 36th (Ulster) Division to pull back to the Somme. To the north Watts's Corps was therefore obliged to follow as soon as, belatedly, they found out what was happening. This has been said to be the result of Gough's lack of clarity in the orders he had issued that morning, though they seem simple enough provided that the 'rear line of rear zone' is a specific location. The order read:

> In the event of serious hostile attack corps will fight rear-guard actions back to the forward line of the rear zones, and if necessary to rear line of rear zone.

More important, perhaps, was the lack of an established lateral chain of communication between neighbouring corps commanders – messages had to pass through army headquarters itself.

Haig recorded in his dairy on 22 March:

> … at 8 pm Gough telephoned 'parties of all arms of the Enemy are through our Reserve Line.' I concurred in his falling back to the line of the Somme and to hold Péronne Bridgehead in accordance with his orders.
>
> I sent at once to tell General Pétain and asked his support to hold line of Somme and Péronne Bridgehead. I expect big attack to develop towards Arras. He [Pétain] had already agreed to send 3 divisions to the Crozat Canal, and to hold that portion of our front.

There had been a tough fight on the British Third Army front that day. On the northern side of the Flesquières Salient a gap had opened up but a counter-attack by twenty-five Mark IV tanks had forced the German 24th Reserve Division to fall back. A British field artillery unit, twenty-six guns, had fired over 20,000 rounds over open sights. General Byng met Gough at Albert and agreed movements of their armies designed to ensure they remained in contact. Unknown to them, Ludendorff was rethinking his tactics.

Rodolphe Rey reported:

> As early as the 23rd the fighting started for our divisions. The reserves, quite rightly sent towards Ercheu and Reiglise to the east of Roye, found themselves face to face with the advancing enemy as soon as they arrived.

General Ludendorff now came to the conclusion that the original concept, to drive up north-westwards from the start line, could not be sustained. He issued orders on 23 March for his most northerly formation, Seventeenth Army, to push for St Pol, beyond Arras, as originally planned, but for the Second Army to head due west astride the Somme towards Amiens and for the Eighteenth Army to work alongside on its left. The major effort was thus an assault on a line from Noyon through Montdidier to Amiens. He had decided that the Seventeenth Army could not get on and that the opportunity open to him was in the south – to take Amiens.

The progress made by the Eighteenth Army appeared, in the hours that followed, to justify the decision. They crossed the Somme at Ham, west of St Simon, opening a gap between Maxse and Butler to the south. Rey's report refers to Butler's contribution:

> On the evening of the 24th a British division held the Oise bridges at Amigny, Condren, Sincecy, Autreville [overlooking the Oise south-west of the junction with the Crozat Canal]. The enemy had forced a crossing of the Somme at Béthencourt, Pargny, Epénancourt [north-west of Ham] on the Fifth Army front.
>
> We made our frontage from Ognes [on the British division's flank on the Oise], Marest-Dampcourt, Cailloël, Guivry, Le Plessis-Patte-d'Oie, Ramecourt [a line towards Ham].
>
> General H[umbert], keeping his centre on Noyon, which he reinforced with a new division, pushed his artillery, his cyclists, and his motor-borne troops towards the dismounted cavalry corps to his west to receive the wave of enemy on his left and to maintain contact with the English retreat north

and to cover the arrival of D[ebeny]'s army from the west of Montdidier. This manoeuvre continued throughout the 25th.

Herbert Sulzbach wrote on 24 March:

> ... the pace is pretty slow up to Ham, a little town I passed through in 1916 when it was a rosy little rear-echelon station. Now it's a pile of rubble; we forage, and find some splendid British supplies. There's really everything you could think of. Plenty of oats for the horses and tinned food, bacon, cheese and wine for us. Thee are huge masses of troops rolling forward again towards Nesle.

Ensign Paul Knoch, fighting on the Seventeenth Army front to the north was in a more sombre mood.

> ... some villages such as Bouchavesnes have disappeared completely... A few splintered stumps is all that remains of the trees. The roads are littered with dead horses, corpses of Germans, Englishmen and Frenchmen.

The old battlefields of 1916 obstructed progress and afforded little forage to sustain the troops.

The coherence of the Allied front was breaking up. The French in the south were struggling to stay in touch, the Fifth Army, pulling out of Péronne, was losing contact with the Third Army which itself was being drawn away to the north. On the night of 24–25 March the Allies reorganised. All British troops north of the Somme were to come under the command of Third Army. Fifth Army was transferred to General Fayolle who thus commanded a frontage manned for three-fifths of its length by British troops and with French troops taking the rest. But the views of the senior commanders were by no means in tune with one another. Pétain had authorised Fayolle to retreat on Beauvais, south of Amiens, if need be, taking him yet further away from the area Haig held most vulnerable, the space on the approach to the Channel ports. On 25 March Haig wrote:

> Lawrence... left me to telegraph to [Sir Henry] Wilson [Chief of the Imperial General Staff, London] requesting him and Lord Milner [Minister of War] to come to France at once in order to arrange that General Foch or some other determined general, who would fight, should be given supreme control of the operations in France ... he was a man of great courage and decision...

While the relationship between Pétain and Haig had not broken down, for it is clear that they held each other in respect, it was also the case that a supreme commander, possessed of both energy and determination, and of a rank superior to both Pétain and Haig, was required to take charge of the Allied force as a whole; indeed, the Americans had been at a loss to understand how the war could be prosecuted in any other way.

On Tuesday 26 March the governments and commanders met at Doullens and Haig records that a decision was made to protect Amiens and to appoint Foch 'to co-ordinate operations'; not exactly a change in command structure of the scale required. It was not until 3 April, at Beauvais, that Foch was given the authority to conduct 'the strategical direction of military operations'. This meeting was attended by the British and French Prime Ministers, Lloyd George and Clemenceau, and by Wilson, Haig, Foch, Pétain and, vitally, by General John J. Pershing, commander of the American Expeditionary Force.

In the meantime, on the field of battle, the German tide rolled onwards. The 28th Division was thrusting west between Maxse's XVIII Corps and the French formation under Humbert to the south, crossing the Roye to Amiens road near Le Quesnoy and through Erches on 25 March; heading south-west as Ludendorff had just directed. The British attacked Bouchoir and Le Quesnoy from the west and north and while the 28th held against the former, the northerly assault pushed them back into Erches and caused them alarm. The divisional report reads:

As strong hostile counter-attacks were to be expected on the 26th [of March], the field and heavy artillery, in spite of the lack of cover on the right flank, had come up in line with the infantry in order to assure cooperation with the infantry in any case. Early on March 26, heavy British counter-attacks were launched against the front and both wings while the right [north] flank was attacked from the direction of Bouchoir and east of that by a French division whose objective was to turn the flank of the 28th Division (prisoners' statements). Attacks against the front and two wings were repulsed with heavy losses to the enemy, as a result of the vigorous cooperation of the elements remaining in Saulchoy. On the other hand the enemy, debouching from Harvillers and Bouchoir, succeeded in temporarily driving back the right wing of the 28th Division as far as Erches and east of Erches. Hostile units were already appearing in rear of the division. Persistent bombardments by hostile aviators were causing appreciable losses to our troops, a part of which were in close formation. Some supply wagons near the east edge of Erches withdrew in haste towards the east.

Gunfire from field artillery with the 28th drove off the assault and a skirmishing party managed to take some prisoners, but clearly, as this annex to the broader memorandum on tactics in the intermediate zone was appended at all, the event was deemed important. The division was withdrawn from the line three days later, having suffered, in some companies, 75 per cent casualties. They needed 2,500 replacements to bring it back to full strength. The rate of loss for the Germans was serious.

The British also took heavy casualties that day. The 7th Duke of Cornwall's Light Infantry, fighting at Le Quesnoy, held the place until evening when the last eleven men managed to get away. The British view was that they had fought a rear-guard action which enabled the XVIII Corps to fall back towards Amiens – the Germans thought they had narrowly avoided being cut off to the rear.

Astride the Somme the line was in jeopardy. Watts's XIX Corps ended the day on a line running south from Bray-sur-Somme but north of the river, Congreve's VII Corps had been planning to withdraw from the continuation of this line to Albert. The new orders from Third Army arrived as this movement was starting, and Congreve wisely decided the disorder ensuing from countermanding the previous plan would be ruinous, so a gap was allowed to open between Bray and Albert. Luckily the German 13th Division was exhausted and halted at Morlancourt, halfway between Bray and Corbie. The Germans entered Albert, but determined fighting by the New Zealand Division to join up with the Australians at Hébuterne prevented the 24th (Saxon) Division getting beyond the old British and French line north of the town.

On 26 March Major-General John Monash, commanding the Australian 3rd Division, had just returned from Paris by way of Doullens to find something close to panic on the front north of Albert. He calmed the situation and then received sudden orders to report to the headquarters of VII Corps. He had trouble finding them, for they had just retired from Corbie in the face of the German advance. He found Lieutenant-General Congreve in a château at Montigny, studying a map with his chief of staff by the light of a candle. Monash wrote home, describing Congreve's orders:

General, the position is very simple. My corps at four o'clock today was holding the line from Bray to Albert, when the line broke, and what is left of three divisions in the line after four days' heavy fighting without food or sleep are falling back rapidly. German cavalry have been seen approaching Morlancourt and Buire. They are making straight for Amiens. What I want you to do is to get into the angle between the Ancre and the Somme as far east as possible.

Congreve told him of a line of old trenches between Méricourt-l'Abbé and Sailly-le-Sec that could provide a defensible line for him. The commander of the Australian 4th Division, Major-General E.G. Sinclair-Maclagen, arrived at that moment and was asked to occupy the high ground above the Ancre, west of Albert. As Congreve himself put it, 'Thank heaven, the Australians at last!'

The energy was draining from the German assault. Their lines of supply were becoming incapable of sustaining the attack, in part because of the distances to be covered by horse-drawn transport and in part because they were attempting to cross terrain they had devastated in 1917 and over which both sides had fought so destructively in 1916. They had, however, managed to out-flank the Allied line on the Somme with the penetration south of Albert. When writing home on 29 March, General von Marwitz remarked:

> … the region is which we are engaged is appalling. It is the area of the earlier Somme battle and is a giant desert. Villages are hardly recognisable as such and topography resembles upland covered with brush and thicket. Our front lines reach the edge of the undestroyed region, but it is not pretty either, for the British have wasted no time in devastating everything. How they will ever make this land inhabitable again is anybody's guess.

General Gough had been tireless in his efforts to coordinate the resistance and retreat south of the Somme. He had been given too few men and whatever mistakes he had made in the static phase, the fluid situation that developed as the Germans advanced suited his talents. Haig noted in his diary on 26 March:

> … I met Milner and Wilson. They spoke to me about Gough, I said that whatever the opinion at home might be, I considered he had dealt with a most difficult situation very well. He had never lost his head, was always cheery and fought hard.

To counter the depletion of his divisions Gough created new formations from whatever units might be to hand, notably, on 26 March, Carey's Force under Major-General George Carey, a grouping that lasted only five days but did vital service in that time. From the support troops working in the Amiens area, railwaymen, engineers, fragmented infantry units and even 300 hospital convalescents, a force of some 2,500 men was pulled together. The American 6th Engineers, 3rd Division, had been building a steel bridge near Péronne when the German operation began, and now B and D companies were in the Amiens area. In spite of the fact that they had no combat training, they, together with 400 men of the 2nd Battalion, Canadian Railway Troops, were grouped with A and B Batteries of the 1st Canadian Motor Machine Gun Brigade and, the next day, with remnants of the 66th (2nd East Lancashire) Division to hold the line to the rear of, and reporting to, Watts's Corps.

North of the river, VII Corps and the Royal Flying Corps opposed the advance of the Germans but on 27 March Walther von Brauchitsch had his 3rd Grenadier and 43rd Regiments plank the blown bridge at Chipilly and cross to Cerisy into the space behind Watts's front line and facing Carey's Force. The Americans were in the centre, north of the Roman road, near Warfusée-Abancourt. With the threat from north of the river the British wished to fall back to the defensive line through Villers-Brettoneux, where the 61st Division were arriving by bus in response to Gough's orders. As the Germans moved into Warfusée-Abancourt, they were attacked by the American Engineers. On 29 March three more companies of the Canadian Motor Machine Gun Brigade joined and Carey was reinforced by what was left of the 1st Cavalry Division. Some survivors of the 16th (Irish) Division also joined the fight and the Germans were stopped at Hamel on the left of the line. On 30 March the remnants of these units were reformed yet again as a smaller force under Lieutenant-Colonel Whitemore, thereafter known as Whitemore's Cosmopolitan Force. They had done their part in halting the German advance and a stable line was formed on the Amiens defence lines, which Gough had had the prudence to leave in place at the start of the year.

Gough, however, was to take the blame for the retreat. Under pressure from above, Haig, over dinner on Good Friday, 29 March, told him:

> … I wanted him and his staff out of the line in order to reconnoitre the Somme Valley from Amiens to the sea. It may be necessary for me to hold such a line if French do not hold on! So a Reserve Army Staff is necessary.

It was poor cover for the act of sacking a scapegoat. The command passed to General Sir Henry Rawlinson, who formally assumed it at 1630 hours on 28 March. Sir Hubert Gough wrote to Field Marshal Haig from England 21 June after he had been sent home and found himself being blamed for much of what had taken place. Haig replied on 6 July, telling him that, in his report of the events of 21 and 22 March, he had stated:

... there was a thick mist. This mist masked the fire of our infantry and machine-gunners, and prevented the signals of batteries and observers being seen. The very dry season had rendered the valley of the River Oise ford-able in many places. There were, moreover, insufficient troops to hold our defences continuously. Under these circumstances, the enemy was able to penetrate our line in certain places unseen...

The failure of the Fifth Army to hold its position on 21 March, even though there are many good reasons why it was forced to fall back, has furnished the Government with a reason for ordering me to send you home. That being the case, I strongly recommend you to remain quiet until more history is made ... Then, I hope, there may be a chance of getting you back to some active appointment.

Gough remained quiet. He was not recalled to an active appointment.

On 27 March Herbert Sultzbach had made an enthusiastic entry in his journal.

We move on to a point beyond Faverolles [east of Montdidier]. It's going at such a pace that I'm afraid our neighbours won't keep up with us. We, that is the 9th Infantry Division, the 7th Grenadiers, the 19th, the 154th, and our own 5th Field Artillery Regiment, maintain our high record of achieve-ment with an infantry assault on Montdidier, and this brings the fighting for 27 March to a close.

The victorious tone soon changed:

Now, however, strong enemy fire started up to make it difficult for our reserves to advance, and a shocking business it was...

28 March... We go into position north of Montdider, and the advance is to be halted for two days until our right and left flank neighbours have come up ... we need a little rest...

30 March, Easter Saturday: It is evening, I'm writing down my impressions of this day, which must have been the nastiest of any blessed day in the whole war, full of many dreadful situations, each one following closely on the one just before...

At 7.30am they had attacked Le Mesnil, just west of the town, and come under heavy machine-gun fire. The French were transformed; reinforcements had come into the line and they were fighting with unwelcome vigour:

> And up there it's a witches' cauldron, compared with which the business we had before was child's play: machine-gun fire and small-arms fire so strong that it might have been thousands and thousands of enemy gun-barrels being trained on one Battery… Our infantry start coming back, in groups or singly, because they can't stand it any more up there at the front, and finally they are lying between the guns… Meanwhile, in spite of bad weather, enemy planes have been appearing over our lines, flying at a low altitude in heavy swarms of twenty or thirty in a bunch… We move back through Montdidier town to the old position…

The French stabilised the line west of Montdidier. Their final fight was at Grivesnes, on the road to Ailly-sur-Noye from Montdidier, north-west of Cantigny. Here elements of the French 127th Infantry Division held the German 1st Guards Division at the château when it attacked on 30 March. The park came under heavy shellfire at 11am for an hour and the assault was launched at noon. The 1st Guards Regiment worked its way through the village, house to house, and were stubbornly opposed every step of the way. The château was taken and retaken by the French 350th Infantry during the night. The 19th Battalion of Chasseurs under Major Ducornez joined the defence. The 350th were relieved by the 355th Infantry before dawn broke on Easter Sunday. Wave after wave of Germans attacked that day, but they could not prevail. Here the line south of Amiens held at last.

North of Albert the Australians prevented any further German advance and, indeed, attacked to establish the front. Further north again, at Arras, the Germans undertook Operation Mars, but without success. The Germans won a salient west of Montdidier, the line then running north past Cantigny, up the valley of the river Avre where, at Moreuil, where they had been stopped on 30 March, it turned eastwards a little towards Villers-Brettoneux and then to Albert beyond the Somme valley. For three days comparative silence descended, during which time the Germans brought up fresh supplies and reinforcements.

Gunner Maurice Burton was pleased to stop at last. They had been moved and moved again since their narrow escape from the first day's confusion as Operation Michael unfolded:

Eventually the Guards came through. It was their boast that they never gave up a position nor failed to take one when so ordered. Certainly it was true in this instance for from the time of their arrival the line held firm. We were able to get the guns properly sited, have a wash and a shave and a properly cooked meal, the first one for days, as I remember. We had not been short of food but it was always biscuits and bully.

Then came the marvellous day, shortly after we had reached the point of no further retreat, when the mail came through... I received a parcel from home. As usual, it had been well packed but its shape bore testimony to the adventures it had had in transit. Inside was a birthday cake, battered and bruised, but tasting like the food of the gods. The letter accompanying it reminded me that I had celebrated my twentieth birthday, although where we were and what we were doing on March 28 ... escaped my memory even then...

Never, as I think back, can I remember hearing anyone even so much as suggesting that we might be defeated. At various times, during the retreat, we met men of many regiments and units, from all parts of England, Wales, Scotland, Ireland and from overseas... They complained of fatigue, of hunger, of inconvenience: they would utter 'Roll on, blighty', which being translated meant 'I shall be glad when all this is over and we can go home.' But despair or defeat seemed not to have been contemplated.

The British had been trying to strengthen their line south of the Somme and Watts now had the 14th Division next to the river, the Australian 9th Brigade under Brigadier-General Charles Rosenthal in the centre and the 18th Division on the right with 6th Cavalry Brigade in reserve. On 4 April, at 0515 hours, the German gas attack began, followed by the assault of the German 228th Division which broke the exhausted 14th and allowed the capture of Hamel. The Australians rallied the fleeing British and, with the 18th Division, held off the German attacks. By the afternoon the British line had been forced back to the outskirts of Villers-Brettoneux. At 1600 hours the German XI Corps launched a violent attack, which pushed the British and Australians back into the town itself. Lieutenant-Colonel J. Milne rallied his own 36th Battalion and other Australians, which encouraged scattered British platoons to join them and thrust the Germans back. The next day the 4th Australian Division endured heavy fighting on the Ancre front, but held firm. Ludendorff ended Operation Michael that day. He said:

On the 4th April 2nd Army and the right wing of the 18th attacked at Albert and south of the Somme towards Amiens. These actions were indecisive. It was an established fact that the enemy's resistance was beyond our strength. We must not get drawn into a battle of exhaustion. This would accord neither with the strategical nor the tactical situation. In agreement with the commanders concerned, G.H.Q. had to take the extremely difficult decision to abandon the attack on Amiens for good.

Not that it was the end of fighting here. On 24 April an attempt was made to take the rest of the ridge overlooking Amiens that the Germans had acquired by moving forward through Villers-Brettoneux. The shelling started at 3am and at 6am four divisions moved on the town, supported by A7V tanks; twelve of these 30-ton monsters were available, under the command of Major Bornschlegel. They had been brought by rail from Charleroi, Belgium, to Wiencourt-l'Equipée on the line to Ham. *Sturm Panzer-kraftwagen Abteilung 1* (Assault Armoured Motor Vehicle Detachment 1) with three machines supported men of 77th Reserve Division in the attack on the town itself, north of the railway line. Hard house-to-house fighting followed, with heavy casualties. A second group, with tanks from Detachments 1 and 2 assaulted the southern side of the town with 4th Guard Infantry Division. The town was soon overrun but one of the tanks, *Mephisto*, fell into a shell hole and had to be abandoned. The Germans also advanced from Marcelcave towards Cachy, south-west of Villers-Brettoneux with four A7Vs from Detachment 2 together with infantry from 77th Reserve Division. Lieutenant Wilhelm Blitz commanded one of the machines, *Nixe*. The clumsy German vehicles rolled down the slope to the south-west of the village at about 9.30am to be met by three British Mark IV tanks. The two female tanks were forced to turn away under fire from the A7Vs, unable to answer with their machine-gun armament. One of the A7Vs, *Elfriede*, blundered into a shallow quarry and slid onto its side; it was abandoned and the crew fought on as infantry. Lieutenant Frank Mitchell was commanding the third British tank, a male, with 6-pounder guns. He wrote:

Opening a loophole, I looked out. There, some three hundred yards away, a round squat-looking monster was advancing; behind it came waves of infantry, and farther away to the left and right crawled two more of these armed tortoises.

So we had met our rivals at last! For the first time in history tank was encountering tank!

The 6-pounder gunners crouching on the floor, their backs against the engine cover, loaded their guns expectantly...

Above the roar of our engine sounded the staccato rat-tat-tat-tat of machine-guns, and another furious jet of bullets sprayed our steel side, the splinters clanging against the engine cover. The Jerry tank had treated us to a broadside of armour-piercing bullets!

Both machines were swaying up and down over the rough terrain, firing and failing to score a serious hit. Mitchell came within feet of crushing one of the British trenches, the yells of the threatened men only just giving him time to turn aside. Then Mitchell saw his gunner had missed Blitz's tank only narrowly and he took the risk of stopping his tank:

The pause was justified; a well-aimed shot hit the enemy's conning tower, bringing him to a standstill. Another roar and yet another white puff at the front of the tank denoted a second hit! Peering with swollen eyes through his narrow slit, the gunner shouted words of triumph that were drowned by the road of the engine. Then once more he aimed with great deliberation and hit for the third time. Through a loophole I saw the tank heel over on one side... We had knocked the monster out!

One shell stuck *Nixe's* turret and the other two the front and side of the machine, killing three crewmen. The tank stalled and the rest of the crew leapt out in case the tank caught fire. Under Mitchell's machine-gun fire they swiftly got back in.

Two more German tanks were advancing, distracting the British and allowing Blitz to escape. As Mitchell's gunners fired on the advancing infantry first one and then the other A7V turned away. Mitchell's joy was short lived. First, a German aircraft shook them up with a bomb and then they stalled the engine in a shell-hole. As they waited for the enemy infantry to swarm over them, rescue materialised. Seven of the new British Medium Mark A Whippets, the new light tank, joined the battle. This was too much for the German infantry and they pulled back to the town. The first tank-against-tank action had cost the Germans one officer and eight other ranks killed, and three officers and fifty men wounded.

That night the Australian 15th and 13th Brigades and a brigade of the 18th Division counter-attacked. The night was misty. There was no artillery preparation to warn the new defenders and the attack went in with bayonet and machine-gun, from one position to another. When day dawned the town was in the embrace of the Australians and by mid-morning the Germans had either been captured, killed or thrown back.

The German advance on the Somme front ceased. It had cost them some 239,000 men. The British had lost 177,739 of whom about 72,000 were prisoners – another burden upon a starving Germany. The Americans had lost seventy-seven men of their small, courageous force. The French had suffered some 60,000 killed or wounded and 17,000 made prisoner. In all, 254,816 Allied troops. In terms of quality, it is probable that the Germans had suffered more greatly, with their crack regiments bearing the brunt of the damage.

Chapter 7

Advance to Victory:
May to November 1918

The German Assaults Continue

The German attacks now moved to other fronts. On 9 April Operation Georgette was launched, the Germans striking through Flanders towards the Channel ports. It was hastily arranged and Colonel Bruchmüller was concerned that he had too little time to plan the bombardment. Even so, the Allied line broke at Laventie, west of Lille, when the unsupported Portuguese 2nd Division was forced back. On 11 April Haig issued his famous 'Order of The Day':

> Many of us are now tired. To those I would say that victory will belong to the side that holds out the longest... There is no course open to us but to fight it out. Every position must be held to the last man: there must be no retirement. With our backs to the wall and believing in the justice of our cause each one of us must fight to the end...

The German advance was halted in front of Hazebrouck on 12 April. The Passchendaele Ridge, so dearly won in 1917, was evacuated on 15 April. The French were pushed off Mount Kemmel on the southern end of the Ypres sector, and their 30th Infantry Regiment was wiped out entirely. The Second Battle of the Lys ended on 29 April when the final attack by thirteen German divisions failed. British losses totalled 76,300, French 35,000 and German 109,300.

On 27 May the next of the series of German assaults started. Operation Blücher-Yorck was a threat directed towards Paris from the Chemin des Dames, first across the Aisne river and then on the Marne. General Denis Duchêne's Sixth Army was driven back and Ludendorff was so pleased with the speed of the advance to the river Ourcq by 29 May that he allocated additional troops to the operation. On 30 May, at 1700 hours, the American 2nd Division was alerted to move to a position west of Château-Thierry on the river Marne, reporting to General Jean Degoutte, commander of the French XXI Corps. The Marine Brigade dashed to Lucy-le-Bocage to oppose the enemy at Belleau Wood and the 3rd Division hastened to prevent a crossing of the Marne via the bridges in the town. They did so and, with men of the French 52nd Colonial Division now south of the river, the bridges were blown on 3 June. The fight for Belleau Wood was bitter and prolonged. The Marines assaulted repeatedly. They were relieved for three days by 7th Infantry, 3rd Division and returned on 22 June to renew their attacks. The wood fell to them on 25 June, by which time they had sustained 5,200 casualties.

On 9 June yet another German operation, Gneisenau, was launched on the river Matz, south of the Montdidier to Noyon line – the result of Operation Michael. The German Eighteenth Army was once again the aggressor, but General Foch had insisted on defence in depth and General Humbert was able to pull his 38th and 15th Divisions back to the edge of the Forest of Laigue, north-east of Compiègne, and von Hutier's army flowed into the space yielded. By the evening of 10 June the Germans held the Lassigny hills and had in the west penetrated as far as Méry and Courcelles, where they were stopped. This left von Hutier's flank exposed to the combative General Charles Mangin who had been allocated an army group of five divisions, including elements of the American 2nd and 3rd Divisions. Mangin moved them into position by motor transport. Two of the divisions were unable to move their artillery that quickly and motorised artillery regiments were provided, as well as the support of 163 Renault light tanks. Mangin encouraged his force with these words:

> Tomorrow's operation must be the end of the defensive battle we have been conducting these last two months; it must signal the halting of the Germans, the renewal of the offensive, and lead to success. Everyone must understand this!

The attack went in at 11am on 11 June, with no preliminary artillery preparation. Progress was slow on the French left, where the German artillery hit their flank, but the 48th Division on the right did well. The Germans lost nineteen guns and about a thousand men made prisoner, and the next day yielded more ground. But there the action ceased; the French wisely judged that no objective

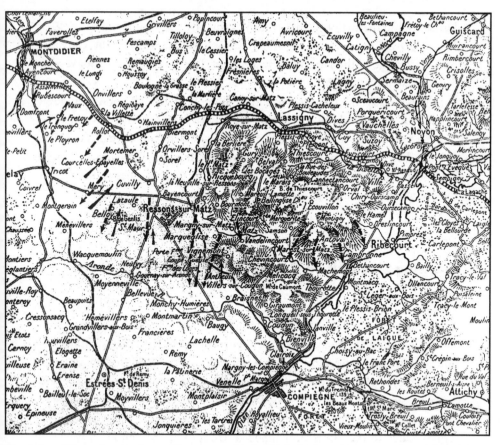

The defeat of Operation Gneisenau. The arrows with dotted shafts show German attacks and the solid arrows Mangin's counter-attack. In the east, south-east of Ribecourt, the French established their new line through Tracey-le-Val. *From* l'Illustration. *(HGG)*

of advantage was open to them and a mere taking back of ground for the sake of it was a costly gesture best not pursued. The Germans, however, had failed in their aims.

On 15 July the last of the great German attacks was attempted on the Marne front, but the French were forewarned by intelligence obtained from prisoners. Their front lines were lightly manned and a counter-bombardment caused their enemy serious damage while his fell on empty positions. The American 3rd Division and part of their 28th Division were east of Château-Thierry and became involved in a tough fight in which they were supported by Colonel William Mitchell's American airmen. The fighting developed into what became known as the Second Battle of the Marne, in which Mangin's Tenth Army, the American 1st, 2nd and 3rd Divisions, and later their 28th and 42nd (Rainbow)

Divisions, and the British 15th (Scottish), 34th, 51st (Highland) and 62nd (West Riding) Divisions, constituting XXII Corps, took part, rolling the Germans back to the line of the river Vesle by 4 August. This was the first major reverse for German forces in 1918.

In these attacks the Germans had inflicted terrible damage upon themselves in their efforts to end the war before the Americans could turn the tide. The number killed came to 227,000 men and the wounded numbered 765,000. The sick numbered an amazing 1,960,000, many suffering from influenza. Of course a proportion of sick and wounded would recover to serve once more, but the losses could not be made good by further conscription.

Growing Strength on the Somme

Fortunately for the British on the Somme, June and July 1918 were comparatively quiet months. Shocked by the closeness of a defeat, the British politicians agreed to reinforce the Army, but only just in time. Foch held that the situation remained precarious until the end of July. The losses of March and April were, however, severe, and the survivors were close to exhaustion. Men on leave or recovering from wounds in England hastened back to France and newly trained troops added to the influx of manpower. Troops who had endured weeks of desperate fighting rested and gathered their strength.

Gunner Burton was weary from the repeated movements of 342nd Battery, Royal Garrison Artillery. Finally they came to rest when Operation Michael stumbled to a halt:

> We found ourselves in the line of trenches from which the British Army had advanced in 1916, in the Battle of the Somme. Then came a brilliantly fine day, with a blue sky and warm sunshine, during which there was no sound of battle that I can remember hearing, perhaps because I spent the afternoon on the fire-step of an old trench, oblivious to the world of man. There was an ants' nest in the parapet of the trench and for what must have been three hours I watched the comings and goings of the ants. It was fascinating beyond my previous experience.
>
> The episode might have ended there except that the first man I talked to was 'Daddy' Hooker, a fellow gunner … I exploded my boyish enthusiasm to

him only to learn that he was a professional lecturer on natural history before the war had dragged him from his bugs and beetles. He listened to me for a few minutes before the suppressed springs of a born teacher burst their banks … from the spring of 1918 onwards there has never been any question of the field of knowledge I wished to explore.

New Tanks and Tactics

The advent of the German tank stimulated the supply of new machines to the Tank Corps in France. In the turmoil of recent events delivery had been difficult to arrange, but now, in May, nearly sixty tanks a week were reaching France. To Frank Mitchell's satisfaction these were of an improved design, the Mark V. It could achieve a speed of 5 miles per hour (8 kilometres per hour) and had a radius of action of 25 miles (40 kilometres). The greatest improvement was its ability to manoeuvre. It had epicyclic gears, which allowed a single man to drive and steer, and the three formerly needed to help with that could now man the guns. It had an observation cab in the roof giving all-round vision. Its armament included Hotchkiss machine-guns, one of which was fitted in the rear wall of the machine. The fuel was carried in a three-compartment tank so, said Mitchell, 'if one was hit by a shell the tank could still keep going on petrol from the others'. His optimism was exemplary. When a number of battalions had been provided with Mark Vs and mastered control of them it was decided to give them a trial run. Mitchell wrote:

> The Australians, who were straining at the leash in front of Villers-Brettoneux, were chosen as companions in this preliminary canter, and the first task was to overcome their prejudices, for ever since the battle at Bullecourt, in 1917, the cry of Australian soldiers had been 'Tanks are no good. We don't want tanks.'

The idea did not enthuse the Australians, but General Rawlinson insisted, so they convened at Vaux, where the training school was located. The 'tankers' and the 'diggers' had a wonderful time. The infantry not only saw everything the machines had and could do, but were able to try their hand at driving them. Then trenches were dug and barbed wire strung in a competition to see if the tanks could be stopped, and when they drove over the obstacles and swivelled to lay their guns on their targets, the Australians were won over to them.

Each unit adopted a tank to work with in the coming attack, and wrote the machine's nickname on it in chalk.

War in the Air

The French and British had been at something of a disadvantage in the air in 1917. During the previous year the Germans had looked for some way to establish dominance of the skies and developed the *Jagdstaffel*, the hunting squadron, a concept proposed by Oswald Boelcke. In August 1916 he had formed the first *Jasta*, or squadron, to operate on these new lines, and recruited, among others, a young pilot named Manfred von Richthofen. They developed a new array of air-fighting tactics, which, together with aircraft innovation such as the Albatros DI biplane and a machine-gun synchronised to fire through the propeller arc, enabled them to inflict serious losses on the Allies. As the war progressed the technical race in aircraft design was a major influence on success, as was the manufacturing capacity of the opposing sides.

In January 1918 a competition for new fighter designs was held by the Germans at Alderhof. The best combat pilots were summoned from the front to take part in the assessment. While many manufacturers attempted to influence them with generous dinners and other delights, Anthony Fokker paid close attention to what they said. As a result he submitted his V-11 prototype to a complete redesign before the next round of competition and his new aircraft, the D.VII, was evidently the best. It had a welded aluminium framework suited to mass production, a Mercedes 160hp engine with a radiator like a motorcar and was both easy to fly and to use as a solid gun platform. It, together with other aircraft, allowed the *Kaiserschlacht* offensives of spring 1918 to benefit from superb air cover. The weather permitting, German aeroplanes flew missions to strafe ground troops, bomb installations, shoot down observation balloons and fight Allied air patrols. The Allies responded by massing fighters in large killer squadrons and by intensifying their bombing missions.

The Allies had also developed highly effective aircraft, notably the Sopwith Camel and the swift S.E.5a. The French had the SPAD XIII, a twin-gunned machine, and the Moraine Saulnier A1, a remarkably modern high wing monoplane. The introduction of these aircraft in appropriate quantity in mid-1918 swung the balance of air power. Von Richthofen complained that his acrobatic Fokker triplane was too slow and that the Albatros D.Va was outdated.

The air arm also benefited from improved organisation, which unified procurement and supply. On 1 April 1918 the Royal Air Force came into existence as a service in its own right; it was no longer a part of either the Army or the Navy. The new service at once ran into trouble when its commander, Major-General Hugh Trenchard, found himself unable to report to the Air Ministry under Lord Rothermere, but that proved to be a blessing when he was later asked to form the Independent Force of the RAF to carry out strategic bombing of German supply lines. On 15 April he was succeeded as Chief of the Air Staff, at the head of the RAF, by Major-General Sir Frederick Sykes. On 14 May the French formed the Division Aérienne, commanded by General Maurice Duval, again independent of Army control.

On 21 April the Red Baron, as von Richthofen was known, led his JG1 formation into a huge aerial dog-fight with 209 Squadron RAF. One inexperienced British pilot became separated from the mêlée and von Richthofen was soon on his tail; but Captain Roy Brown was on his. As Australian troops opened up with Lewis guns, Brown opened fire. The red triplane went into a glide, an indication of the pilot being hit. The airman's body was accorded a funeral with full military honours by the Australians.

Locating the Enemy Guns

A major task of the artillery was the suppression of enemy guns, and for that it was necessary to be able to target them exactly. Various methods of locating and mapping German guns were developed, but by 1918 the best results were to be had from sound ranging. Walter von B. Roberst was an American engineer, but closely associated with artillery work, as he was a member of a Flash and Sound Ranging unit. Both are methods of locating enemy artillery in order to be able to strike back. He produced a detailed explanation of sound ranging in a letter to his family:

After March 26 I was assigned to Sound Ranging and since this service is not much heard of nowadays it may be worth while to describe it sufficiently to make its purpose and method clear. Briefly, its object was to locate a source of sound, particularly the big boom of a gun or explosion of a shell, by means of sound alone. Thus the method worked equally well at night or in fog, and could not be fooled by putting camouflage over a gun. The Germans understood the possibility of doing this and even tried it in a crude way with stop watches, but the British and French had developed highly sophisticated equipment which made results accurate and fast. Their equipment could be used simply to locate on a map the spot where an enemy gun was located, or where one of our shells landed. But its best trick was to combine the two so as to help our gunners knock out an enemy gun. This was called 'Counter Battery' work. It was possible to tell our gunners very accurately whether their shells were going over or short, right or left, and how much, even when vagaries of wind or temperature prevented accurate location of the enemy gun itself, since these vagaries effected the locations of shell and gun equally.

First imagine yourself in the central station dug-out of one of our sound ranging sections. On one side there is a table with a detailed map of the territory extending several miles around glued to the top. On this map there are six spots marked at intervals of about one kilometer along or close behind our front line trenches. Each spot represents a microphone designed to be responsive to big booms of sound but not very sensitive to the lighter and sharper sounds of rifle fire. Each microphone is connected to the central station by wires laid along the ground or sometimes strung on little posts. When an enemy gun fires, the sound reaching the nearest microphone causes a pulse of current to flow to the central station along its connecting wire line. A little later the sound reaches the next nearest microphone and similarly produces a little pulse of current over its particular line. In this way, each big bang reaches the central station in the form of six current pulses, one in each of the six lines. These pulses are photographed on moving film or paper as little jogs in six otherwise fairly straight lines running the length of the film. In addition to these lines there are cross lines produced by a rotating wheel with a thin slit in it to expose the film once every one hundredth of a second. The film reader can determine the time difference of arrival of the sound at any pair of microphones by counting the number of cross lines between the jogs produced by the two microphones. Finally there is at least one forward outpost man, out in the trenches, or in any case a hundred yards or so ahead of the microphones, with a telephone and a switch (all connected to the central station) which he closes when he hears a sound that he judges to be worth recording. This turns on the film motor so that by the time the sound reaches the nearest microphone the film is moving and ready to make the record.

(If the machinery were kept going all the time would waste a lot of film). So far we have shown how the sound of a gun or shell burst is recorded on film in such a way that the time intervals between its arrival at the second microphones can be accurately measured, to the hundredth of a second or less. To achieve this result involves a lot of delicate equipment including the string galvanometer, mentioned previously, and the automatic developing and fixing machine for the film developed in Palmer Laboratory at Princeton (although semi-manual methods were used during most of the war).

He then went on to explain that the difference in time between one microphone receiving the sound and the next one picking it up enabled the operator to calculate the difference in distance between the locations of the microphones and the enemy gun. This allows a curve to be used on the map indicating the distance of the gun from a pair of microphones, and multiple curves like this home in on the true position:

But if we make several locations, using different groups of microphones, and get the same result, we are confident that it is correct. We actually used five time intervals, but the five corresponding hyperbolas cross each other at ten different places, thus giving ten different locations for the gun. If the ten spots so plotted fell within 25 yards of each other the location of the mean was considered very reliable. Usually, due to wind or temperature affecting the speed of sound differently at different places, some of our spots were likely to be 150 or more yards apart, and our result not very accurate.

In practice we found that in the region on the map where enemy guns were located, these imaginary hyperbolic, curves were fairly straight lines, each of which if extended passed through a point mid way between the microphones giving rise to the curve in question. So we bored a little hole in the table half way between each two adjacent microphone locations and ran a thread up through it with a lead weight on the table and another below the table to keep it taut. Around the edge of the table were scales of time intervals. All the computer did was to put the string coming from between A and B onto the AB scale on the table edge at a reading (AB), then do the same for the string coming from between B and C, C and D, etc. until all five strings crossed (supposedly) at a single point on the map and there the gun must be. In practice they did not often cross at the same point so we took the center of the bunch of crossings as the best we could do...

It proved to be a system quick to use and accurate enough to yield very satisfactory results.

A fresh enemy, a threat to both sides, appeared in June – the influenza pandemic. By May 1919, 200,000 British were to die of the disease, but the Germans, deprived of food supplies by the Allied blockade, were weakened and lost over 400,000 civilians. The disease spread among the fighting forces as well. The Americans lost more men to influenza than in battle during this war.

Cantigny

The United States had now been at war for a year. In that time the American Expeditionary Force's fatal casualties in action had been a mere 163 men, and training of the first troops to arrive in France was scarcely complete. It was, however, essential that General John J. Pershing took a greater share of the load, and yet more important that he gained the confidence of his allies and raised the morale of his troops by making, and succeeding in, an attack. The fighting spirit of the men was not in doubt, but the competence of the regimental officers and staff was. The place chosen for this first American offensive was the village of Cantigny, west of Montdidier, where the German advance had been halted in March. The US 1st Division had entered the line here at Villers-Tournelle on 23 April, overlooked by the Germans from the village on the ridge opposite. A deep valley lay in between the front lines. Raymond Austin, of the 6th Field Artillery wrote to his mother in May:

> The German drive advanced so rapidly that the people... left in great haste. Their houses and their household goods were abandoned – china, bed linen, clocks, furniture, pianos and everything... My dug-out is very novel – a wine cellar cut from pure, white chalk...

This section of the front was, in terms of this war, quiet, but Austin's battery was firing some 1,500 rounds a day and the Germans were no less energetic. Earl D. Seaton, 16th Infantry, was checking the food issue in Broyes when shells started to fall:

> At first at the edge of the town, then closer and closer the shells landed... We heard the 'whomp', then the topoff as the shell reached its highest and started

down, growing louder and louder. Then the sharp crack as it hit the tile roof and exploded before entering the ground... Several men were killed, one was gone completely ... he was in right where the shell hit... I saw a leg with shoe and puttee leggings on it, cut off above the knee. One fellow told me he was walking down the street with his mess kit when the fellow in front of him was cut off at the hips. The legs stood for a moment, as the blood oozed out, then collapsed.

Captain Jeremiah M. Evarts, 18th Infantry, was concerned about one of his men, Private Jackson. Every time the shelling started up the boy shook uncontrollably. He threw himself flat in the bottom of the trench and when Evarts pulled him up the tears were pouring down his mud-streaked face:

That night I made him go the rounds with [Sergeant] Shea and myself. I walked first and Shea last. Poor Jackson was frightened most of the time and if a shell came within 200 yards, he was flat on the ground. It was still raining and Shea was greatly annoyed after he had fallen over Jackson several times in the dark.

The French provided the greater part of the artillery support for the coming attack. The preparations were made with immense care – the American staff, including Captain George C. Marshall, Jr, were determined that everything should go perfectly. A model of the objective was made for the officers and NCOs to study, and well to the rear, the target zone was replicated by tracing it out on the ground so that troops could practise their tasks. The mission was described and repeatedly emphasised: Cantigny was to be taken and held against all counter-attacks. The assault on 28 May fell to the 28th Infantry Regiment. Raymond Austin wrote home on 1 June:

We adjusted our rolling barrage, etc., as discreetly as possible the day before, and everything was ready that evening... H hour would be at 6.45am – the time when the infantry would go over the top... At 4.45 all batteries ... began their final adjustments all along the line and at the first shots the Boche's sausages [observation balloons] went up in a hurry to see what was going on... Then at 5.45 all batteries began a heavy raking fire throughout the zone to be covered by our advance. The ground was pounded to dust by our shells... At 6.40 the preparation ceased, the heavy batteries shifted over to cover the flanks of the attack or pounded the enemy rear trenches and batteries, and the

75s [shells from French 75-mm field guns, the famous 'Soixante-Quinzes'] dropped into place on the line of departure of the rolling barrage ... until along the whole front of the attack there was a perfect, even line of bursting shells a mile long. Then at 6.45 ... the barrage moved forward at a rate just fast enough for the infantry to keep up with it at a walk. At the same time ... the infantry suddenly appeared on the slope of the ridge close behind our barrage - a long brown line with bayonets glistening in the sun... They walked steadily along ... accompanied by the [French] tanks which buzzed along with smoke coming out from their exhausts and their guns. As the line reached the crest and was silhouetted in the morning sun ... it looked like a long picket fence. Occasionally a shell would strike among them and a gap would appear among the pickets, then quickly close.

The Americans were soon in the enemy's third line trenches, having carried the first and second lines. As the shellfire passed beyond Cantigny, Germans emerged from the cellars where they had sheltered, either of their own volition or flushed out by flamethrower or grenade, and a flurry of fights saw them either killed or captured. Now the 28th had to hold the ground. Counter-attacks were not long in coming – the German shelling was immediate. Lieutenant Daniel Sargent, 5th Field Artillery, saw the clouds of yellow smoke rising from the ruins of the town and, as they began to fall nearer to him and his companions, a French officer and another American lieutenant, the latter asked him the date of his commission. 'September, 1917' Sargent replied. 'But,' came the reply, 'my commission was dated August, 1917, which makes me your senior, in which case I suppose this foxhole falls to me.' With that the speaker occupied the only available cover. The Frenchman witnessed this exchange with total incredulity before departing. The French artillery had been called away, for, only a few hours before, the Germans had launched their next great assault – Operation Blücher-Yorck – this time on the Chemin des Dames above the valley of the Aisne, and every French gun was needed to oppose them.

There were two counter-attacks that day and the 28th fought both of them off. Two companies of the 18th Infantry reinforced the position that night, and Captain Evarts took his men forward as part of a further reinforcement the night after. Jackson shook, did not cry, and managed to stay with his buddies. Evarts was proud of him. In all there were seven attempts by the Germans to regain the ground. All failed. Some fifty casualties had been the price of taking Cantigny, but holding it cost the Americans 199 killed, 652 wounded, 200 gassed and 16 missing. Raymond Austin wrote:

The attack on
Cantigny, from
*American Armies and
Battlefields in Europe,*
Center of Military
History, Washington
DC, 1995.

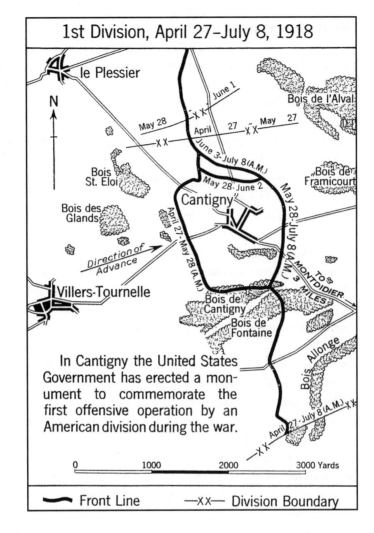

1st Division, April 27–July 8, 1918

le Plessier

N

Bois de l'Alval

June 1

May 28

April 27   May 27

X X

June 3-July 8(A.M.)

Bois
St. Eloi

May 28-June 2

Bois de
Framicourt

Cantigny

Bois des
Glands

April 27-May 28 (A.M.)

May 28-July 8 (A.M.)

Direction of
Advance

TO MONTDIDIER 3 MILES

Villers-Tournelle

Bois de
Cantigny

Bois de
Fontaine

Bois Allonge

In Cantigny the United States
Government has erected a monument to commemorate the
first offensive operation by an
American division during the war.

April 27-July 8 (A.M.)

0   1000   2000   3000 Yards

━ Front Line   —xx— Division Boundary

Casualty lists of an attack like this don't look very large beside those of a
German 50 mile front drive, but when you see fine, young American boys
lying dead in heaps of six or eight or twelve here and there it's more than
enough, but it must be if we're going to whip Germany and the sooner people
realize it in America the better – and we may be able to finish the job sooner.

It was, as Austin points out, a minor action, but it made its point. The Americans
had proved not only that they could organise and carry out an attack, but also
that they could hold their ground.

The Action at Le Hamel

The Germans were still too close to Amiens, but before attempting to drive them back it was necessary to adjust the line where the little village of Le Hamel gave the enemy an enfilading position on troops making an advance from Villers-Brettoneux to the south-west. The task of taking it was given to the Australians under Lieutenant-General Sir John Monash, as he now was. King George V had visited the Australian Corps on 12 August at Bertangles Château. There various displays of weapons, a guard of honour and a number of captured guns and vehicles were arranged for him to see. A guard of honour one hundred strong, and the same number of men from each division, were paraded and inspected by the king:

> The King then had my name called and I stepped up before him and, at his behest, knelt and received the accolade of knighthood, and, when he had bidden me to rise, he presented me with the insignia of a Knight Commander of the Bath. He shook hands most warmly and made me a little speech, commending my work and that of the Australian troops.

It was a considerable and memorable day for a territorial officer.

Monash was of the opinion that, in the attack, the infantry should be able to advance under the maximum protection that technology could provide, not having to fight their way forward, but proceed to the objective in order to hold it. An engineer by training, he was meticulous in his staff work, and the operation at Le Hamel was to be recognised as a classic. Monash later set out the principles that governed the use of tanks in this operation; principles that would be adopted generally by the British thereafter:

> Firstly, each Tank was, for tactical purposes, to be treated as an Infantry weapon; from the moment that it entered battle until the objective had been gained it was to be under the exclusive orders of the Infantry Commander to whom it had been assigned.
>
> Secondly, the deployed line of Tanks was to advance, level with the infantry, and pressing close up to the barrage. This, of course, subjected the Tanks, which towered high above the heads of the neighbouring infantry, to the danger of being struck by any of our shells which happened to fall a little short. Tank experts, consulted beforehand, considered therefore that it was not practicable for Tanks to follow close behind an artillery barrage. The battle of Hamel proved it was.

The plan for the heavy artillery creeping barrage at Hamel on OS map
parts of 62nd N.W., N.E., S.W. and S.E. The infantry start line is on the left
and the artillery start to its right. The village of Le Hamel is on the next of
the continuous lines (marked +28 H.A. Halt). The final objective line runs
along the ridge and the H.A. Protective barrage line to the right is marked
+93; the time of completion of the operation. (TM Accn 107.5)

The principal force was the 4th Australian Division, with the addition of the
machine-gun battalions of the 2nd, 3rd and 5th Divisions. Sixty Mark V tanks and
600 artillery pieces were to be used. Finally, eight companies from the American
forces training in the Australian sector were to be included. Their unit, the 3rd
Division, was commanded by Major-General John Bell. Each unit was allotted
specific tasks. The creeping barrage was precisely defined. The preparations

were complex, detailed and, at the last minute, endangered. General Pershing objected to his troops serving under anything other than American command. Monash argued strongly for their retention in the operation; they could not be replaced in so complicated a plan at the last minute; the attack must either proceed with them or be cancelled entirely. The American commanders of the units involved added their voices to protest being excluded from the fight. The matter had to be considered higher up the chain of command, by Field-Marshal Haig himself, from whom the order came to proceed as planned. He had spoken to Pershing earlier that day and heard that the American commander thought the 3rd Division was insufficiently trained; as a result six companies had been withdrawn, but Haig was not prepared to jeopardise the operation because of the remaining four. Pershing was not pleased and later protested, but accepted the logic of the decision.

On the auspicious date of 4 July the attack was mounted, both here at Hamel and, by a battalion of the 15th Brigade at Dernancourt on the Ancre, by way of distraction. The tanks advanced with the infantry through morning mist, close to the creeping barrage. The smoke intended to conceal the advance was scarcely needed. The machine-gunners followed to secure the positions taken against counter-attack. The greed of machine-guns for ammunition made supply a problem for men advancing on foot. The problem was solved with the first air-drop of munitions in history – the Royal Air Force delivered 100,000 rounds. Of the sixty tanks engaged only three broke down. The whole action was over in ninety-three minutes. An Australian officer, nursing an arm with two machine-gun bullets in it, remarked afterwards:

> The tanks were great. They kept right on the barrage and each time a machine-gun nest held us up, we only had to signal the tank and it just waded in and shot up the gun crew and all was serene again. We'll never go over without tanks again.

Forty-one German officers and 1,431 other ranks were captured, two field guns were taken, 171 machine-guns and 26 trench mortars. Australian casualties numbered 775 and American 134. The British published the complete battle plan as a staff brochure. Le Hamel was a model for future combined operations.

The Battle of Amiens

Preparations for the attack on the Somme to roll the Germans back from Amiens were now complete. On the north bank of the river the British III Corps was to secure the left flank from Dernancourt southwards with the 12th, 18th and 58th Divisions. South of the Amiens–Roye road the French First Army would do the same service on the right, with XXXI Corps (42nd, 159th, 37th and 66th Regiments) holding a front reaching south as far as Moreuil. The four Australian divisions under Monash had the segment between the river Somme and the Amiens–Nesle railway line and the four Canadian divisions (2nd, 1st and 3rd from north to south in the front line, 4th in reserve) under Lieutenant-General Arthur Currie the segment between the Australians and the French. The tanks were there in force. Three hundred and twenty-four Mark V battle tanks supported by 184 supply tanks and two battalions of Whippet light tanks – ninety-six machines, would take the field. There were also a number of the new Mark V (Star) tanks, these were stretched versions of the Mark V which were capable of carrying infantry – two complete three-man Lewis gun detachments, for example. In the event they were not a great success, as the Canadian official history states:

> But this scheme to transport foot-soldiers in tanks did not work out well. Jolted about in their cramped quarters, the men suffered severely from the unaccustomed heat and fumes from the engines; many became sick, and a number fainted. More than half the infantry detachments were obliged to seek fresh air and follow on foot.

In the process they certainly gained a new insight into the challenge the tank crews faced as a matter of routine.

The balance of power in the air was heavily tipped in favour of the Allies. The RAF had 239 heavy bombers, 376 fighters and 185 reconnaissance machines available and the French 1,349 aircraft. On the first day of the battle the Germans had merely 365 aeroplanes on this front as much of their strength was still in the Champagne theatre.

The French had 780 field guns and 826 heavy guns deployed and the British had 1,386 field guns and howitzers and 684 heavy guns. The enemy artillery positions had been plotted by the new technique of sound ranging combined with the reconnaissance work of the Royal Air Force. The field artillery had been organised so that only a part of the strength would be in action at zero hour, the rest being ready to advance with guns limbered up and wagons and lorries at the ready to move as soon as the first objective had been taken. The 'leap-frog' approach was described by Private Edward Lynch, acting as runner for the Australian 45th Battalion. The plan was for the 2nd and 3rd Australian divisions to advance 3,000 yards (2,750 metres) to the first object, which was called the Green Line, and to hold there. Then Lynch's division, the 4th, together with the 5th come through and advanced to the Red Line, another 5,000 yards (4,750 metres). Finally the other brigades of these two divisions would take the final objective, known as the Blue Line.

In all this, secrecy had been preserved. The Germans were not aware of the Canadian presence and the deception had been supported by the obvious appearance of a Canadian unit at Orange Hill, east of Arras, and a flow of false radio signals that suggested a build-up of the rest of the Canadian Corps in the Calais area apparently destined for Flanders. Once it was evident the Germans had taken note, the unit was rushed to the Somme by train. The subterfuge may not have fooled the Germans completely, but it did confuse them.

A surprise attack by the Germans north of the river on 6 August pushed the British III Corps back and they had to struggle to regain their ground the following day. This did not delay the schedule for the main Allied offensive. At 4.20am on 8 August the guns opened fire. The pre-targeted German batteries were heavily shelled and the first line of the creeping bombardment lasted for a mere three minutes before lifting by 100 yards (90 metres) and, as it did so, the advance began.

In the morning mist the attack went precisely according to plan. The Germans had been taken by surprise with no preliminary bombardment to alert them to the threat. Moreover they were not in occupation of positions carefully prepared and fortified over many months as they had been on 1 July or had created in the Hindenburg Line. Ludendorff was not, however, dissatisfied with the preparations to defend this position:

At my special request General von Kuhl proceeded to the 2nd Army, in order to discuss once again the defensive measures on the line Albert–Moreuil. In this area two divisions that had been a long time in line, and seemed specially tired, were relieved by fresh ones. In this storm-centre the divisional fronts were narrow, artillery was plentiful and the trench system was organised in depth. All experience gained on the 18th of July [the Second Battle of the Marne] had been acted upon. Only as regards construction of works, the 2nd

216

From OS sheet 62D S.W. and S.E. The Australian front at the Battle of Amiens, from the operational
map of the officer commanding B Company, 2nd Tank Battalion. The Roman road runs across through
Lamotte-en-Santerre and the company front also passes through that town as far as the line chalked across the
road: the Green Line. The railway, which divided the Australian assault from the Canadian, passes diagonally
between the letters P and V at the foot of the map, left. (TM Accn. 4760)

Army had not done as much as the 18th, for example, which had captured its
positions at a later date.

The British Fourth Army and the French XXXI Corps were faced by the
German Second Army with nine divisions on this front. The front to the south,
held by the French First Army and part of their Third Army, was facing the
German Eighteenth Army, which had its centre on Montdidier.

By 7am the Australians had taken their first objective, the ridge from
Warfusée-Abancourt to Cerisy-Gailly near the river, and by 10.30 their second
objective, including the villages of Morecourt and Harbonnières, had also
been achieved. Private Lynch was in that second wave. His battalion moved off

towards the Green Line at 8am and then they set off for the Red Line. Together with the tanks they hurried forward through the thinning fog. A machine-gun nest stopped them for a while and then Lynch's commanding officer took a flanking party to the left while Lynch led a four-man party in a rush towards the gun. Two of his comrades were hit, but the remaining man sent a lucky shot through the machine-gunner's shoulder and the remaining crew fled straight into the line of fire of the flank party. On they went. Suddenly:

> Behind galloping horses, an Australian 18-pounder battery races through us. Ahead of the racing guns, an artillery officer slides to a propping stand-still and his hand goes up as he bellows, 'Halt!' The gun-carriage horses are pulled hard back on steaming haunches, breeching-straps sinking deep into the sweat-lathered hind legs of the gallant animals. 'Action Front!' roars the officer. The guns are swung round, horses unharnessed and galloped back, and *Bang! Bang! Bang!* Six guns are pouring shells somewhere ahead.

Onwards through a wood they went, Germans either defiantly fighting or throwing their hands up with cries of '*Kamerad!*' Then they were digging. The Red Line had been reached. It was 10.20am. The 48th Battalion came through and took up the task of advancing to the Blue Line, which they took and where the 45th, Lynch with them, relieved them that night. In the morning they were re-supplied. Lynch remarked approvingly of the Allied aircraft dropping ammunition to them.

The Canadian line started further west but by 11am they had come up level with the Australians. The infantry was not excessively burdened; Rawlinson's staff had devised a 'fighting order' which consisted of a haversack, 250 rounds of ammunition (100 in bandoliers), a gas mask, water bottle, 'iron rations' of corned beef and biscuits, an entrenching tool, two Mills bombs and two sand-bags. On the left, alongside the Australians, the Canadian 2nd Division had easier ground than their comrades on their right. They were on the plateau north of the little river Luce – rolling cornfield terrain. On the left the 19th Battalion was assisted by Lewis-gun fire from the 21st Australian Battalion on the other side of the railway. The Canadians had reached the Green Line by 8.20am and, as the next wave came through, the thinning mist allowed German field guns to engage the tanks. Taking evasive action made some of them run short of petrol. The resistance encountered from Guillaucourt early in the afternoon was suppressed by three batteries of the 5th Brigade, Canadian Field Artillery, which had moved forward to support the infantry as planned. In the centre the 1st Canadian Division had to deal with the valley of the river Luce, with its trees and hidden side-valleys from which the Germans were able to lay down effective fire. However, they pressed forward in the mist with such speed that the first and second waves became somewhat spread out in small formations, and the following platoons had to mop up points of resistance bypassed by the first wave. Some 2,500 yards (2,285 metres) into their advance they ran into the trench line the Germans had dug in front of their main artillery emplacements. Two Victoria Crosses were won there by Private J.B. Crook and Corporal H.J. Good who, in separate actions, accounted for seven machine-gun nests between them, and Good added to that the capture of an entire battery of 5.9-inch guns. As the fog dispersed, permitting the tanks to see the enemy clearly, progress improved and the Green Line was reached at 8.15am. Similar progress was made to the Red Line which they gained by 11.30.

On the right, 3rd Division packed into the front line and moved ahead quickly. Rifle Wood was overrun within the hour, but here again the mist hampered the progress of the tanks, which had the additional hazard of shattered woodland to deal with, and the link with the infantry broke down. North of the Luce, 1st Canadian Mounted Rifles outran their tanks and took Cemetery Copse in forty minutes. The tanks came up and assisted in the taking of Hangard and the establishment of a bridgehead over the Luce at Demuin. This was followed by a swift advance to the Red Line by 10am. Of the forty-two tanks they had started with, only eight remained serviceable. Finally the 4th Division passed through to secure the Blue Line.

To the south, on the west bank of the river Avre, the French First Army under General Debeney was poised to advance. The overall command had been allocated to Haig by General Foch, so that the whole of the action on the Somme front came under a single, coherent command structure. After a forty-five minute bombardment, the First Army advanced on a 2.5-mile (4-kilometre) front. By 11am the next day they had secured the Hangest-en-Santerre plateau, with their front at Arvillers.

The tanks performed well, but their losses were considerable. More than one hundred were knocked out by enemy action and twice as many broke down or were immobilised in accidents. The German field artillery clung stubbornly to their positions and managed to inflict considerable damage. At Le Quesnel, on the Canadians' southern flank, ten tanks were reduced to a single survivor by field guns and the Canadian advance was held. On the extreme north the Australian advance slowed because the setback suffered earlier by the British III Corps left their flank exposed as they approached the limit of their advance.

The British did not take their objective, the Chipilly Spur around which the river swung, until the next day.

The heavy guns had fallen silent early in the day; the advance had out-stripped their range. By 1.30pm the Allies had gone further than planned, having made between 6 and 8 miles (10 and 13 kilometres). The freedom of movement that the speed and distance of the advance permitted came as a surprise to troops habituated to trench warfare. A plan to have the light tanks and cavalry fight in tandem proved unworkable; where they faced machine-guns the cavalry could not operate, though the tanks were effective and where speed was possible the horses soon outran the tanks. By themselves, each was able to achieve fine results. *Musical Box*, for example, did excellent service.

The Light tank, the Medium Mark A, known as the 'Whippet', weighed 14 tons against the Mark V's 35 tons, and was said to be capable of 8.3 miles per hour (13.4 kilometres per hour) on the road, outpacing the battle tank by nearly 4 miles per hour (6.5 kilometres per hour). The crew of three had four Hotchkiss machine-guns at its disposal. Lieutenant C.B. Arnold, Gunner Ribbans and Driver Carney were going along in *Musical Box* next to the railway line that divided the Australian from the Canadian sector when they saw two Mark Vs hit by a four-gun field battery between Warfusée and Bayonvillers. Arnold turned half-left and ran across the front of the battery, firing with two machine-guns. The return fire missed. He then did a U-turn around some trees and came at the battery from the rear. The gunners tried to run, but Arnold and Ribbans shot them. The Australians took full advantage of the battery's demise. Arnold then dealt with two groups of Germans who were troubling his cavalry further down the railway line at Guillaucourt before cruising off between Bayonvillers and Harbonnières where he strafed a crowd of Germans packing up to leave. Ribbans counted more than sixty dead and wounded. At this point in his report Arnold breaks off to suggest that, in future, no fuel is carried on the outside of a tank; the cans he had were being hit by enemy fire and were filling the tank with fumes. This comment made, he continues his account. Further east, at about 2pm, he opened fire on retreating transports, motor and horse-drawn, on the roads crossing the railway before turning to engage another target. Suddenly there was a loud bang and the tank burst into flames. The crew got out, on fire, but Carney was immediately shot. Arnold and Ribbans rolled on the ground to put out the flames and were surrounded by Germans. 'They were' observed Arnold, 'furious'. This was real mobile warfare.

The cavalry at last had the chance to charge. Beaucourt-en-Santerre was taken by the Canadian Cavalry Brigade and the Queen's Bays almost secured

Harbonnières, but had to leave it to the Australians to finish the job. The 5th Dragoons captured an 11-inch railway gun and 600 prisoners while 15th and 19th Hussars charged 2,000 yards (1,828 metres) ahead of the cheering Canadians in Guillaucourt to seize the trenches beyond and hold them until the Whippets and infantry came up. It was 'worth all the years of waiting', said an officer of the 15th.

The RAF fared less well, losing forty-four aircraft and suffering fifty-two seriously damaged in 205 sorties flown. At the start of the day they were hampered by the mist, but later in the morning they flew valuable support actions coordinated with infantry attacks. As the day went on the possibility of cutting the Germans off by destroying the Somme bridges led to their being given bombing missions. They were fiercely attacked by German aircraft, including those of the late Baron von Richthofen's squadron, now commanded by one Hermann Göring. 'Richthofen's Circus', as it was known, was virtually destroyed in the process.

Ludendorff was later to say:

August 8th was the black day of the German Army in the history of this war. This was the worst experience I had to go through...

The report of the Staff Officer I had sent to the battle-field as to the condition of those divisions which had met the first shock of the attack on the 8th, perturbed me deeply. I summoned divisional commanders and officers from the line to Avesnes [his HQ] to discuss events with them in detail. I was told of deeds of glorious valour but also of behaviour which, I openly confess, I should not have thought possible in the German Army; whole bodies of our men had surrendered to single troopers, or isolated squadrons. Retiring troops, meeting a fresh division going bravely into action, has shouted things like 'Blackleg,' and 'You're prolonging the war,' expressions that were to be heard again later. The officers in many places had lost their influence and allowed themselves to be swept along with the rest...

A battalion commander from the front, who came out with a draft from home shortly before August 8th, attributed this to the spirit of insubordination and the atmosphere which the men brought back with them from home. Everything I had feared, and of which I had so often given warning, had here, in one place, become a reality. Our war machine was no longer efficient. Our fighting power had suffered, even though the great majority of divisions still fought heroically.

Five German divisions were broken. The Australians had taken nearly 8,000 prisoners and 173 guns while the Canadians took over 5,000 prisoners and 161 guns. Total Allied losses were about 6,500. The German Official Monograph estimates their losses at about 30,000, and described the battle as the greatest defeat the German Army had suffered since the beginning of the war.

The Australians said 'It was a très bon stunt.'

Retaking the Somme

To a command used to handling large numbers of troops in a small area, the extent of the advance on 8 August presented new problems. Communication by a web of telephone wires became impossible and radio was still at an early stage of development, dispensing with the need for wires but still depending on largely immobile radio positions. The hope for a breakthrough could not be realised. The Tank Corps had no reserves available and the pace of progress was limited to the speed attainable by the infantry. The Canadians advanced another 3 miles (5 kilometres) and, with American help, the British took the Chipilly Spur on the second day.

On the northern flank the Australian progress had been slowed by flanking fire from the German positions that they had secured on 6 August, and action had to be taken by III Corps to free them for a further advance. The British 58th Division was reinforced by the 131st Infantry of the US 33rd Division on 9 August for the recovery of the Chipilly Spur and Gressaire Wood. The assault began at 5.30pm and by nightfall, with the help of the Australian 4th Division coming over the river from the south, the spur itself and half the wood were taken. Corporal Jake Allex, 131st Infantry, took over command of his platoon when the officers were wounded and, finding his men pinned down by machine-gun fire, worked his way forward to the German strong-point. Having killed five men with his bayonet, the weapon broke, so he reversed arms and clubbed the remaining fifteen into surrender. He was awarded the Congressional Medal of Honor. The 33rd remained in the area long enough to be recognised, congratulated and have some of their number decorated by King George V on 12 August. Will Judy witnessed the ceremony.

At eleven on this sunny morning the heralds came up the hill and soon the royal car shone in the sunlight as it moved between the two rows of poplars that for a quarter mile border the road to the chateau at the top of the hill. An American soldier near me rushed back and called to his comrade: 'Hurry, here comes the king.' 'What king?' 'George King.' We crowded the sideways, silent in expectancy. The long limousine, black and sleek, drew near and one American called out loudly – 'So that's the big stiff!'

King George V of England led the procession to the green back of the chateau. General Pershing walked on his left; then came General Bliss, General Henry Rawlinson and General Bell [Major-General George Bell, Jr, commanding 33rd Division], and after them a host, including myself. About twenty officers and men of the 131st and 132nd Infantry stood at attention. The movie cameras clicked, the king pinned an English medal on each, the band played 'God Save the King,' and then the 'Star Spangled Banner;' the procession returned to the chateau, the band played 'Illinois', and the little white-bellied donkey that wanders around our headquarters every day, stood nearby half asleep thru it all, ready to kick King George in the rear side as readily as a soldier of the ranks.

Then the division left to join the American First Army in the east.

German resistance was increasing on the Canadian and Australian front, and Haig decided to have Byng's Third Army push forward further north, towards Bapaume. The battlefield of July 1916, still strewn with the débris of that conflict, cut with old trenches and wrapped in rusting barbed wire, offered a foul place to fight; Haig planned to pass to the north of the Ancre. Foch was all for extending the attack both north and south while maintaining it in the centre, but was dissuaded by the men closer to the action. Allied indecision was matched by German hesitation. The reserves arriving to relieve the defeated divisions were shocked to be accused of needlessly prolonging the war, by their demoralised comrades. Local commanders wanted to fall back once more to better positions, but Ludendorff demanded that they stood where they were. The German Army was starting to crack in spite of having forty-two divisions to the Allies' thirty-two on the Somme front.

The French First Army had occupied the flanks of the Montdidier salient on 10 August and the town was liberated the next day. Further south, Humbert advanced to recover much of the terrain lost in Operation Gniesenau in June.

On 14 August the German Supreme Command met at the headquarters, now returned to Spa in Belgium. The position they reviewed was extremely serious, they concluded. The Austro-Hungarian armies were collapsing, the Bulgarians were a spent force and Turkey could assist no longer.

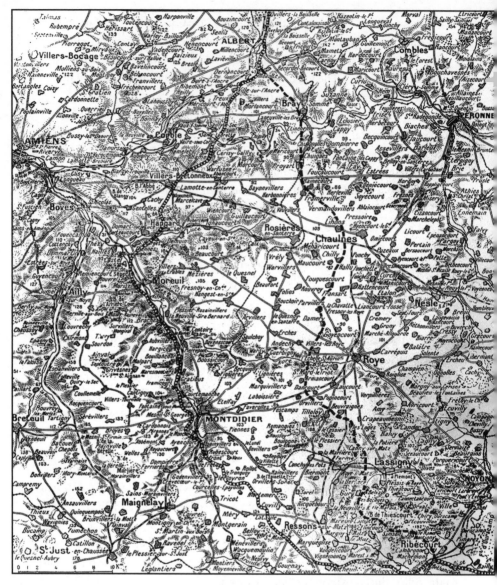

The Somme theatre, with the front line of 8 August 1918 shown to the left and the line attained by 13 August indicated by the dotted line to the right. From *l' Illustration*, 17 August 1918. *(HGG)*

1 *Above Left*: Visitors tour the preserved British trenches at the Newfoundland Memorial Park and explore the German positions at Y Ravine.

2 *Above Right*: The huge memorial to the missing at Thiepval, on the site of the former château, overlooks the French and British graves, symbolic of the alliance. Beyond is the British front line of 1916.

3 *Below*: The Commonwealth War Graves Commission cemetery at Beaumont-Hamel, seen from the edge of Hawthorn Crater.

Opposite: 4 The site of the windmill at Pozières is now a memorial to the Australian troops that took it at such cost. The Thiepval Memorial is on the skyline, left of the flagpoles, at the end of the ridge that took so long to wrest from German hands.

5 A German machine-gunner's-eye view of the former front at Mametz. Seen from the corner of the village graveyard, the railway halt and the slope rising towards Mansell Copse.

6 The River Somme at Curlu, seen from the belvedere at Vaux. In June 1916 this viewpoint was in French hands and the village was held by the Germans. The marshy, meandering river valley divided the battlefield north and south.

This Page; Right: 7 The vast crater of Lochnagar, near La Boisselle, is preserved as a memorial.

Below Left: 8 The Riqueval Bridge, taken in September 1918, over the St Quentin Canal still stands, now surrounded with trees. The canal was an integral part of the German Hindenburg Line defence system.

Below Right: 10 The St Quentin Canal, now lined with trees, running south from the tunnel mouth. The tunnel itself was used to shelter the defensive troops.

10 The statue of a 'doughboy' commemorates the men who took Cantigny, and held it against determined German counter-attacks.

11 The American memorial at Cantigny.

12 The village of Cantigny, seen from the American start line on the edge of the plateau stretching back to Villers-Tournelle to the south-west. The nature of the challenge that faced the US 1st Division on 28 May 1918 can be appreciated in full.

13 At Bony, where the Americans and Australians broke through the Hindenburg Line above the St Quentin Canal, lie the fallen of the American Expeditionary Force in the Somme theatre.

14 Serre Road Cemetery No. 2 is thronged with the graves of British soldiers who fell in the great Somme battles of 1916.

15 Caix, south-east of Villers-Brettoneux, is the last resting place of soldiers of many nations killed as the battles swept to and fro across the Santerre region of the Somme. The Commonwealth War Graves Commission cemetery is witness to the British retreat during Operation Michael in March and April 1918 and to the Canadian attack of the following August.

16 The German cemetery at Caix, with 1,264 graves, lies in a shady grove.

17 The French fallen, including men from North Africa, are buried in the annex to the village graveyard at Caix. The majority were killed between February and November 1916.

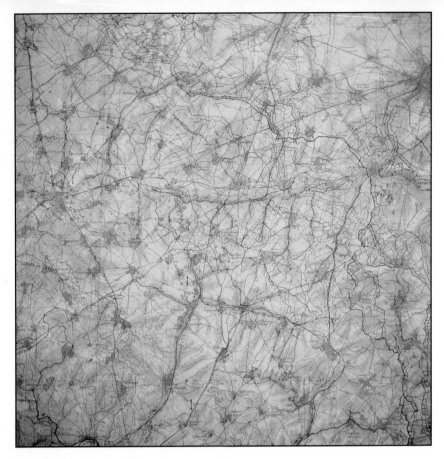

18 A German map of the front line from Bullecourt in the north-west to Bony and Bellicourt in the south, dated 1 March 1918. Bapaume is to the left with the Roman road running to Cambrai, top right. Mont St Quentin, outside Péronne, is on the left at the foot of the map. The thinness of the red, i.e. British, defences is evident in the southern part of the front line, around Epéhy, for example. (USAMHI)

19 Sketch map prepared by Lt Col (Rtd) Martin P. Korn, formerly of 301st Tank Battalion, illustrating the route of his battalion in the attack on the Hindenburg Line. (USAMHI WWI Survey)

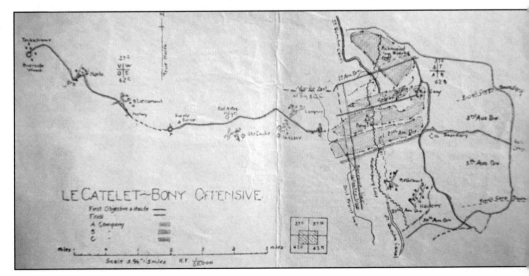

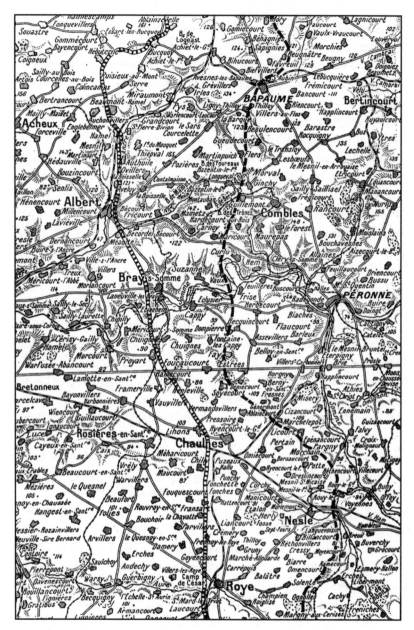

The line on 21 August is shown on the left and that of 28 August on the right.
Bapaume is at the top of the map and Roye at the bottom. Péronne is centre right.
From l'Illustration. *(HGG)*

Their allies had nothing further to contribute. On the Western Front, therefore, they had no alternative but to pull back to the Hindenburg Line again and see what sort of peace could be negotiated while they resisted here as best they could.

Between Arras and Beaumont-Hamel and rolling eastwards towards the Hindenburg Line, the country was still unscarred by war, providing, it was thought, an opportunity to use the remaining tanks. For the rest of August, however, the weather was very hot and tanks – noisy, smelly and oppressive enough at the best of times – became fume-filled ovens. The Whippets' Hotchkiss guns jammed and the crews passed out. The wonder-weapon showed its limitations once more, and the infantry's speed again set the pace. Byng attacked on 21 August and made some progress, but not enough to satisfy Haig. Rawlinson's men retook Albert the next day. The names of terrible memory appeared on the reports once more, but with less cost and at shorter intervals: Thiepval, 24 August; Mametz Wood, 25 August; Delville Wood, 27 August. On 26 August the First Army opened the Battle of the Scarpe, east of Arras. It became clear to Ludendorff that another retreat to the Hindenburg Line was inevitable, and that troops would have to be transferred from Flanders, abandoning all hope of taking the Channel ports to stiffen resistance further south.

Bapaume fell to the New Zealanders on 29 August and the steady, bloody rolling-back of the German line continued. Although the prospect of losing the war was now apparent to them, their will to fight and to extract the maximum cost from the Allies for every gain remained formidable. To the west of Péronne, above the marshy Somme river valley and embraced by the Canal du Nord which curves around the town, the German positions on Mont St Quentin commanded the approaches not merely to the town, but to the country to the east. The land near the waterways was a mass of barbed wire entanglements surviving from 1916, with breaches in them, but still formidable, and was overlooked from Mont St Quentin over which the road from Bapaume passes. The importance to the Germans attempting to establish a line of defence from north to south was such that the crack 2nd Prussian Guards Division was allocated to the defence of the position. The Australians facing this obstacle were now seriously depleted. The task fell to Brigadier-General Martin's 5th (New South Wales) Brigade of the 2nd Division under Major-General Charles Rosenthal. There were no tanks available, given the heavy losses and the fatigue of both men and machines. The attackers had the support of a sixteen-gun machine-gun company, five brigades of field artillery and one of heavy artillery. The infantry strength was about seventy officers and 1,250 other ranks. Using their superiority in artillery and charging forward in the dawning light of

31 August, the Australians swarmed into the defences and harried the Germans from one strong-point to the next. The centre battalion gained the hill and the village to the left, Feuillaucourt, fell to the battalion on that flank, but on the right German machine-gun fire slowed the advance of the remaining battalion.

The Germans then counter-attacked in the centre and the Australians were driven back over the road to occupy old trenches and hold them. By 8am General Monash was able to report to General Rawlinson that they had gained a position on the hillside. Meanwhile the number of river crossings the 2nd Division had secured made it possible for the 14th (New South Wales) Brigade to cross the Somme and threaten, by a movement to the south-east, the Germans in Péronne itself. It took a long time for the 14th Brigade to cross the broken country and heavily shelled river crossing, and the 7th Brigade arrived at much the same time. The night saw elements of both 2nd and 5th Divisions preparing to renew the assault on 1 September.

The fighting to secure the summit of Mont St Quentin was particularly hard and bloody. The 6th (Victoria) Brigade took the position trench by trench with bomb and bayonet. 14th Brigade went for Péronne. One battalion headed for St Denis while another pushed towards the town centre, and two battalions were in reserve. By the end of the day the western part of town had been taken, but the broken brickfields and tangled wire still delayed the fall of the hamlet of St Denis. Lieutenant Harold Williams of the 5th Division recalled:

> Word came through that the 54th Battalion [14th Brigade] had gained a foot-hold in the town of Péronne. Small parties were rushed across footbridges raked with machine-gun fire, in which many men were killed, but the few who lived to reach the bridgehead attacked the German machine-gunners and cleared the way for other parties to cross the footbridges. Once a hold was gained on part of the town, it was exploited to the utmost, and the Germans were rooted out of cellars and other cover.

The next day, 15th Brigade supplied reinforcements to finish the job and push east to take Flamicourt. On the left of this action the 3rd Division was working its way along the Bouchavesnes spur to the north-east. Rawlinson sent a congratulatory message:

> The capture of Mont St Quentin by the Second Division is a feat of arms worthy of the highest praise. The natural strength of the position is immense, and the tactical value of it, in reference to Péronne and the whole system of

the Somme defences, cannot be over-estimated. I am filled with admiration at the gallantry and surpassing daring of the Second Division in winning this important fortress, and I congratulate them with all my heart.

The assessment of Private Edward Lynch after he marched from Biaches, which his unit had entered on 7 September, to Stable Wood and then went sight-seeing was less enthusiastic, though no less amazed at the achievement. He saw a narrow opening in the enemy wire which had tempted men to rush through; there were fourteen dead men who had fallen into the trap and become victims of German machine-guns:

> Crossing a little ditch of water we reach a great earthen mound in front of Péronne town where enemy machine-guns were fired. Hundreds of empty cartridge shells are scattered around each position. No wonder Fritz stopped our men…

August was a bad month for the Germans on the French front as well. The persistently aggressive Mangin had won new victories on the Aisne and at Noyon. September would see the first independent action by the Americans at St Mihiel and other German defeats. On the Somme front the next challenge was the Hindenburg Line.

Breaking the Hindenburg Line

The defensive complex constructed by the Germans in the autumn and winter of 1916 was viewed with respect and not a little apprehension by the Allies. The Germans believed that the Allies had a limited understanding of the nature of the Line. It was based upon the concept of defence in depth. Rather than a single trench or a series of trench lines, the area it covered was occupied by numerous redoubts and strong-points, reinforced machine-gun emplace-ments, a web of trenches and carefully disposed blocks and rows of barbed wire to funnel attackers into pre-determined lines of fire for the guns. The Wotan Position, which the British called the Drocourt–Quéant Switch Line, ran south from Lille to join the Siegfried Position near Cambrai. This, the strongest part of the Line, was 10 miles (16 kilometres) deep and went as far south as La Fère on the river Oise. The plans of the entire layout of the Siegfried Position had been acquired by the British with the capture of a German command post on 6 August. Every last detail of the dispositions of the defences from Bellicourt to La Fère was known. (See Map p.153)

Less robust, the Wotan Position was the first to fall. The First Army, under General Sir Henry Horne, moved against it on 2 September. The Canadian Corps smashed their way through. Ludendorff gave orders for withdrawal both on the Somme and in Flanders. All the territory gained in the spring was abandoned.

Haig realised that a crucial moment had arrived. Back in London the government was still talking of the campaigns to be mounted in 1919. Here, on the front, the troops were steadily being eroded by the succession of attacks, successful though they were, and the Germans were slowly, very slowly, crumbling before them. It was vital to strain every sinew to achieve victory soon, while the tide of war was flowing in favour of the Allies. On 9 September Haig went to London to press his view that reserves in England should be regarded as reserves for the front in France. He was regarded with suspicion as a dangerous optimist given the losses over which he had presided in the past, but coming events would support Haig's analysis and he had at least prepared the ground for a change of attitude. The despair of the German commanders was not even guessed at in London.

The local actions to gain positions from which the major effort could be launched continued. The village of Havrincourt, last taken during the Battle of Cambrai, fell to the British once more on 12 September, in spite of significant moves by the Germans to reinforce the defenders. Rawlinson improved his position further south with an attack on 18 September to take the Hindenburg outpost line. It was necessary to conserve the tanks for the principal effort, so only eight machines were used together with artillery support, without a preliminary barrage but by concentrated targeting and a creeping barrage. The number of machine-guns was doubled by bringing up the weapons and crews from 3rd and 5th Australian Divisions. The village of Epéhy was stubbornly defended and III Corps made poor progress, but the Australians with their 1st and 4th Divisions achieved an advance on a front 4 miles (6.4 kilometres) wide of over 2.5 miles (4 kilometres) in length, taking 4,243 prisoners, 76 guns, 300 machine-guns and 30 trench mortars for the loss of 1,260 of the 6,800 men committed to the action. The final objective was taken at 11pm that night after the troops had been rested at dusk. Among the Germans, the Australians were now considered to be their most formidable adversaries.

Private Edward Lynch and the 45th Battalion, 12th Brigade, took part in the attack:

Eyes are glued to watches. Three minutes to go! Two minutes to go! Barely a minute! A tense silence, a tightening of jaws, or little fixing of equipment that have already been fixed a dozen times. Right on the tick of 5.20 am comes the tremendous crash of a hundred batteries blazing into action in one awful all-shattering roar of explosion.

They moved forward and crossed the taped line from which the 48th had set off in front of them. A shell fell amongst them, but when they clambered to their feet once more they found that no one had been hit. In the smoke and fog they blundered forward, and suddenly German soldiers appeared, running the other way – prisoners taken by the 48th, thirty men with a single Australian guard.

On we go, capturing more and more Fritz; cringing, crawling, cowardly fellows, those we meet now. Poor broken-spirited beggars, they've had the pluck knocked out of them… Many of them are just kids; poor, frightened, skinny little codgers of fifteen to seventeen, a pathetic sight…

They fought on through the day, now sheltering and regaining breath, now rushing German guns and bayoneting the enemy. The grand view Monash could take of the day was diminished to the reality of serial combat, lost comrades and relief at still being alive.

For the first time the Allies were in a position to launch coordinated offensives on chosen segments of the Western Front. The French and Americans, the latter being switched in remarkably short time from St Mihiel, assaulted the German line in the Argonne on 26 September and a long, hard slog it proved to be. The next day the British were to go in towards Cambrai and on 28 September the armies in Flanders were to attack. On 29 September the Siegfried Position was the target.

The approach to Cambrai was barred by the Canal du Nord, a half-finished construction still waterless in places. To the east marshy land gave way to hills from which the Germans could observe and lay down fire. This daunting situation was to be faced by Currie's Canadians. Currie selected the dry section of the canal to the south for his attack, passing two divisions through the gap he intended to make and then spreading them out beyond while pushing a third division through in support. Only sixteen tanks could be provided to him, so the artillery plans had to be precise and excellently managed. Over 1,000 aircraft were to support the attack, dropping 700 tons of bombs and firing some

26,000 rounds from their machine-guns. It was a scheme of a sophistication that could scarcely have been contemplated a year earlier.

It worked perfectly. At 5.30am on 27 September the action started and by the end of the day the Canadians had taken all of their objectives and more. German resistance was ferocious, but by the end of the second day the advance had penetrated 6 miles (10 kilometres) on a 12-mile (19-kilometre) front. Slowly fatigue overcame the offensive; 1 October saw a further advance of only a mile. Another 7,000 prisoners and 205 guns were added to the Allies' trophies.

The Siegfried Line

Now it was the turn of the main Siegfried Position to benefit from the Allies' attentions. Here the German defences made use of the St Quentin canal which curves around the town from the east to Bellenglise, where it heads north to Riqueval to enter a tunnel under Bellicourt and Bony before coming into the open once more to make its way towards Cambrai. South of the tunnel, it passes through a deep cutting and was fortified with concrete pill-boxes and barbed-wire entanglements both on the banks and in the canal itself. Closer to St Quentin it was almost waterless, but still full of mud. Evidently the open country over the tunnel was the only place tanks could be of use, but here the depth of the defences was greatest and here the Allies were still well to the west.

Above the tunnel, Monash and the Australians were once more given the tough assignment: that of breaking the German line, but by now they were deeply fatigued and short of men. The 1st and 4th Divisions were withdrawn from the line and replaced by the fresh, though inexperienced, American 27th and 30th Divisions under General George W. Read. These divisions, with eighty-six tanks, were to overcome the German forward positions, and the Australians, with seventy-six tanks, would pass through them to smash through the main line. An attempt was made to compensate for the lack of American combat knowledge by seconding 200 Australian officers and NCOs to them, but it was a dangerously optimistic arrangement. An additional proposal was submitted to Rawlinson by Lieutenant-General Sir Walter Braithwaite for an assault further south by the 46th (North Midland) Division with the 32nd Division in support and this was added to the battle plan.

Detail from OS map 62C N.E. & S.E. and 62B – The Siegfried Position from Bellicourt in the north to Bellenglise in the south. The density of the obstacles above the canal tunnel in the north is in great contrast to that on the canal section where the waterway itself was relied upon. (TM Accn 442, 6/8(3))

Private J. Walter Strauss, with the 102nd Engineers, 27th Division, described the Siegfried Line:

These defenses consisted generally of three strong lines of trenches, protected by an extraordinary mass of wire... There were 25 barges in the main tunnel and these were used by the Germans as billets for reserve troops... Along the easterly side of the tunnel there had been sunk through the ground above a number of approaches to the tunnel towpath... In similar manner passageways had been excavated from the westerly side of the canal to the main line of resistance constructed in the ground above and a short distance westerly of the line of the tunnel. No bombardment, no matter how severe, could affect reserve troops... [The] trenches had been perfected with dugouts, concrete machine-gun and mortar emplacements and underground shelters. They were protected by belt after belt of barbed wire entanglements ...

What was more, these obstacles were sited so as to channel attackers into the path of fixed aim machine-guns, while field guns were dug in and concealed to shell tanks similarly beguiled into the line of fire.

The outposts of the Siegfried Line ran from north to south just east of the villages of Lempire, Hargicourt and Villeret. For the assault, the northern sector, Lempire–Hargicourt, was assigned to the 27th Division while the 30th took over the southern half. At 5.30am on 27 September the 106th Infantry, 27th Division, supported by twelve tanks of the British 4th Battalion, Tank Corps, moved to take strong-points: the Knoll north-west of Bony, Guillemont Farm west of the village and Quennemont Farm to the south-west. Smoke shells added to the obscurity of that foggy morning. The regiment was seriously short of officers and of experienced non-commissioned officers, and as the casualties among their commanders mounted, confusion set in. Acts of bravery were numerous. Lieutenant William Bradford Turner led an attack against the Knoll, taking two machine-gun posts and then pushing forward over four lines of trenches. He died in the counter-attack that followed. Sergeant Reidar Waaler risked his life saving men from a burning British tank. But the heroism of individuals was not enough. By the next morning it had become evident that the 106th had failed in its attack and had taken heavy losses, 1,540 casualties in all. It was also probable that many men were isolated in no-man's-land, directly in the path of a further offensive. To their right the 30th Division had also suffered, though not on the same scale.

On the morning of 29 September they attacked again. Fearful of killing their own men, maybe wounded men not retrieved after the previous attack, they put their barrage 1,000 yards (914 metres) ahead of the advancing troops and chased to catch up. With the American 301st Tank Battalion, 2nd Tank Brigade, in British Mark V tanks in support, the 27th and 30th Divisions pushed forward through thick fog. Once again they were met with lethal machine-gun and artillery fire. Their courage was beyond doubt, but skill was lacking. Again their casualties were heavy and their progress slow, while the tanks fell victim to the new sophistication of the way the German field guns were deployed. Of 141 tanks engaged, seventy-five were hit, some of them destroyed while crossing an old British minefield.

Private Strauss reports that his F Company, 102nd Engineers, was used as a combat unit that day, moving towards a machine-gun post near Guillemont Farm:

> As we were advancing, a sudden shower of shells hit us and I dove into a shell hole. As I did so, I felt a thud in my side from a machine-gun the Germans had at the knoll. I crawled back into a trench for better protection and found a German machine-gun bullet had gone through a first aid packet on the right side of my pack, then on into my Bible (New Testament) and lodged there. A quarter of an inch to the right would have punctured my lung and I would have died quickly. This was the Bible given to me by our Camp Mother, Mrs Ella Hight, back in May (9th) 1918 at Belvoir, Virginia... We kept pushing the Germans back and they kept shelling us with gas shells, phosgene and mustard gas.

Private Edward L. North, 102nd Field Signal Battalion, 27th Division, had little time to write home that morning. He stuffed the letter he had just received from his brother (Charles, who was serving with 302nd Field Signal Battalion) into an envelope and scrawled a note: 'Going out for a long hike this a.m. for the day. Rec'd letter from Charlie last night. Will enclose it as he requested. Love to all, Edward.' A long hike it was.

Pushing towards Bellicourt, the 30th Division's progress, at first encouraging, was slowed by the elaborate system of tunnels that allowed the Germans to emerge in their rear once the attackers had passed over, rushing up from their secure shelters by the underground canal to man machine-guns afresh. Private Willard M. Newton of the 105th Engineers, 30th Division, was eighteen years old. His company was in a trench with the 117th Infantry before the attack started:

> We are all full of cheer and anxiously waiting for the shelling to start. The infantrymen are as full of cheer as we. They are anxious to get a whack at Fritz. When asked by the doughboys what we are going to do, we say 'build and repair roads', not really knowing what we would do before the day is

over... At last we are at the beginning of a real battle between Prussianism and Democracy!

Scores of dead Americans, Australians and Germans can be seen lying here and there, some covered with raincoats and overcoats and others lying just as they fell. Walking wounded are going back in twos and threes, while those unable to walk are being carried off of the field as rapidly as possible under the circumstances. Men with arms shot off, with slight shrapnel wounds and gassed victims are being helped to the rear by German prisoners and by other men similarly wounded... Packs, rifles, cartridge belts, wrecked ammunition wagons, hand grenades, and ammunition of every size and kind are scattered everywhere in great quantities.

Newton spent the better part of the day in shell holes and captured bunkers, waiting for orders. At about 3pm he was detailed with seven others to carry two wounded men to the rear. It was sunset before they got back. One of the men had died on the way and all of the carriers were badly gassed.

The Australians formed the second wave of attack, intended to pass through the positions the Americans had taken and go forward from there. But both the Australian 3rd Division, behind the American 27th, and the 5th Division, moving up to the 30th, found their allies still struggling against their early objectives. The Americans refused the relief. Side by side the two nations fought on, doggedly reducing the German strong-points until, as darkness fell, the line was finally broken. The victory had been expensively bought. The 27th had 3,500 men killed, wounded and missing and their Australian friends of the 3rd Division, 1,000. The 30th took 1,881 casualties and, by 2 October the Australian 5th had lost 1,500 officers and men. On 3 October Strauss wrote: 'Rested. Bath in p.m. at Templeux la Fosse. Clean underwear. Wow!'

Bellenglise and Riqueval

The attempt to break the Hindenburg Line at Bony and Bellicourt had been slow and costly, but it was not the only attack in progress on 29 September. Formidable though the obstacle might be, extensive plans had been made to master the St Quentin Canal. This task fell to the Territorials of 46th (North Midland) Division.

The Royal Engineers devised a series of gadgets. Mud mats of canvas and reeds were to provide footing over the miry shallows, ladders would be available to scale the steep canal banks and collapsible boats would ferry troops across. The cross-Channel steamers were plundered of their life-belts. Experiment showed that a fully-armed man could rely on a life-belt to keep him afloat and that the boats could be unfolded and on the water in twenty seconds. This was not only prudent and practical but also excellent for morale.

As the Americans launched themselves against the line to the north, the 1st/6th South Staffordshire Regiment advanced behind a creeping barrage from the positions secured by the division's 138 Brigade two days earlier. In the fog, and organised into small groups, they worked their way up to the enemy positions then rushed in with the bayonet. The west bank was soon in their hands and they waded across to overwhelm the allegedly impregnable positions opposite. By 8.30am Bellenglise was in their hands. On their left the 1st/5th South Staffords made use of the boats to cross the waterway, also exploiting the advantage of the poor visibility.

Close to the southern end of the tunnel the Riqueval bridge strides over the canal opposite the junction with the Le Cateau road to give the local farmers access to the fields on the western bank. The Germans had, of course, prepared charges so that it could be blown up in case of attack.

In the fog of the morning of 29 September, Captain A.H. Charlton had to navigate by compass to find the bridge at all. As his company of the 1st/6th North Staffords emerged from the mist they came under fire from a machine-gun sited in a trench on the western side. A bayonet charge put an end to that. Alerted by the firing, the demolition party of four men appeared from the German bunker beyond the bridge and ran to blow the charges fixed to the structure. Charlton and his men beat them to it, killing all four and cutting the wires to the explosives. The rest of the company dashed over the bridge and cleared the trenches and bunkers to secure passage for the brigade.

The supporting troops moved up and through the successful assault force to continue the advance. To the rear the fog persisted, causing confusion among units attempting to move up and great difficulties for those wounded seeking the dressing stations behind the line. The tanks became targets as the fog dispersed in front, but the progress continued and great columns of prisoners started their journeys to the cages. By the time, early in the afternoon, that the commanders could see clearly they were rewarded with the most heartening sight of this long war – a genuine breakthrough.

The 46th Division took 4,200 prisoners that day, 80 per cent of the total to fall into Allied hands on this front. They had done this at the cost of fewer than 800 casualties. But most remarkable of all, against the strongest defensive system

The Allied advance from 18 July to 26 September on the Somme front and regions eastward. Arras and Valenciennes are at the top, and Verdun is shown on the right. The shaded area shows the terrain captured and the broken situation on the German front shows clearly. *From l'Illustration, 5 October 1918.* (HGG)

the Germans had been able to construct, they had advanced nearly 3.5 miles (5.5 kilometres).

In the days following the momentum was maintained. The 49th Division and the Australian 2nd Division took Ramicourt and Montbréhain, to the right of the Le Cateau road, to complete the conquest of the Siegfried Position and by 5 October the entire Hindenburg Line had been broken. Ahead lay green fields and unblemished countryside, and an enemy now doomed to defeat.

The Final Weeks

The need to sue for an armistice was now undeniable. A new administration under Prince Max of Baden took power in Germany. As the events of the next few weeks unfolded the unity and reliability of the German armed forces crumbled, but the Army remained a serious adversary and the Allies still had hard fighting before them. In the east the French and the Americans battled on in the Argonne and in Champagne. In the north, September had seen the Germans rolled back in Flanders. On 14 October the last shell fell on Ypres and, two days later, the British occupied Menen, a town that had been their objective four years previously.

The open, undamaged landscape appealed to enthusiasts of wars of movement; it looked perfect for cavalry or tank deployment. The efforts of the cavalry were, for the most part, futile; the machine-gun still dominated the field. As for tanks, there were scarcely any of them left but, more importantly the Tank Corps had lost approximately one third of its men, and skilled, well-trained specialists were required for these weapons. The speed of advance thus depended, as always, on the infantry and on the ability of the Army to supply them. The supplies, of course, had to be brought up over that very country that had been fought over for the last four years – over shattered roads and tortured and denuded fields, past heaps of stone where villages had once stood and the few stumps that indicated that here once was a wood. Finally the troops themselves found the environment strange. After years of closely controlled action over distances measured in tens of yards they were unprepared for the demands of open warfare.

Although these factors slowed the advance, and although German resistance persisted in the face of defeat, the advance continued. Lille was liberated on

17 October and Douai on the same day. On 17 October the Fourth Army was fighting on the river Selle, north-east of Cambrai, in worsening weather. In three days they took 5,000 prisoners. On the same day Le Cateau, scene of the noted rearguard action by the British in 1914, was liberated. As the armistice negotiations continued, so did the steady advance.

Lance-bombardier Maurice Burton, as for the time being he was ranked, found a strange new environment:

We moved northeastwards into territory occupied by civilians... We pulled into a scattered village and were billeted in the houses, the French making us welcome. They showed us the empty cowsheds, the hides still lying where enemy troops had hastily slaughtered their cattle, skinned the carcasses and absconded with them. They showed us where they had buried their potato crop to save it and we saw that each meal for them was baked potatoes only, with a pile of salt on the bare wood at the centre of the table into which each man, woman and child dipped a portion of potato before eating it.

The last of the Bushmills men died on 4 November. Joseph Thompson had emigrated to New Zealand in 1913 to join his brother. Both of them enlisted, and Joseph became a Lance-Corporal in the New Zealand Rifle Brigade. He was going forward with the Medical Officer and the Chaplain to establish a regimental aid post on the road from Romeries to le Quesnoy, east of Cambrai, at about 8am when a machine-gun opened fire. They took cover, but Thompson had been hit. The Chaplain buried him nearby later that day. That same day the Manchester Regiment was making an opposed crossing of the Sambre and Oise Canal and a 25-year-old captain, the poet Wilfred Owen MC, was killed. The Canadians were at a scene of a famous action of 1914 on 11 November – Mons. One of their number, Private George L. Price, was shot dead at 10.58am

Maurice Burton wrote:

Then ... on November 11, the word got round that an armistice would be declared at eleven o'clock that damp, misty morning. We could hardly believe it. The guns were slamming away still, the machine-guns were still rattling, as the seconds ticked by up to that magic hour. Then, suddenly, everywhere was silence.

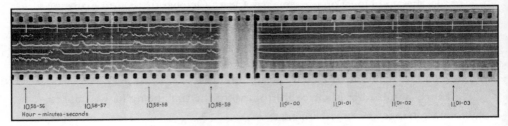

Sound Ranging film at 11.11.1918 showing activity on the American front near the river Moselle. The cessation of activity to a flat-line signal shows the end of shellfire. *(USMHI)*

Today countless people speed along the autoroutes from Calais to Reims and from Lille to Paris. If they can spare a second or two to glance at the countryside they may catch a glimpse of a cemetery or see some unidentified monument silhouetted against the sky. They give no thought to the thousands who suffered and died here. For those who take the slower country roads the evidence of sacrifice is more easily discovered, and those who choose to walk in the footsteps of the brave will find memories more resonant than words can describe and questions to which we still seek answers.

Chapter 8

Hindsight

The story of the war in the Somme region illustrates important aspects of the First World War as a whole. As new historians carry out fresh research yet further insights are to be expected, and so to draw conclusions would not be appropriate. However, some kind of oversight must be attempted if the impact of events on humankind is to be respected. In exercising hindsight various dangers present themselves.

The breadth of view can influence opinion. Some scholars have concentrated on one, major battle and formed their opinions in that light. In doing so they lose sight of the facts that gave context to the events they study. It was a world war. For example, when, in October 1914, the 'race to the sea' was as yet unresolved, Colonel Solomon Maritz was starting a revolt in South Africa, the Russians were crossing the river Vistula, Turkey was launching an attack upon Russia, the Indian Expeditionary Force was sailing from Bombay (Mumbai) to Mesopotamia (Iraq) to begin the Baghdad Campaign, the German East Asiatic Squadron was closing on the British squadron in the Pacific off the coast of Chile, the Australian cruiser *Sydney* was in pursuit of the German raider *Emden* near the Cocos Islands in the Indian Ocean, and the German cruiser *Königsberg* was being confined to the Refugi Delta in East Africa. Events in Flanders were part of this larger picture, but it is easy to forget it. It is possible to think in terms of the war in Europe, or the war on the eastern or western front, of the war in Belgium, at Verdun or on the Somme, or on 1 July 1916, the first day of the great Somme battle, to the exclusion of all else, but it is vital to be aware of doing so. To some extent each time and theatre influences the other.

It is also possible to allow nationalities to dominate, either by concentrating on just one country's experience or by imposing a single, simple characterisation on the people of a given nation. The experiences of the men of all sides in the front line varied little; they were deeply unpleasant although relieved by intervals out of the line or by the stimulation that combat can bring. Emotion, reason, ingenuity, laziness, courage and cowardice were demonstrated on all sides; these were human beings, not national stereotypes. The people involved were not just those with weapons in their hands. The vast supply chain required many more than those who fought, and in the battle areas the conflict raged over lands and through villages, erasing everyday life. There were thousands of Mme Demarolles thrown out of their homes. Love, too, stubbornly persisted, both in letters to and from the front and in the plaintive voice of the young woman whom Maurice Burton pretended not to understand when, in his final weeks in France, she whispered to him, 'Je t'aime, Maurice.'

Assuming we are capable of putting into effect these lofty warnings, what emerges from the story told in this book? Perhaps the first thing that strikes one is the great enthusiasm with which people went to war in 1914 and how old-fashioned their kind of warfare seemed only four years later. What was almost a sport became a grim form of business. Then the technological developments impress. Where men and horses vied with machine-gun and artillery in a war of movement, now tanks, aircraft and poison gas are added and orchestrated in precise and complex manoeuvres using radio communication and sound-ranged targeting. Lines of infantry charging to confront their enemies are replaced by skilled units of diversely specialised practitioners of war, outflanking and enfolding their opponents while supported by their comrades in the sky. This complexity requires, of course, a previously undreamed-of level of staff work by the high command. In short, the whole art and science of warfare changed, almost beyond recognition.

The change came in response to new conditions and new weapons. Artillery, machine-gun and aircraft had all existed before the war began, but the formation of a continuous line of fortification, the trench, across the whole of the western front gave them a new significance. How to overcome a fortification thus equipped was a problem not to be solved in a matter of days or even months. Moreover, the technology did not stand still, so invention could be overtaken by innovation. The war was not simply a learning process, it was a succession of lessons expensively bought in blood and suffering.

Faced with the evidence of the appalling suffering and losses that, for example, the battles of Verdun, the Somme and Passchendaele inflicted, it is tempting to castigate national leaders for failure to bring the conflict to a halt. If, however, one considers the situation at the time and the natural, human response to it, such criticism is less reasonable. Germany was in occupation of almost all of Belgium and a major part of French territory which included a crucial proportion of her raw materials and industrial installations. To ask the French and Belgians to accept this, even after the cost of these battles was obvious, was clearly entirely out of the question. The Allies were where they were, and had to get on with it.

How they got on with it is the subject of this work and will be the subject of new books to come. It is not easy work. The facile triviality of *Oh What a Lovely War!* is as useless and as patronising as gung-ho nationalism. People made mistakes. The same people may also have demonstrated courage and creative insight. The study of these events is thus fascinating and rewarding, even if crisp, clear conclusions escape us.

Some lessons can be seen to have been learned. Both sides had grasped the need to perfect combined operations. The Allies managed to integrate the operations of a wider range of weapons than their opponents; tanks, for example, were discounted by the German high command. The Allies also learned to stop. Throughout the war attackers enjoying initial success were lured into out-reaching themselves, but in 1918 an enlarged version of the 'bite and hold' strategy was practiced. The technology to sustain what would become known as 'blitzkrieg' tactics just did not exist. Certain technical innovations can be seen to have contributed to, rather than guaranteed, success. Sound-ranging made counter-battery work practicable. Radio made working with aircraft effective. Others were found to be defective. Gas, for example, was so uncertain a weapon that its use was avoided in the next war; hindsight has its benefits.

If a conclusion is to be attempted it is this. It is clear that, in the end and on the battlefield, the resources the Allies were able to bring to bear in men, minds and materials, all three, overcame those of the German armies.

Bibliography

The literature of the Somme is extensive, and that of the First World War is vast. In the preparation of this book I have consulted and, on occasion, quoted from the works listed below. The list does not pretend to be more than a personal one. Materials from archives are annotated with the abbreviations HGG for the Historial de la Grande Guerre, Péronne and IWM for the Imperial War Museum, London, where the text has not previously been published. Contemporary American texts from the USA Military History Institute, Carlisle, PA, have been taken from my own work, *American Voices of World War I*. Passages by British men that are not found in the author listing are from the relevant volume of Lyn Macdonald's works.

Unpublished works

Bardon, Lt, *Letters*, HGG, Naslin collection.

Browne, Eric Gore, DSO, OBE, Croix de Guerre, *Letters* (deposited IWM, London), by permission of Fanny Hugill.

Burton, Maurice, *Memoir*, by permission of Robert Burton.

Charlet, Roger, *Letters*, HGG 28999.

Demarolles, Mme, *Douilly pendant l'Occupation, Journal du 24/12/16 au 21/2/17*, HGG, Charlet collection.

Gain, René, *Letters,* HGG 34505.

Le Poitevin, Maurice, *Journal de Guerre Août 1914 à Novembre 1918*, HGG.

Marix, Georges, *Album*, HGG 021436.

Naslin, Emile, *Letters*, HGG 25823, 26826, 25827, 25841 and 25972.

Rey, Rudolphe, *Comment l'Armée a barré la Route de Paris*, HGG 03585 – 1/4.

— *L'Attaque Allemande du 30 Mars 1918*, HGG 035384 –1/6.

Riser, Marcel, *Letters*, HGG 22553.

Books

Anon., *American Armies and Battlefields in Europe*, Center of Military History, Washington DC, 1995.

Anon., *An Der Somme,* Piper, Munich, 1917.

Anon., *An Der Somme,* Dümmlers, Berlin, 1918.

Anon., *Les Armées Françaises dans le Grande Guerre, Pt IV,Vol. 1*, Paris, 1927.

Anon., *Kamerad im Westen*, Societäts-Verlag, Frankfurt a.M., 1930.

Anon., *The Western Front Then and Now*, C.Arthur Pearson, London, 1938.

Ashworth,Tony, *Trench Warfare 1914–1918:The Live and Let Live System*, Macmillan, London, 1980.

Audoin-Rouzeau, Stéphane, *Men at War 1914–1918*, Berg, Oxford, 1992.

Banks,Arthur, *A Military Atlas of the First World War*, Leo Cooper, London, 1989.

Barker, Stephen, and Christopher Boardman, *Lancashire's Forgotten Heroes*, The History Press, Stroud, 2008.

Barton, Peter, with Jeremy Banning, *The Battlefields of the First World War:The Unseen Panoramas of the Western Front*, Constable, London, 2008.

Beauchamp, K.G., *A History of Telegraphy*, Institution of Electrical Engineers, London, 2000.

Bloem,Walter, *The Advance from Mons 1914*, Helion & Co., Solihull, 2004.

Boraston, J.H. (ed), *Sir Douglas Haig's Despatches*, Naval & Military Press reprint, 1919.

Burness, Peter, *Amiens to the Hindenburg Line:Australians on the Western Front – 1918*, Department ofVeterans'Affairs, Canberra, 2008.

Chappell, Michael, *The Somme 1916: Crucible of a British Army*,Windrow & Greene, London, 1995.

Cook,Wilfred, ed. Audrey Larkins, *Mens' Horses, Mud and Stew*,Tommies Guides, Eastbourne, 2009.

Corcoran,A.P., 'Wireless in the Trenches', *Popular Science Monthly*, May 1917.

Corrigan, Gordon, *Mud, Blood and Poppycock*, Cassell, London, 2003.

Cross,Tim (ed.), *The Lost Voices ofWorld War I,* University of Iowa Press, Iowa City, 1988.

Cutlack, F.M. (ed.), *War Letters of General Monash*,Angus and Robertson, London, 1935.

Denizot,Alain, *La Bataille de la Somme*, Perrin, 2002.

Doyle, Peter, *Geology of the Western Front, 1914–1918*, Geologists'Association, London, 1998.

Falkenhayn, Erich von, *General Headquarters 1914–1916 and its Critical Decisions*, Naval & Military Press, Uckfield, 2004 (reprint of 1919 edition).

Fletcher, David (ed.), *Tanks and Trenches*, Grange Books, London, 1994.

Gilbert, Martin, *First World War*, Weidenfeld & Nicolson, London, 1994.

—— *Somme: The Heroism and Horror of War*, John Murray, London, 2007.

Gliddon, Gerald, *The Battle of the Somme: A Topographical History*, Sutton, Stroud, 1994.

Glover, Michael, *A New Guide to the Battlefields of Northern France and the Low Countries*, Michael Joseph, London, 1987.

Gosse, Philip, *A Naturalist Goes to War*, Penguin Books, London, 1943.

Gray, Randal, with Christopher Argyle, *Chronicle of the First World War, Volume I: 1914–1916, Volume II: 1917–1921*, Facts on File, New York, Oxford and Sydney, 1990.

Graves, Robert, *Goodbye to All That*, Berghahn Books, Oxford, 1995.

Griffith, Paddy, *Battle Tactics of the Western Front: The British Army's Art of Attack 1916–18*, Yale University Press, New Haven and London, 1994.

Hadley, Frédérick, 'L' Offensive de la Somme', *14–18, le magazine de la Grande Guerre No. 33*, August/September 2006.

Hogg, Ian V., *Allied Artillery of World War One*, Crowood Press, Ramsbury, 1998.

Holmes, Richard, *The Oxford Companion to Military History*, Oxford University Press, Oxford, 2001.

——, *Riding the Retreat. Mons to Marne: 1914 Revisited*, Jonathan Cape, London, 1995.

Holt, Tonie and Valmai, *Battlefields of the First World War*, Pavilion, London, 1993.

——, *Battle Map of the Somme*, Holt's Battlefield Tours, Sandwich, 1995.

Judy, Will, *A Soldier's Diary*, Judy Publishing, Chicago, IL, 1930.

Kitchen, Martin, *The German Offensives of 1918*, Tempus, Stroud, 2001.

Laurent, André, *1918 en Picardie – Les Dernières Batailles*, Martelle, Amiens, 1998.

Lawson, Eric, and Jane Lawson, *The First Air Campaign, August 1914–November 1918*, Combined Books, Conshohocken, PA, 1996.

Liveing, Edward, *Attack on the Somme*, Spa/Tom Donovan Military Books, Stevenage, 1986.

Ludendorff, Erich, *My War Memories 1914–1918,* Hutchinson, London, 1929.

Lynch, E.P.F., ed. Will Davies, *Somme Mud*, Doubleday, London, 2006.

McCarthy, Chris, *The Somme: The Day-by-Day Account*, Arms & Armour Press, London, 1993.

Macdonald, Lyn, *1914: The Days of Hope*, Michael Joseph, London, 1987.

——, *1915*, Headline, London, 1993.

——, *Somme*, Michael Joseph, London, 1983.

Malins, Geoffrey, *How I Filmed the War*, Herbert Jenkins, London, 1920.

Mangin, Charles, *Comment Finit la Guerre*, Plon, Paris, 1920.

Marix Evans, Martin, *1918: The Year of Victories*, Arcturus, London, 2002.

——, *American Voices of World War I*, Fitzroy Dearborn, Chicago and London, 2001.

——, *Battles of World War I*, Airlife, Ramsbury, 2004.

——, *Battles of WW I*, Arcturus, London, 2008.

——, *Retreat Hell! We Just Got Here!: the AEF in France 1917–1918*, Osprey, Oxford, 1998.

Masefield, John, ed. Peter Vansittart, *Letters from the Front 1915–17*, Constable, London, 1984.

——, *The Old Front Line*, Heinemann, London, 1917, reprinted Pen & Sword, Barnsley, 2003.

Middlebrook, Martin, *The First Day on the Somme*, Penguin Books, London, 1984.

——, *The Kaiser's Battle*, Allen Lane, London, 1978.

Mitchell, Frank, *Tank Warfare*, 1933, reprinted Spa Books & Tom Donovan, Stevenage, 1987.

Monash, Sir John, *The Australian Victories in France in 1918*, 1920, reprinted IWM, London and Battery Press, Nashville, 1993.

Nicholson, G.W.L., *Canadian Expeditionary Force 1914–1919*, Queen's Printer, Ottawa, 1962.

Palmer, Alan, *Victory 1918*, Weidenfeld & Nicolson, London, 1998.

Parker, Ernest, *Into Battle 1914–1918*, Longmans, Green, London, 1964.

Pope, Stephen, and Elizabeth-Anne Wheal, *Dictionary of the First World War*, Macmillan, London, 1995.

Quarrie, Bruce, *Encyclopedia of the German Army in the 20th Century*, Patrick Stephens, Wellingborough, 1989.

Ratinaud, Jean, *La Course à la Mer*, Fayard, Paris, 1967.

Renz, Irina, Gerd Krumeich and Gerhard Hirschfeld, *Scorched Earth: The Germans on the Somme 1914–1918*, Pen & Sword, Barnsley, 2009.

Richards, Frank, *Old Soldiers Never Die*, Faber and Faber, London, 1933, reprinted Naval & Military Press, Uckfield.

Rickard, J. (15 September 2007), *The Race to the Sea, September – October 1914*, http://www.historyofwar.org.

Samson, Charles Rumney, *Fights and Flights: A Memoir of the Royal Naval Air Service in World War I*, The Battery Press, Nashville, 1990, reprint of original 1930 edition.

Schmidt, Capt., General Staff, 28th Infantry Division, *The Battle in the Intermediate Zone*, GHQAEF, Chaumont-en-Bassingy, August 19, 1918.

Sheffield, Gary, *Forgotten Victory: The First World War, Myths and Realities*, Headline, London, 2001.

——, *The Pictorial History of World War I*, Bison Books, London, 1987.

——, *The Somme*, Cassell, London, 2003.

Sheffield, Gary, and John Bourne (eds), *Douglas Haig: War Diaries and Letters 1914–1918*, Weidenfeld & Nicolson, London, 2005.

Sheldon, Jack, *The German Army on the Somme, 1914–1918*, Pen & Sword, Barnsley, 2005.

Smith, Aubrey ('A Rifleman'), *Four years on the Western Front*, Odhams, London, 1922, reprinted Naval & Military Press.

Spears, Sir Edward, *Liaison 1914: A Narrative of the Great Retreat, 2nd Edition*, Eyre & Spottiswoode, London, 1968.

Strachan, Hew, *The First World War. Volume I: To Arms*, Oxford University Press, Oxford, 2001.

Stallings, Laurence (ed.), *The First World War: A Photographic History*, Daily Express Publications, London, 1933.

Sweeting, C.G., 'Tank Versus Panzer', *MHQ: The Quarterly Journal of Military History*, Leesburg, VA, Winter 2010.

Terraine, John, *To Win a War: 1918, the Year of Victory*, Macmillan, London, 1986.

Thompson, Robert (ed.), *Bushmills Heroes 1914–1918*, Thompson, Bushmills, 1995.

Trask, David F., *The AEF and Coalition Warmaking 1917–1918,* University Press of Kansas, Lawrence, 1993.

Travers, Tim, *The Killing Ground*, Allen & Unwin, London, 1987.

Tuchman, Barbara W., *August 1914*, 1962 and Constable, London, 1993.

Vaughan, Edwin Campion, *Some Desperate Glory*, Frederick Warne, London, 1981.

Walker, Jonathan, *The Blood Tub: General Gough and the Battle of Bullecourt*, Spellmount, Staplehurst, 1998.

Zabecki, David T., 'Colonel Georg Bruchmüller and the Birth of Modern Artillery Tactics', *Stand To!*, No. 53, September 1998.

Zabecki, David T., *Steel Wind*, Praeger, Westport CT, 1994.

CDs and DVDs

Imperial War Museum, *Trench Map Archive*, Naval & Military Press, Uckfield, 2004.

National Archives, *Captured German Trench and Operations Maps,* Naval & Military Press, Uckfield, 2003.

Index

Note: References to illustrations are in italic type. References to colour plates are shown as *col* and the black and white plates as *b/w*.

Accrington Pals, *see* BEF, York and Lancaster
Aircraft, 76, 204, 215
Aisne, River, 28, 162
Agins, Cpt. Arthur, 103
Albert, 81, 190, 226
Albert of the Belgians, King, 16
Allenby, Lt-Gen. Sir Edmund, 19, 20, 100
Amade, Gen. Albert d', 16, 18, 21, 25, 31
American Expeditionary Force, 172, 208, 230
  1st Division, 48, 201, 208, 211
  2nd Division, 200
  3rd Division, 192, 200, 201, 213
  27th Division, 231, 233-5
  28th Division, 201
  30th Division, 231, 233-5
  33rd Division, 222-3
  42nd Division, 201
  5th Field Artillery, 210
  6th Field Artillery, 208
  16th Infantry, 48, 208
  18th Infantry, 208
  28th Infantry, 208-9
  106th Infantry, 233
  117th Infantry, 234
  131st Infantry, 222-3
  132nd Infantry, 223
  11th Engineers, 171
  102nd Engineers, 234
  105th Engineers, 234
  301st Tank Bn, 234, *col. 19*

US Marine Corps, 200
Amiens, 189, 196
  Battle of, 215-22
Ancre, 36
  River, 36, 147
Ancre Heights, Battle of, 145
Antwerp, 21, 25, 38, 40
Arnold, Lt A. E., 139
Arnold, Lt C. B., 220
Arras, 38, 159, 187, 194, 226
artillery, 74
  barrage, 55, 129, 144, 160, 170, 174
    creeping, 75, 131, *213*
    lifting, 52, 75, 131
    rolling, 75
    standing, 75
    spotting, 76-7, 205-7, *240*
  See also BEF: Royal Regiment of Artillery
Ashurst, Cpl. George, 88
Asquith, Raymond, 138
Aston, Brig-Gen. Sir G., 34
Aubers Ridge, 53, 54-5
Auchonvillers, 85
Austin, Raymond, 208-9, 211
Autille, 36
Avoca valley, 81

Balfourier, Gen. Maurice, 107
Bapaume, 81, 223, 226
Bardon, Lt., 118, 123
Barleux, 143
Barnsley Pals, *see* BEF York and Lancaster
barrage, *see* artillery
Bayonvillers, 220

Bazentin-le-Grand, 119
Bazentin-le-Petit, 119, 120
Beadle, Lt F.W., 121
Beaucourt en Santerre, 220
Beaumont Hamel, 69, 85-90, *86*, 147, 149, 226
Belgian forces, 16
Bell, Major-General John, 213
Bellenglise, *232*, 236
Bellicourt, 229, *232*, 234
Belloy en Santerre, 114, 143
Below, Gen. Fritz von, 74, 77, 112, 119, 147
Below, Gen. Otto von, 176
Bernafay Wood, 105, 113
Biaches, 114, 126, 156, 228
Bidon, Gen., 26
Bloem, Hauptmann Walter, 27
Bony, 180, 233, *c. 13*
booby traps, 155-6
Bradford Pals, *see* BEF: West Yorkshire
Braithwaite, Lt-Gen. Sir Walter, 231
Bram, Lt-Col, 98, 100
British Expeditionary Force (BEF), 16, 23, 35, 38, 59
  New Armies, 59, 67-8
  First Army, 52, 159, 229
  Second Army, 164-5
  Third Army, 160, 176, 188, 223
  Fifth Army, 124, 147, 165, 176, 188
    reconformed as Fourth, 217, 238
  Cavalry Corps, 19, 145, 170, 176

I Corps, 19, 22, 23
II Corps, 19, 20, 23, 141, 144, 149
III Corps, 141, 143, 144, 170, 176, 182, 184, 215, 216, 229
IV Corps, 52, 54, 63, 170, 175
V Corps, 148, 175
VI Corps, 175
VII Corps, 175, 190, 192
XIII Corps, 109, 148
XIV Corps, 143, 144, 147
XV Corps, 119, 121, 122, 141, 143, 144
XVII Corps, 160, 175
XVIII Corps, 176, 184, 186, 190
XIX Corps, 175, 190
Australian and New Zealand Army Corps
    (ANZAC), 68, 123, 134, 149, 161, 164, 166
    Canadian Corps, 53, 68, 134, 141, 143, 144, 159, 167, 229
Indian Corps, 38, 52, 54
1st Cavalry Division, 117
2nd Cavalry Division, 117, 186
2nd Indian Division, 117, 121
Guards Division, 63, 134, 138, 165, 171
1st Division, 63, 124
2nd Division, 150, 213
3rd Division, 20, 119, 124, 148, 175, 213
4th Division, 20, 90, 175
5th Division, 20, 124, 213
6th Division, 38, 138, 170, 175, 178
7th Division, 38, 106, 119
9th (Scottish) Division, 63, 122, 175, 178
11th Division, 144
12th (Eastern) Division, 113, 170, 215
14th (Light) Division, 138, 140, 185, 195
15th (Scottish) Division, 61, 136, 139, 175, 202

16th (Irish) Division, 133, 175, 180
17th (Northern) Division, 113, 115, 175
18th (Eastern) Division, 108, 144, 195, 197, 215
19th (Western) Division, 112, 124
20th (Light) Division, 170
21st Division, 63, 119, 144, 175
23rd Division, 114, 145
24th Division, 63, 175
29th Division, 98, 170
30th Division, 104, 124, 127, 176
31st Division, 90, 148
32nd Division, 94, 98
33rd Division, 121-2
34th Division, 81, 175
36th (Ulster) Division, 96, 170, 176, 184
37th Division, 149
38th (Welsh) Division, 115, 165
39th Division, 146, 149
41st Division, 139
46th (North Midland) Division, 100, 231, 235-6
47th (1/2nd London) Division, 139, 145, 175
48th (South Midland) Division, 124
49th (West Riding) Division, 98, 238
51st (Highland) Division, 124, 148, 150, 165, 170, 175, 178, 202
56th (1/1st London) Division, 100
58th Division, 215, 222
59th Division, 175, 178
61st Division, 124, 176
62nd (West Riding) Division, 161, 170, 202
63rd (Royal Naval) Division, 148, 175
66th Division, 175, 192
1st Australian Division, 124, 215, 229

2nd Australian Division, 124, 215, 226, 238
3rd Australian Division, 215, 229, 235
4th Australian Division, 191, 195, 213, 215, 229
5th Australian Division, 123, 229, 235
1st Canadian Division, 215, 219
2nd Canadian Division, 139, 215, 218
3rd Canadian Division, 139, 215, 219
4th Canadian Division, 215, 219
New Zealand Division, 139, 190
1 Guards Brigade, 138
2 Guards Brigade, 138
34 Brigade, 145
64 Brigade, 144
87 Brigade, 89
89 Brigade, 127
100 Brigade, 122
101 Brigade, 81
102 (Tyneside Scottish) Brigade, 81
103 (Tyneside Irish) Brigade, 82
107 Brigade, 97
109 Brigade, 96
110 Brigade, 180
115 Brigade, 115
138 Brigade, 236
6 Australian (Victoria) Brigade, 124, 227
9 Australian Brigade, 195
13 Australian Brigade, 197
14 Australian (NSW) Brigade, 227
15 Australian Brigade, 197
Canadian Cavalry Brigade, 176, 220
South African Brigade, 122, 178
Royal Regiment of Artillery
    Royal Field Artillery, 20, 23

XXVIII Brigade, 20

Royal Garrison Artillery, 181

Machine Gun Corps (Heavy Section) (later Tank Corps), 139, 161, 165, 170, 215-22, 233-4

4th Dragoon Guards, 21

7th Dragoon Guards, 121

2nd Dragoons (Royal Scots Grays), 23

11th Hussars, 16

15th Hussars, 221

19th Hussars, 221

12th Lancers, 23

Queen's Bays, 220

11th Argyll and Sutherland Highlanders, 136

2nd Bedfordshire, 104, 127

4/5th Black Watch, 146

6th Black Watch, 70

11th Border (Lonsdale Bn), 96

1/1st Cambridgeshire, 146

10th Cameronians (Scottish Rifles), 136

10th Cheshire, 145

Coldstream Guards, 138

9th Devonshire, 106

1st Duke of Cornwall's Light Infantry, 133

7th Duke of Cornwall's Light Infantry, 190

10th Durham Light Infantry, 130, 140-2

15th Durham Light Infantry, 145

8th East Lancashire, 150

11th East Lancashire (Accrington Pals), 92

1st Essex, 89

4th Gloucestershire, 155

12th Gloucester (Bristol), 133

2nd Green Howards (Yorkshire Regiment), 104

Grenadier Guards, 138

1/9th Highland Light Infantry, 122

16th Highland Light Infantry (Glasgow Boys' Brigade), 150

17th Highland Light Infantry, 94

17th King's (Liverpool) (1st Liverpool Pals), 104, 127

18th King's (Liverpool) (2nd Liverpool Pals), 104

19th King's (Liverpool) (3rd Liverpool Pals), 127

20th King's (Liverpool) (4th Liverpool Pals), 104, 127

1/5th King's (Liverpool), 129

1/8th King's (Liverpool) (Liverpool Irish), 129

1st King's Own Scottish Borderers, 89

7/8th King's Own Scottish Borderers, 136

6th King's Own Yorkshire Light Infantry, 138

8th King's Royal Rifle Corps, 138

17th King's Royal Rifle Corps (British Empire League), 146

1st Lancashire Fusiliers, 87, 88

15th Lancashire Fusiliers (1st Salford Pals), 93

2nd Lincolnshire, 55

7th Lincolnshire, 113

10th Lincolnshire (Grimsby Chums), 68, 81

1/3rd London (Royal Fusiliers), 103

1/5th London, 79

1/6th London, 62

1/7th London, 62

1/8th London (Post Office Rifles), 58, 61

1/12th London (The Rangers), 102

16th Manchester (1st Manchester Pals), 68, 127, 183

17th Manchester (2nd Manchester Pals), 104, 127

18th Manchester (3rd Manchester Pals), 104, 127

19th Manchester (4th Manchester Pals), 104

Middlesex Regiment, 61, 88

9th Norfolk, 138

1/5th North Staffords, 102

1/6th North Staffords, 102, 236

2nd Northamptonshire, 55

1st Northumberland Fusiliers, 119

16th Northumberland Fusiliers (Newcastle Commercials), 93

20th Northumberland Fusiliers (1st Tyneside Scottish), 81

21st Northumberland Fusiliers (2nd Tyneside Scottish), 81, 84

22nd Northumberland Fusiliers (3rd Tyneside Scottish), 81

23rd Northumberland Fusiliers (4th Tyneside Scottish), 81

24th Northumberland Fusiliers (1st Tyneside Irish), 82

25th Northumberland Fusiliers (2nd Tyneside Irish), 82

26th Northumberland Fusiliers (3rd Tyneside Irish), 82

27th Northumberland Fusiliers (4th Tyneside Irish), 82

1st Queen's Royal, 122

1st Rifle Brigade, 90

2nd Rifle Brigade, 54

7th Rifle Brigade, 132

8th Rifle Brigade, 138

13th Rifle Brigade, 114, 148

1st Royal Dublin Fusiliers, 88

2nd Royal Fusiliers, 88

Royal Irish Rifles, 55

9th Royal Irish Rifles (West Belfast), 97

11th Royal Irish Rifles, 96
1st Royal Inniskilling
Fusiliers, 89
2nd Royal Inniskilling
Fusiliers, 184
9th Royal Inniskilling
Fusiliers (Tyrone Volunteers),
96, 97
10th Royal Inniskilling
Fusiliers, 96
Royal Munster Fusiliers,
181
Royal Newfoundland, 89
15th Royal Scots (1st
Edinburgh), 81
16th Royal Scots (2nd
Edinburgh), 81
2nd Royal Scots Fusiliers,
104
2/6th Royal Warwickshire,
177
8th Royal Warwickshire,
90, 155
17th Royal Warwickshire,
124
Royal Welch Fusiliers,
60, 112, 115
1st Sherwood Foresters, 55
10th Sherwood Foresters,
113
1/5th South Staffordshire,
102
1/6th South Staffordshire,
102, 236
2nd South Wales Borderers,
89
11th Suffolk
(Cambridgeshire), 81
Welsh, 38
1/6th West Yorkshire, 79
1/7th West Yorkshire, 98
16th West Yorkshire (1st
Bradford Pals), 93
18th West Yorkshire (2nd
Bradford Pals), 93
2nd Wiltshire, 104
6th Wiltshire, 112
10th Worcester, 112
12th York and Lancaster
(Sheffield City), 92

13th York and Lancaster (1st
Barnsley Pals), 93
14th York and Lancaster
(2nd Barnsley Pals), 93
20th Deccan Horse (Indian
Army), 121
2/3 Gurkha Rifles, 55
Bouchavesnes, 142, 227
Bourlon Wood, 170-1
Bridges, Major Tom, 21
Bruchmüller, Col. Georg,
167-8, 174, 199
Brugère, Gen., 31, 39
Brusilov, Gen. Alexei, 74, 118
Bullecourt, 16, 178
Bülow, F.M. Karl von, 15, 19
Burton, Gunner Maurice, 181,
194, 202, 239, 242
Bushmills, Co. Antrim, men of,
99, 239
Butler, Lt-Gen. Sir Ricard,
176, 187
Byng, Lt-Gen. Sir Julian, 159,
170, 175

Cambrai, 20, 169-72, 229
Canal du Nord, 230
Cantigny, 194, 208-11, *c. 10-12*,
b/w. 37-8
Caporetto, Battle of, 169
Carey's Force, 191-2
Casino Point, 104
Cassel, action at, 26
Castelnau, Gen. Noël de, 16,
29, 34
casualties, 1914, 46
  Arras, 40
  Le Cateau, 21
  'Race to the Sea', 45
casualties, 1915
  Aubers Ridge, 55, 56
  Neuve Chapelle, 53
casualties, 1916, 152
  1 July, 110
    Gommecourt, 103, 104
    La Boisselle, 84
    Thiepval, 100
  July, 127
    Delville Wood, 123
    Pozières, 126

Verdun, 67
casualties, 1917
  Bullecourt, 162
  Cambrai, 171
  Chemin des Dames, 163
  Vimy Ridge, 160
  Ypres, 167
casualties, 1918
  March, 185
  Amiens, 198, 222
  Bony, 235
  Cantigny, 210
  Epéhy, 229
  Hamel, 214
  Kaiserschlacht, 202
  St Quentin Canal, 236
Cateau, Le, 18, 20-21
  battle of, 20-21
Cavan, Lt-Gen. the Earl of,
128, 147
Charlet, Roger, 15, 126, 142-3
Charlton, Capt. A.H., 236
Château-Thierry, 28
Chauchat machine-gun, 48
Chaulnes, 33, 49
Chemin des Dames, 159,
162-3
Chipilly Spur, 220, 222
Churchill, Winston, 34
Clemenceau, Georges, 189
Cléry-sur-Somme, 126, 142
Combles, 143
Congreve, Lt-Gen. Walter, 109,
175, 180, 190
Contalmaison, 35, 113
Cook, Wilfred, 119-20
Crozat Canal, 175, 184, 186
Courcelette, 139
Curlu, 44, 107
Currie, Lt-Gen. Sir Arthur, 230

Debeney, Gen., 219
Delmensingen, Gen. Konrad
Kraft von, 31
Delville Wood, 119, 122,
130-1, 138
Demarolles, Mme, 154
Drocourt–Quéant Switch
Line, 159
Douai, 34, 37-38

Douaumont, Fort, 66
Doullens, 189
Douilly, 154
Dubail, Gen Auguste, 16
Dunkirk, 22, 25, 34

Easton, Pte. Tom, 84, 112
Epéhy, 175, 180, 229
Escant, river, 20
Esperey, Gen. Louis Franchet
d', 22, 23, 28
Estrées, 114
Evarts, Cpt. Jerimiah, 209-10

Falkenhayn, Gen. Erich von,
28, 38, 58, 63, 65-6, 112, 119,
132
Fanshawe, Lt-Gen. Sir Edward,
175
Fayolle, Gen. Marie Emile, 37,
73, 106, 113, 188
Fergusson, Lt-Gen. Sir Charles,
175
Feste Staufen; see Stuff Redoubt
Festubert, 55
Flers, 138, 139
Flesquières, 175, 178
Foch, Marshal Ferdinand, 23,
28, 39, 113, 163, 189, 219
Fokker E1, 76
Foster & Co, Lincoln, 135
Frankfort Trench, 85, 149
Franz Ferdinand, Archduke, 15
French forces
First Army, 16, 165, 215, 217,
219
Second Army, 16, 31, 34,
39, 43
Third Army, 16, 185, 217
Fourth Army, 23, 142
Fifth Army, 16, 22, 23, 163
Sixth Army, 21, 23, 31, 73,
106, 114, 132, 163, 200
Ninth Army, 23
Tenth Army, 39, 43, 106, 127
Territorial Divisions Group,
16, 31, 39
Conneau's Cavalry Corps,
31, 34

1st Colonial Corps, 107
I Corps, 22, 132, 142
III Corps, 22
V Corps, 142
VII Corps, 142
X Corps, 22, 28, 39
XIII Corps, 31
XIV Corps, 29, 31, 32
XVIII Corps, 22
XX Corps, 31, 35, 107, 114,
127, 132
XXI Corps, 32
XXXI Corps, 215, 217
XXXII, 146
XXXV Corps, 108
2nd Colonial Division, 108
3rd Colonial Division, 108
7th Division, 28
8th Division, 32
11th Division, 34, 35
19th Division, 37
20th Division, 37
31st Division, 39
39th Division, 104
41st Division, 127, 142
45th Algerian Division, 53
45th Division, 34
55th Division, 23
56th Division, 22
61st Division, 21, 23, 25
62nd Division, 21, 23
70th Division, 37
81st Division, 16, 25, 37, 39
82nd Division, 16, 25, 37
84th Division, 16, 25, 37
87th Division, 53
88th Division, 19, 25, 37
Barbot Division, 37
3rd Moroccan Brigade, 31
Regiments
61st Artillery, 143,
85th Heavy Artillery,
b/w. 28-32
30th Chasseurs Alpins,
107
97th Chasseurs Alpins,
37
159th Chasseurs Alpins,
37

Rég. De Marche, Foreign
Legion, 144
Infantry Regiments
1st, 132,
37th, 107, 215
42nd, 215
45th, 31
66th, 215
67th, 118, 123
87th, 15, 142
124th, 32
137th, 56
153rd, 127
159th, 215
205th, 44
329th, 15, 35, 78
350th, 194
355th, 194

French, Gen. Sir John, 16, 17,
21, 35, 38, 63
Freyberg, Lt-Col. Bernard, 149
Fricourt, 35, 44, 51, 69, 116
Fromelles, 54, 123
Fuller, J.F.C., 169

Gain, René, 143
Gallieni, Gen. Joseph, 28
Gallwitz, Gen. Max von, 119
Gas, 53, 60-1, 165, 177-8
German Army
Army Group Gallwitz, 119
Armies:
First, 15, 21, 28, 38, 119
Second, 15, 28, 74, 112,
119, 176, 187, 216
Third, 16, 28
Fourth, 16
Fifth, 16
Sixth, 16, 29
Seventh, 16, 38
Seventeenth, 176, 178,
187
Eighteenth, 176, 187,
200, 217
Corps:
Richthofen Cavalry, 23
I Bavarian, 32, 40
II, 21

II Bavarian, 32
IV, 21, 25, 38
XI, 195
XIV, 31, 38
XIV Reserve, 37
XVII, 112, 184
Divisions:
Prussian Guards, 38, 40, 56
1st Bavarian, 186
1st Guards, 194
2nd Guards, 18
13th, 190
19th, 18
26th Reserve, 43, 56
28th, 177, 182, 189
39th, 146
50th, 183
52nd, 56
54th Reserve, 171
70th, 146
228th, 195
Brigade:
51st Reserve, 36
Regiments, Artillery:
22nd Field, 105
26th, 97
63rd (Frankfurt) Field, 184
Regiment, Cavalry:
26th Württemberg Dragoons, 31
Regiments: Infantry/ Fusilier/Grenadier:
1st Grenadier Guards, 45
9th Grenadier, 113
10th Grenadier, 108
11th, 107
24th, 190
27th, 162
38th Fusilier, 108
60th, 49
62nd, 104, 105
63rd, 104, 107
73rd Fusilier, 133
110th, 83
118th, 183
121st, 107
126th, 147

164th, 133
169th, 92
170th, 56, 103
180th, 98
186th, 113
Bavarian Infantry:
Leibregiment, 33, 51
1st, 43
6th Reserve, 104, 107
8th Reserve, 97, 98
16th, 32
17th, 136
Reserve Infantry:
7th, 108
40th, 35, 43, 44
55th, 103
60th, 108
77th, 120, 126
91st, 102, 116, 120
99th, 79, 96, 98
110th, 51
111th, 44, 113
119th, 70, 88, 98
121st, 90
269th, 49
George V, King, 212, 222-235
Gerster, Lt M, 70, 78
Gibraltar, 124
Ginchy, 127, 129, 134
Glasgow Tramways battalion, *see* BEF: 15th Highland Light Infantry
Glory Hole, the, 50
Goering, Hermann, 221
Gommecourt, 69, 100, *101*
Gore Brown, Cpt. Eric, 58, 60-62
Gosse, Philip, 116
Gough, Lt-Gen. Sir Hubert, 124, 147, 164, 175, 180, 185, 186, 191, 192
Granathof, La, 50
Graves, Robert, 60-1, 116
Griffith, Paddy, 63
Grimsby Chums, *see* BEF: 10th Lincolnshire
Gueudecourt, 141
Guillaucourt, 218, 221
Guillaumat, Gen. Marie Louis, 132

Guillemont, 127, 129, 133, 143
Guynemer, Georges, 77

Haig, Gen. Sir Douglas, 19, 52, 59, 64-5, 148, 160-4, 172, 188, 192, 199, 214, 229
on Somme plans, 72, 111, 117
Haldane, Lt-Gen. Sir Aylmer, 175
Hall, Pte. E.G., 79
Ham, 187, 188
Hamel, 192, 195, 212-14
Hangest-en-Santerre, 219
Harbonnières, 78, 220
Harper, Gen. G.M., 170, 175
Hausen, Gen. Max von, 16
Havrincourt, 229
Hawthorn Crater, 88-9
Redoubt, 87, 147
Ridge, 85
Heeringen, Gen. August von, 16
helmets, steel, 58
Herbécourt, 108, 155
High Wood, 120
Hindenburg, Field Marshal Paul von, 151
Line, 151, *153*, 169, 226, 228-38
Hinkel, Cpl. Freidrich, 79
Holnon, Forest of, 183
Horne, Gen. Sir Henry, 159, 229
Humbert, Gen. Georges, 185, 187
Hutier, Gen. Oskar von, 176, 200

influenza pandemic, 208
Ingouville-Williams, Maj.-Gen. E.C., 81

Jacob's Ladder, 85, 87
Joffre, Gen. Joseph, 21, 22, 29, 39, 66

Kaiserschlacht, 176-200
Kern Redoubt, 104
Kettle, Tom, 133

Kinematographer, Official
  W.O., 85
Kircher, Felix, 97
Kitchener, Field Marshal Lord,
  23
Kluck, Gen. Alexander von, 15,
  19, 21, 25, 38
Koehler, Lt, 36
Kuhl, Gentleman, 216
Kyler, Sgt. Donald D., 48

La Boisselle, 44, 50, 69, 112
La Fère, 229
Laffargue, Cpt. André, 168
Lais, Cpl. Otto, 92
Langdale Cary, Gen. Fernand
  de, 16
Lanrezac, Gen. Charles, 16, 17,
  21, 22
Leibrock, Col., 105
Leipzig Redoubt, 93, 132
Le Poitevin, Maurice, 15, 44,
  56, 78, 114
Le Quesnoy, 189
Le Sars, 145
Lesboeufs, 143
Leuze Wood, 133, 134
Lille, 25
Liveing, Lt. Edward, 102
Liverpool Pals, *see* BEF: King's
  (Liverpool)
Lloyd George, David, 172, 189
Lochnagar Crater, 82, 112
Longueval, 78, 119, 127
Loos, 58, 60–63
Ludendorff, Gen. Erich, 132,
  173, 187, 196, 216
  strategy 1917, 151–2
  on Amiens and morale, 221
Lynch, Pte Edward, 216, 217,
  229

McDowell, John, 85
machine-guns, 47–49, *b/w.*
  12-16
  aerial, 76
Malins, Geoffrey, 85, 126, 136,
  143, 145
Mametz, 35, 36, 44, 69, 104,
  106

Mametz Wood, 113, 115–6
Manchester Hill Redoubt, 183
Manchester Pals, *see* BEF:
  16th, 17th, 18th and 19th
  Manchester
Mangin, Gen. Charles, 163,
  200
Maricourt, 106
Marix, Major Georges,
  b/w. 28-32
Marix, Flight Lt. Reggie, 25
Marne, First Battle of, 28
  River, 28
Marshall, Cpt. George C., 209
Martin, Cpt. D. L., 106
Martinpuich, 136, 139
Marwitz, Gen. Georg von der,
  21, 176, 191
Masefield, John, 145, 146
Mash Valley, 81
Maubeuge, 25
Maud'huy, Gen. Louis
  Comtede, 37, 39
Maunoury, Gen. Michel-
  Joseph, 21
Maurepas, 133
Max of Baden, Prince, 238
Maxse, Lt-Gen. Sir Ivor, 176,
  186
Mazel, Gen., 163
Messines Ridge, 164
Micheler, Gen. Alfred, 106, 162
Milner, Lord, 188
mines, *see* tunnels
Mitchell, Lt. Frank, 196
Moltke, Field Marshal
  Helmuth von, 24, 28
Monash, Lt-Gen. Sir John, 190,
  212, 227, 231
Mons, Battle of, 18–19
Montauban, 35, 43, 104, 109
Montdidier, 193, 194
Mont St Quentin, 226–7
Moran, Lord, 122
Mormel, Forest of, 19, 20
Morval, 143
Mouquet Farm, 93, 129, 144,
  145
Möy-de-l'Aisne, action at, 23
Munich Trench, 149

Musgrave, Major Herbert, 76
Musical Box, 220
mutiny, of French troops, 1917,
  163

Namur, 15
Naslin, Emile, 126
Neumann, Lt. E., 77
Neuve Chapelle, 52, 54
Nieuport fighter, 76, 77
Nivelle, Gen. Robert, 159,
  162–3
Noyon, 187

O'Caffrey, Cavrois, 25
Oise River, 22
Operation Alberich, 154–7
Operation Blücher-Yorck,
  199, 210
Operation Georgette, 199
Operation Gueisenau, 200, *201*
Operation Michael, 176–198
Ovillers la Boisselle, 112
Owen, Cpt. Wilfred, 239

packs, 79
Paris, Major-General Sir
  Archibald, 38
Parker, L/Cpl. Edward, 130,
  141–2
Parker, Pte Reg, 93
Passchendaele, 199, *see* Ypres,
  Third Battle of
Péronne, 21, 35, 143, 156, 188,
  226, 227
Pershing, Gen. John J., 189,
  208, 214
Pétain, Gen. Philippe, 59, 163,
  172, 188
photography, aerial, 76, *b/w. 21*
Plan XVII, 15
Plantey, Gen., 34
Plumer, Gen. Sir Herbert, 164,
  166
Pozières, 81, 114, 129
  Ridge, 123, *125*
Price, Pte. George, 239
Princip, Gavrilo, 15

Quadrilateral, the, 90

'Race to the Sea', 29–40
radio, *see* wireless
railways, 29, *30*, 52
Rancourt, 147
Rawlinson, Lt-Gen. Sir Henry,
    38, 52, 72, 110, 146, 192, 227
Raynal, Maj. Sylvain-Eugène,
    67
Read, Gen. George W., 231
Redan Ridge, 90
Rey, Rodolphe, 185
Richthofen, Freiherr Manfred
    von, 204-5, 221
Riga, 168
Riqueval, 20
    bridge, 236
Riser, Marcel, 35, 106
Robertson, Gen. Sir William,
    127
Rohr, Cpt. Willy, 168
Rosenthal, Major-General
    Charles, 226
Royal Air Force, 214, 215, 221
Royal Flying Corps, 70, 73, 77,
    128, 139, 161, 192
Royal Marines, 21, 30, 34
Royal Naval Air Service, 21,
    25, 76, 135
Roye, 32, 35
Ruffey, Gen. Pierre, 16
Rupprecht of Bavaria, Crown
    Prince, 16, 29, 31, 40, 119,
    132, 147

St-Pierre-Divion, 93, 147
St Quentin, 19, 23, 29
    Canal, 231, *col. 8, 9*
Sailly Saillisel, 146
Salford Pals, *see* BEF: 15th
    Lancashire Fusiliers
Sambre, river, 20
Samson, Commander Charles,
    21-2, 25-6, 30, 34, 37, 76
Sargent, Lt. Daniel, 210
Sarajevo, 15
Sassoon, Siegfried, 116
Sausage Valley, 81
Scarpe, river, 160
Schilling, Xavier, 44
Schlieffen Plan, 15, 24

Schwaben Redoubt, 93, 96, 98,
    144, 145
Seaton, Earl D, 208
Seeger, Alan, 114
Selle, river, 20
Serre, 56, *57*, 90-93, *91*, 148
shells, British, 55; *see also*
    artillery
Siegfried Line, 231-236, 232
Smith, Aubrey, 79-80
Smith-Dorrien, Gen. Sir
    Horace, 19, 54
Snow, Lt-Gen. Sir Thomas,
    20, 100
Soden, Lt-Gen. Freiherr von,
    98
Somme, First Battle of, plans, 72
    river, 20, 25, 67, 106, 175
Sopwith Strutter, 76
Sordet, Gen. Jean, 21
Souville, Fort, 67
Spears, Lt. Edward, 16-19
Stencerwld, Lt W., 120
Stokes mortar, 120
Stuff Redoubt (Feste Staufen),
    97, 144, 145
Sulzbach, Herbert, 184, 188, 193
Swinton, Lt-Col. Ernest, 73,
    134, 169
Switch Line, 122, *137*, 139

Tactics, defensive, 69-70, 172-3
    offensive, 128, 134, 158-9,
    168, 182-3, 212
tanks
    British, 73, 134, 140, 160,
    166, 170-2, 173, 174, *b/w.*
    23-6, 196, 203, 212, 215 *see*
    also BEF: Machine Gun
    Corps (Heavy Section)
    French, 163, *b/w. 24*
    German, 196, *b/w. 27*
Tara-Usna line, 81, *82*
taxicabs, use of, 28
Thiepval, 36, 43, *b/w. 22*, 79,
    93-100, *94-5*
    Memorial, 93
    Ridge, 144
    Wood, 36, 93
Transloy Ridge, Battle of, 145

Trenchard, Major-General
    Hugh, 77, 128
trenches, 41-2, *b/w. 7-11*, 43, 49,
    51, 54, 58, 157
Trônes Wood, 117
truce, 44, 45, 110
Tudor, Brig-Gen. H.H., 170
tunnels, 50-1, 160, 164
Turner, Lt. William Bradford,
    233

U-boats, 164
USA, 152

Vaquette, Boromée, 36
Vaughan, Edwin, 155
Vaux, 44
Vaux, 67
Verdun, 65-7
Villers Bretonneux, 194
Villers-Carbonnel, 143
Villers-Tournelle, 208
Vimy, 39
    Ridge, 54, 56, 159-60

Warfusée Abancourt, 220
Watts, Lt-Gen. Sir Herbert, 175
Weber, Karl, 32
Western Front, *46*
Whitemore's Force, 192
Wilhelm of Prussia, Crown
    Prince, 16
Willock, Sir James, 52
Wilson, Gen. Sir Henry, 189
wireless telegraphy, 77, 131-2
Wotan Position, 159
Württemberg, Albrecht,
    Grand Duke of, 16

Y Ravine, 89, 149
Y Sap, 82
Ypres, 38
    First Battle of, 40
    Second Battle of, 53-4
    Third Battle of
    (Passchendaele), 164-7
Zeppelin ZIX, 25
Zollern Redoubt, 144